A Political Analysis of Deviance

The University of Minnesota Press
gratefully acknowledges the support for its program
of the Andrew W. Mellon Foundation.
This book is one of those in whose financing
the Foundation's grant played a part.

A Political Analysis of Deviance

Pat Lauderdale, *Editor*

Department of Sociology, University of Minnesota

UNIVERSITY OF MINNESOTA PRESS Minneapolis

Published by the University of Minnesota Press,
2037 University Avenue Southeast,
Minneapolis, Minnesota 55414

Library of Congress Cataloging in Publication Data

Main entry under title:

A Political analysis of deviance.

    Bibliography: p.
    Includes index.
    1. Deviant behavior — Addresses, essays, lectures.
2. Deviant behavior — Political aspects — Addresses,
essays, lectures, I. Lauderdale, Pat.
HM291.P62   302.5   79-27057
ISBN 0-8166-0931-4

Preface

The conventional wisdom of American society and much of the professional knowledge within the social sciences assumes a clear and distinct line between political and deviant activity. This distinction has become increasingly blurred by sociological and historical studies that reveal the political nature of deviance. Although overt political conflict between economic groups, status groups, and professions has received much attention, the present work goes beyond such studies to examine the subtle political dimensions of deviance for which clear historical episodes of political conflict have not been found. Those dimensions are most evident when new categories of deviance are being created or old categories being transformed. The chapters in this book examine aspects of political life and their relationship to the study of deviance that are typically ignored or suffocated before they become public.

In essence, this volume suggests that all definitions of deviance are in some sense political. The major problem we address is under what conditions does a form of action come to be defined as deviant or conversely redefined as normal.

□□□□□□□□

This book exists because a number of friends survived the five-year period from inception to completion. The friends are Gerald Larson,

Mary Jane Lehnertz, Steve McLaughlin, Phil Smith-Cunnien, and Jeff Stitt. Their support went beyond cheerful encouragement and editorial comments regarding the manuscript. The book emerged from extensive conversation with these people and included their continued search for useful material. It was not an easy task for them because I initially proclaimed that the book would take only five months to complete. In addition, they managed to convince me that it would be impossible to include all relevant studies, especially those that came out during the processing of the book. I am disappointed that the time involved in processing the final copy precludes the integration of the most recent work. I am responsible for the embarrassing length of time it took to finish as well as those parts of the book that assume a kaleidoscopic quality; my friends did all they could.

It also happens that I have had the good fortune throughout the revisions of the book to work closely with James Inverarity. Although we disagree on a number of intellectual issues, and I imagine we will continue to disagree, his critical reviews and substantive additions to all parts of the book are greatly appreciated. He is, in fact, responsible for the better portions of the text.

Mike Cruit, Dan Doyle, Hal Finestone, Charles Lakin, and Paul Reynolds are scholars who read sections of the manuscript in one or another state of preparation and contributed much to its style and content. I also thank Marilyn Pindroh, Peggy Saunders, and Karen Smith for typing the manuscript. The people in my department here at the University of Minnesota were supportive, and I especially appreciate the commitment of Rich Abel and the skill of Beverly Kaemmer from the University of Minnesota Press.

For helping me diminish the prattle of my own work, I owe special thanks to Buzz Zelditch. Unfortunately, there is still much to be done.

Finally, I want to acknowledge five people who have continually protected me from the associated stigma of everyday life. I appreciate the warmth and steady understanding of Almeta, Dick, Mike, Rett, and T. E.

P. L.

Contents

Introduction

A Power
and Process Approach
to the Definition
of Deviance

Pat Lauderdale

In the midst of the human rights campaign of the Carter administration, Andrew Young, at that time the United States ambassador to the United Nations, declared that there are "hundreds, perhaps thousands of persons in the U.S. I would call political prisoners." There followed a presidential reprimand, demands for Young's dismissal, a partial retraction on the part of Young, and a brief discussion in the mass media of "political prisoners" and whether the United States had any.[1] Young seemed to include under this rubric anyone who had failed to receive justice in the criminal courts. Persons convicted because of race or class bias could thus properly be called political prisoners, but not exactly in the same sense as dissidents imprisoned in the Soviet Union for offenses such as criticizing the regime. This brief controversy enflamed a smoldering issue and produced an insight into the definition of the nature of deviance that has so far eluded most analysts in both nonacademic and academic circles.

POLITICAL VERSUS APOLITICAL DEVIANCE:
STANDARD DISTINCTIONS

The concept of political crime has usually been narrowly defined as an offense against the state such as espionage, treason, assassination, terrorism, or sedition (Kircheimer, 1961; Packer, 1962). The distinction between political and "normal" criminals, deviants, and prisoners has traditionally been made in terms of the attitudes and articulations of individual actors. Political deviants are typically viewed as individuals who challenge or deny the legitimacy of rules, laws, or norms because of some commitment to a higher or, at least, different moral order. Apolitical deviants, on the other hand, are conventionally viewed as accepting the existing order as valid but seeking to circumvent its restrictions for their personal gain. Angela Davis, for example, argues that

> There is a distinct and qualitative difference between one breaking a law for one's own individual self-interest and violating it in the interests of a class of a people whose oppression is expressed either directly or indirectly through that particular law (1971: 29).

At the other end of the political spectrum Ernest van den Haag argues that

> the aim of his crime determines whether or not the criminal is political; the offender who intended personal enrichment cannot become a political criminal independently of his actual intent . . . (1966: 135).

Sociologically, this position is embodied in Merton's (1968: 414-17) distinction between two types of deviant behavior—*nonconformity*, which challenges the legitimacy of the social norms openly and disinterestedly, and *crime*, which seeks to evade social norms for personal ends. Such conceptions view political deviance as behavior that is not fully legitimate but at the same time is exempt from the usual stigma attached to illegitimate behavior by virtue of the intent of the actors.

This approach to political deviance and its variations are strikingly similar to legal criteria, even though they do not explicitly refer to legal constructions. Thus, an act is criminal in the law generally only if there was criminal intent (*mens rea*) on the part of the actor. If Jones runs over Smith in his automobile, the death of Smith is typically defined as murder only if Jones planned the event in advance with full knowledge of the consequences of his action. Without such intent we have accidental homicide, Jones-not-guilty-by-reason-of-insanity, or some other legal definition of the event. For Merton et al., however, whether Smith's untimely end was a result of nonconformity or crime on the part of Jones depends upon the *political intent* of Jones. Did Jones have a higher moral cause?

Nontrivial examples of this problem fill history books. Is, for example, the leader of loose-knit bands of hit-and-run killers of British soldiers a "homicidal maniac," a "crazed cult killer," or a "bandit?" Or is George Washington a revolutionary hero? Is Nat Turner, who executed Virginia slave owners and their families in 1830, in the same category? Is the Jewish terrorist in Palestine in 1948 distinguishable from the Palestinian terrorist in Israel in 1978? Societies continually face such questions of definition. *Intent* of the actors is a central ingredient in the construction of these definitions. Merton's emphasis on the role of intent, however, has an unintended negative consequence of injecting into sociological analysis all of the conundra associated with the use of the *mens rea* criterion of crime in the law. Note, for example, the controversy in law surrounding one exemption from *mens rea*, the insanity defense. Jones running over Smith may not be a crime because Jones was incapable of discerning right from wrong and/or was driven by an uncontrollable impulse. An uncontrolled impulse may be momentary, making it extremely difficult to distinguish between sane and temporarily insane actors. The net result has been that the insanity plea has turned into a bargaining device, the status of sanity being something to be negotiated.[2]

The lesson here is transparent. What is and what is not politically deviant cannot be determined solely by an examination of an actor's intent, because intent is socially negotiated. Consider the statement by Charles Manson:

> Mr. and Mrs. America—you are wrong. I am not the King of the Jews nor am I a hippie cult leader. I am what you have made of me and the mad dog devil killer fiend leper is a reflection of your society . . . (Bugliosi, 1975:561).

Manson goes on to claim that he was created as a deviant (i.e., a scapegoat) by American society for its political ends when, in fact, his commitment to a higher political moral order led to his actions (cf. Sanders, 1972; Bugliosi, 1975). Manson's proclamations illustrate some of the problems with previous conceptualizations of political deviance. Reliance on individual verbalizations leaves a heavy burden of proof upon observers to determine whether the actor's justifications are legitimate indicators of constructive ideals or simply machinations. Even if observers are able to discern the underlying motives behind the words, we are still left with a partial analysis of political deviance. The fact, for example, that labor organizers did not have criminal intent does not help to explain why their activities continued to be criminalized. For example, in 1878 the founder of the Pinkerton detective agency stated:

> Every trades-union has for its vital principle, whatever is professed, the con-
> centration of brute force to gain certain ends. Then the deadly spirit of
> Communism steals in and further embitters the workingman against that
> from which his very livelihood is secured, and gradually makes him an
> enemy to all law, order, and good society . . . And it will be found true
> the world over, that in just the proportion that all classes of workingmen
> refuse to be coerced and embittered by these pernicious societies, in just
> that proportion do they rise above their previous conditions, and reach a
> nobler and happier condition of life (Pinkerton, 1878: xi-xii).

Reading this indictment of labor unions a century later starkly reveals the ambiguous relationship between politics and deviance. Avowal and imputation of intent is an important variable in the creation of deviance, but it is not a sufficient condition.

A second conception of political deviance commonly encountered conceives of the actions of the deviants as intrinsically political or apolitical. For example, Gouldner suggests that

> the kinds of researches that are undertaken by [the labeling school of
> deviance] tend to exclude a concern with *political* deviance, in which men
> do actively fight back on behalf of their values and interests. We thus find
> relatively few studies of people involved in the civil rights struggle or in the
> peace movement. For however much these deviant groups are made to
> suffer, no one could easily conceive of them as mere victims well under the
> control of bureaucratic officialdom. It is not man fighting back that wins
> Becker's sympathy but, rather, man-on-his-back that piques his curiosity
> (1973: 39).

Related to this position is the view of Liazos (1972), Pepinsky (1974), and Schwendinger and Schwendinger (1977) that deviance in general is a property inherent in the act. (Recall Becker's [1963] keynote of labeling theory, that deviance is a property conferred upon rather than inherent in the act.) These writers argue that certain acts are inherently criminal or deviant depending upon the magnitude of harm they cause; the "real crimes" (exploitation, sexism, racism, imperialism, the profit motive, consumer fraud) are objectively defined by their harmful consequences. It is a paradox of this viewpoint that, while neither legislature nor appellate court in the United States would consider the question of whether it is criminal for a motion picture magnate to spend $20,000 on a birthday party for his daughter while people are starving a few blocks from the night club he rented for the occasion (Chambliss, 1976: 80).

Such episodes lead to asking:

> Isn't it time to raise serious questions about the assumptions underlying the definition of the field of criminology when a man who steals a paltry sum can be called a criminal while agents of the state can, with impunity, legally reward men who destroy food so that price levels can be maintained while a sizable portion of the population suffers from malnutrition? (Schwendinger and Schwendinger, 1970: 149).

Although these writers fail to explicitly address the phenomenon of political deviance, their positions would seem to suggest that the distinction between apolitical and political deviance should be made in terms of the objective consequences of the action. If the action (for example, a collective disturbance) is "progressive" in its consequences, then it is revolutionary or political; otherwise, it is deviant.

TOWARD A POLITICAL PROCESS APPROACH TO THE DEFINITION OF DEVIANCE

Although the works above shed light on two important aspects of the definitional process—intent of the actors and behavioral consequences of their actions—the understanding of definitional processes they provide is only partial. Merton et al. fail to recognize that intent is socially negotiated. Although Gouldner and others are heuristic, they do not give adequate attention to the role of nondeviant factors (social movements, public opinion, agencies of control) in determining social perception of the deviants' actions and their consequences.

To study social definition, we must first set aside the preoccupation with intent and consequences of behavior. Through a variety of societal mechanisms, most of the diversity of individuals is categorized as normal variation, a small fraction as apolitical deviance, and an even smaller fraction as political deviance. The problem this book addresses is how the boundaries of these categories are drawn and what determines the placement of specific actors and acts in any

Table 1. Conflict Situations: Dimensions of the
Character and Relations of Parties in Conflict

Resulting Popular Definition of the Conflict Situation	Size and Organization of Party Feared	Relative Power of Party Feared	Degree to Which Opposing Party Feels Fearful or Threatened
Deviance ("crime," etc.)	Individuals or small, loosely organized group	Almost none	Very high
Civil uprising or disorder	Small, loosely organized minority	Relatively low	Very high
Social movement	Sizable organized minority	Relatively low	Mild
Civil war	Large, well-organized minority	Relatively high or almost equal	Very high
Mainstream party politics in the United States	Large, organized minority	About equal	Mild

Source: Lofland (1969: 15), adapted.

given category. The creation of categories (or enactment) and assignment of individuals (or enforcement) are viewed here as two basic processes of social definition, processes that are outcomes of political variables.

An analysis of the social organization of the definition of deviance requires an examination of how criminal or political intent is socially negotiated and how objectively harmful social actions are rendered conventional or necessary (cf. Blum and McHugh, 1971). Lofland (1969) was the first sociologist to lay out, albeit in a schematic fashion, such an approach. As seen in table 1, Lofland views deviance as one outcome of social definition arising from a configuration of three aspects of social organization: size, threat (relative power), and degree of organization.

To develop a more complete political analysis of deviance, one that addresses the question of when acts or actors will be seen as deviant versus political, this book examines how various political entities construct and dismantle definitions of deviance. Following Lofland's lead, we examine variations in group organization ranging from nascent, inchoate protest groups through highly organized professions. Our approach to the study of deviance suggests that:

(1) actors (e.g., groups, organizations, states) with varying resources create, maintain, or transform definitions of deviance; and (2) these ensuing processes require delineation at various stages. For example, the processes need to be examined during the conditions under which the definitions are created, the initial consequences of those definitions, the routinization of the definitions, and the application of sanctions to those definitional changes.

Chapter 1 examines how the political analysis of deviance can clarify important issues in the field of deviance and integrate this field with theory and research in conflict, social change, and sociology of law. Rather than emphasizing the motivations of deviant action, the discussion centers on the sources of changing definitions of deviance. It examines how theory and research in the field of deviance have historically ignored most of the political aspects of deviance and then examines some consequences of the dominant apolitical approach in sociological research. The chapter further considers why sociologists, with different perspectives and approaches (e.g., consensus, pluralistic, conflict, critical, etc.), have largely ignored or rejected one another and attempts to move beyond the rather sterile debate now dominant between conflict and consensus sociologists. The chapter concludes with an examination of the maintenance or transformation of definitions of deviance stemming from a variety of political processes that occur at multiple levels of analysis.

Two emergent themes are pursued by dividing the book into two general sections. Part I looks at the role of collective interaction and social movements in creating, removing, or altering definitions of deviance, and part II discusses the role of organizations and, in particular, the state.

Part I concerns the general issue of hegemony (cf. Bates, 1975; Anderson, 1977) and its role in the definition of diversity as deviant or political. The basic concept of *hegemony*[3] refers to

> an order in which a certain way of life and thought is dominant, in which one concept of reality is diffused throughout society in all its institutional and private manifestations, informing with its spirit all taste, morality, customs, religious and political principles, and all social relations, particularly in their intellectual and moral connotations (Williams, 1960: 587).

This section of the book explores the nature of two forms of hegemony in contemporary American society, legal and cultural. Chapter 2 examines legal hegemony manifested in antiwar trials. The study shows how adversarial procedures and due process legitimations create barriers to defendants who attempt to define their activities as political. It emphasizes the role of the deviants in changing the definitions imposed upon them and suggests that, when their definitions are supported by an organized movement outside the courtroom, legal hegemony can be penetrated. Particular attention is given to status degradation ceremonies in antiwar trials as models of the interactionist view of political deviance.

Chapter 3 investigates the role of cultural hegemony in constraining the political definition of acts. It examines two questions: (1) under what conditions will an event be reported; and (2) given that the event is covered, what influences the way the event is depicted? The chapter focuses upon the news coverage of one particular event, the anti-Bicentennial march planned and executed by the July Fourth Coalition. The participants' definition of this historical event as protest is contrasted with 18 major newspapers' depiction of the same event. The discrepancies between the two conceptions of the event, especially in judgments of the event's importance and the particular labels applied to the event, are traced to various causes—the cultural context, social system linkages, organizational dimensions of both newspapers and the march participation, and the event itself. By drawing on theoretical perspectives and studies from diverse fields—social movements, deviance, political sociology, and the media—this paper constructs a general approach to the study of public events and their portrayal to a public. This work explores the process of acquiring a deviant label rather than simply studying only those already stigmatized with the label.

Part II moves from the level of collective behavior and social movements to more institutionalized arenas (viz., formal organizations, professional associations, and the state) in which definitions of political deviance are created and imposed. Chapter 4 begins this discussion with a consideration of roles of professional associations and the state in criminalizing violence in professional hockey. The study demonstrates that sport in general and hockey in particular present peculiar definitional problems since potentially "violent" acts are intrinsic to legitimate sport activity. The study shows that the legal status of athletic violence is a product of delicate negotiations between professional hockey organizations and the state, both of which are subject to changing pressures over time. Research into the history of the sport institution reveals that earlier in this century it was characterized by violence, extreme injury, public indignation, and official reform action. Changes in the definition and legitimation of violence in hockey and the consequences of those changes in maintaining the autonomy of the occupation in relation to the criminal justice system are explored. The threat to the profession lies in the possibility that official reform action will reduce or destroy autonomy. This conflict leads to a variety of responses. For example, individual players may be scapegoated or "sacrificed" to an external system in order to avoid open conflict over the possible collective nature of the deviance, thereby maintaining the mandate of the particular institution.

Chapter 5 suggests that another form of deviance definition arises when the state intervenes in local protest and politics. For example, the Watts, Newark, and Detroit race riots of the mid-sixties can be interpreted as the actions of local law enforcement officials protesting the intrusion of the federal government into their local affairs. Data indicate that violence initiated by civilians occurs during the early stages of the riot and violence by the police and the National Guard comes later. The data analysis reveals that most of the people who died were black civilians, killed by police officers and National Guardsmen. Officials became increasingly indiscriminate in their killings as the riot progressed and civilian violence ceased. Thus, "racial violence" was at least as much a protest by whites as by blacks. In an attempt to generate a more general theory, chapter 5 draws upon earlier riots in eighteenth-century France, where the people protested the coming of the revolutionary regime and the centralization of local life. Similarly, local whites in south Boston and other large American cities protested the intrusion of the central state into their affairs much as their Parisian counterparts did some two hundred years earlier.

Chapter 6 explores alternative theoretical conceptions of the political bases of deviance definition. It maintains that, in general, theories of the political processes underlying the definition of deviance have been fragmentary and incomplete. The major single theory that addresses these issues is the American conflict theory, developed by Quinney, Chambliss, Platt, and Turk. That approach has concentrated primarily on the politics of interest group manipulations of the law. This chapter examines several impasses of the current conflict theory approach to political processes in the definition of deviance and turns to classical sociological theory as a source of an alternative conception. In particular, Marx's contrast between feudal and bourgeois law and Durkheim's contrast between repressive and restitutive law are used to develop hypotheses about the political and social organizational factors that underlie the definition of deviance. The chapter presents a structural approach to the definition of deviance, especially via criminal law, and seeks to explore the nature of particular institutional arrangements of a society and the constraints that these institutions create on the criminal law.

The afterword explores the general political dimensions of deviance definition and provides a research agenda for future work. It focuses upon studies in conflict, social change, and the sociology of law as well as a brief consideration of interdisciplinary work relevant to changing definitions of behavior.

NOTES

1. The mass media in the United States consequently became unsure of the meaning of "political prisoner." The *Christian Science Monitor* News Service (July 30, 1978) initially stated that the number of such prisoners in the United States appeared negligible compared with an estimated 10,000 to 20,000 in Soviet labor camps, 5,000 to 20,000 in Argentine jails, or 50,000 in the Philippines in the preceding four years. Later, however, the *Monitor* noted that there may be substantial numbers of political prisoners in the United States if the term is construed as described in recent studies (some by the federal government). These studies indicated that many, perhaps even a majority, of the prisoners in American local jails are there because they lack money for bail, fines, or legal defense. The *Monitor* was not sure whether these conditions fit the description of "political"; however, the *Washington Star* (July 28, 1978) ran a column suggesting that it is ambiguous to state that political prisoners are people incarcerated for acts directed against the political system. The *Star* contended that if Anatoly Scharansky and Alexander Ginsburg were considered by Americans to be political prisoners in the Soviet Union, then a number of previously defined common criminals in the United States should be designated as political prisoners (e.g., members of the Wilmington Ten).

The controversy in this case started by Ambassador Young reflects the importance of considering the status of the definer (e.g., Young's relatively high status gave some credence to a debate that is typically glossed over in the United States), the historical period during which the debate emerges, and the ideological differences between the parties (e.g., although Aleksandr Solzhenitsyn was considered a political hero when he arrived in the United States, he was designated a political deviant by the Soviet Union).

2. Engels (1961: 59) presents one of many analogous dilemmas by observing that

for everyday purposes we know and can say, e.g., whether an animal is alive or not. But, upon closer inquiry, we find that this is, in many cases, a very complex question, as the jurists know very well. They have racked their brains in vain to discover a rational limit beyond which the killing of the child in its mother's womb is murder. It is just as impossible to determine absolutely the moment of death, for physiology proves that death is not an instantaneous, momentary phenomenon, but a very protracted process.

3. Antonio Gramsci (1971) introduced the notion of hegemony to deal with peculiar characteristics of advanced capitalist society. Widespread consensus about the seriousness of criminal offenses (cf. Rossi et al., 1974) and about the apolitical character of deviance cannot from this perspective be understood as simply "false consciousness" in Engel's sense. False consciousness denotes a situation in which the ruling class is aware of its interests while

the working class remains ignorant of its true interests. In Marx's terms, the ruling class is a class-for-itself, while the working class is a class-in-itself. Gramsci argues that this characterization is not adequate for the present situation. Rather, the working class in advanced capitalistic society believes that the ruling class interest is the same as the interest of the larger society. The problem is to account for the persuasiveness of hegemony.

REFERENCES

Anderson, Perry. 1977. "The antinomies of Antonio Gramsci." *New Left Review* 100: 5-78.

Bates, Thomas R. 1975. "Gramsci and the theory of hegemony." *Journal of the History of Ideas* 36: 351-56.

Becker, Howard S. 1963. *Outsiders: Studies in the Sociology of Deviance.* New York: Free Press.

____. 1973. Outsiders: *Studies in the Sociology of Deviance.* 2nd ed. New York: Free Press.

Blum, Alan F., and Peter McHugh. 1971. "Social ascription of motives." *American Sociological Review* 36: 98-109.

Bugliosi, Vincent. 1975. *Helter Skelter: The True Story of the Manson Murder.* New York: W. W. Norton.

Chambliss, William. 1976. "Functional and conflict theories of crime: The heritage of Emile Durkheim and Karl Marx" In William Chambliss and Milton Mankoff (eds.). *Whose Law? What Order? A Conflict Approach to Criminology.* New York: John Wiley.

Davis, Angela. 1971. *If They Come in the Morning.* New York: New American Library, Signet Books.

Engels, Friedrich. 1961. "Socialism: Utopian and scientific." In Arthur P. Mendel (ed.). *Essential Works of Marxism.* New York: Bantam Books.

Gouldner, Alvin. 1973. *For Sociology: Renewal and Critique in Sociology Today.* New York: Basic Books.

Gramsci, Antonio. 1971. *Selections from the Prison Notebooks.* New York: International.

Kirchheimer, Otto. 1961. *Political Justice: The Use of Legal Procedure for Political Ends.* Princeton: Princeton University Press.

Liazos, Alexander. 1972. "The poverty of the sociology of deviance: Nuts, sluts, and perverts." *Social Problems* 20: 103-120.

Lofland, John. 1969. *Deviance and Identity.* Englewood Cliffs, N.J.: Prentice-Hall.

Merton, Robert K. 1968. *Social Theory and Social Structure.* New York: Free Press.

Packer, Herbert. 1962. "Offenses against the state." *Annals of the American Academy of Political and Social Science* 339: 77-110.

Pepinsky, Harold E. 1974. "From white collar crime to exploitation: Redefinition of a field." *Journal of Criminal Law and Criminology* 65: 225-33.

Pinkerton, Alan. 1878. *Strikers, Communists, Tramps and Detectives.* New York: G. W. Carleton.

Reasons, Charles. 1973. "The politicizing of crime, the criminal and the criminologist." *Journal of Criminal Law and Criminology* 64: 471-77.

Rossi, Peter, et al. 1974. "The seriousness of crimes: Normative structure and individual differences." *American Sociological Review* 39: 224-37.

Sanders, Ed. 1972. *The Family.* New York: E. P. Dutton.

Schafer, Stephen. 1974. *The Political Criminal: The Problem of Morality and Crime.* Englewood Cliffs, N.J.: Prentice-Hall.

Schwendinger, Herman, and Julia R. Schwendinger. 1970. "Defenders of order or guardians of human rights?" *Issues in Criminology* 5: 123-57.

____. 1977. "Social class and the definition of crime." *Crime and Social Justice* 7: 4-13.

Turk, Austin. 1977. "Class, conflict and criminalization." *Sociological Focus* 10: 209-20.

Van den Haag, Ernest. 1966. "No excuse for crime." *Annals of the American Academy of Political and Social Sciences* 423: 133-41.

Williams, Gwyn A. 1960. "The concept of 'egemonia' in the thought of Antonio Gramsci: Some notes on interpretation." *Journal of the History of Ideas* 21: 586-99.

Chapter 1

From Apolitical to Political Analyses of Deviance

Pat Lauderdale and **James Inverarity**

INTRODUCTION

This chapter examines the shift in the social sciences from the traditionally apolitical conception of deviance to increasingly political analyses. It suggests that in the evolution of the social sciences the study of deviance became the province of psychology and that the psychologistic orientation has preoccupied generations of researchers. We briefly discuss how this historical evolution has been reinforced by patterns of professional specialization and government funding. Then, we outline the emergence in the sixties of a nascent recognition of the role of political processes involved in the creation of deviance in the forms of labeling and conflict theory. The final section of the chapter examines the political processes underlying the creation, maintenance, and change of deviance definitions and the necessity of considering various levels of analysis in which those political processes operate.

ROOTS OF THE APOLITICAL ORIENTATION TOWARD DEVIANCE

The present field of deviance is primarily a product of a succession of theories. To understand its apolitical orientation it is necessary to examine how the field evolved and how most succeeding orientations have been influenced by their predecessors. Detailed accounts of this development have been published elsewhere;[1] for present purposes it will be sufficient to consider the following schematic summary of the development of approaches toward deviance and their respective focuses or causal agents.

1. Aristotelian (antiquity). Deviance was associated with punishment inflicted on individuals by the gods. Logic revealed that some individuals were by nature deviant.

2. Medieval Scholastic. Deviance was thought to have been created by the devil (or some similar religious or spiritual entity). The demonic entity possessed or manipulated the deviant.

3. Physiological. Deviance was felt to be related to the surface characteristics (exterior) of individuals, regardless of whether the researcher thought the cause was biological or psychological. Physiognomy, craniology, cranioscopy, phrenology, or a general conception of ugliness served as the frame of reference.[2]

4. Biological. Deviance was thought to be rooted in the biochemistry of the person. The emphasis was on the inner characteristics (interior) of individuals.

5. Economic. Deviance was related to economic conditions. For example, drunkenness was associated with prosperity and burglary with depression.

6. Psychological. Deviance was initially viewed as a consequence of events in the individual's biography, be it situational frustration or an arrested stage of psychosexual development. Recent views propose a modified frustration-aggression perspective, a series of reinforcement theories, or a modeling explanation of deviance.

The peculiar development of the study of deviance has thus traditionally been psychologistic, centered on attempting to explain the problematic behavior of the isolated individual. This is the primary reason for the failure to develop a political perspective on the phenomenon of deviance. For example, the phrenologists, while rejecting the demonological approach, remained prisoners of the medieval perspective. The novelty of the phrenologists' contribution was to show that what the demonologists had attempted to explain could be better accounted for in terms of natural rather than supernatural causes. The new generation of psychologists took as problematic the same issues about deviance that had occupied the phrenologists, but they offered a new, more adequate set of causal factors to account for the same observations. Since the problem of deviance was essentially dictated by a research tradition that took individual personality as the unit of analysis, the role of social organizations in separating deviance from normality could not be seen as an important issue. Each new set of researchers was content to modify the psychological tradition in the study of deviance without considering how the behavior being studied first came to be defined as deviant.[3]

The assumption that deviance is a property of acts or actors that has individualistic, identifiable causes has not only a long history but also a wide range of contemporary manifestations. Recently, low blood sugar or XYY chromosomal arrangements have been proposed as causes of at least some forms of deviant behavior; an explanation of the Salem witchcraft episode contends that bread contaminated with a parasitic fungus induced hallucinations in the bewitched pre-pubescents. Some, all, or none of these causal factors may ultimately be shown to cause variations in behavior that then becomes labeled deviant. None of these investigations, however, can tell us why such behaviors are defined as deviant. Furthermore, looking at deviance as an individual phenomenon, taking the deviant *behavior* as problematic, as the thing to be explained, creates a myopia that has prevented and continues to prevent sociologists from considering the power dimensions of deviance.

Even when sociologists took up the study of deviance, eager to illustrate its "social" aspects, they remained tied to key assumptions from the psychologistic approaches. The commitment to explaining individual motivation provided sociologists with a research agenda that excluded definitional issues despite the attention they paid to such structural variables as stratification and subculture.

It is instructive to review how social class entered as a variable into the sociological study of deviance. Merton's (1938) anomie theory, for example, took as the key problem to be explained the social class distribution of crime. Merton explained this distribution in terms of a general typology of individual adaptations to social strain. Burglary, for example, might be motivated by a combination of commitment to goals of material success and an inability to achieve those goals through legitimate means of occupational roles. The fact that this condition was empirically more frequent among the unemployed and marginally employed accounted for the observed (or assumed) relationships between burglary and social class.

The relationship between deviance and social class was also critical for Sutherland (1940 and 1948). His theory of differential association, however, began with a picture of the social class distribution of crime diametrically opposed to that of Merton. Sutherland supposed that deviance is common among all social classes and that the same process—differential association—underlies deviance regardless of its social class location. Sutherland was thus led to study white-collar crime to demonstrate that becoming a burglar involved the same basic learning and social support processes that led to becoming a price fixer. What is interesting, from our standpoint, about Sutherland's work is that it raised in a serious way the political issues of definition. Why is it, Sutherland asked in passing, that offenses committed by higher-status members of the society are lightly sanctioned (e.g., corporate offenses are dealt with by civil rather than criminal law), but, on the other hand, offenses committed by lower-class individuals receive not only a harsher (criminal) sanction but in many instances a sanction vastly disproportionate to the relative harm of the offense.

This concern with explaining the societal reaction to the deviance, as opposed to the motivation, of the deviant actor received more explicit consideration by labeling theory in the 1960s. Becker (1963), Erikson (1962), Kitsuse and Cicourel (1963), and Scheff (1966) suggested that the critical factor to consider was the reaction to deviance. This reorientation, in turn, gave impetus to a rebirth of the sociology of law, out of which this volume has grown. The labeling theorists, however, despite their revolution in perspective, remained partially tied to the traditional concern with motivation. In particular, most of them took as their primary task to demonstrate that sanctioning and the associated stigma serve to reinforce and stabilize the deviant behavior of the individual. Labeling theorists tended to take as their central mission the exorcism of explanations of deviance in terms of individual characteristics. Becker's battle cry was that deviance is a property conferred upon rather than inherent in the actor. In fighting this war with their predecessors and focusing on the consequences of stigma, labeling theorists often overlooked the sources of the deviant labels being imposed by social control agencies, the ways in which such labels changed, and especially the political processes underlying the development and imposition of labels.[4]

It may be instructive to compare these developments with contemporary developments in the sociological field called "stratification." The research in stratification also took the direction of emphasizing individual motivational issues at the expense of political and structural questions. The field became consumed with the process of status attainment by individuals, tracing out the career trajectories of individuals in the occupational structure, and with the rather precise estimation of the role of achievement versus ascription in career development. Coser pointed out that this exclusive concern with the distributive aspects of stratification directs attention away from the sociopolitical mechanisms through which members of different strata monopolize chances by reducing the chances of others . . . It is one thing to investigate the ways in which, for example, people manage to attain the status position of medical practitioners in American society; it is quite another to analyze the institutions that help the American Medical Association to monopolize the market for health care by restricting access. What needs analysis is not merely the ladder to medical success but those institutional factors that contribute to the maintenance of a system of medical services that effectively minimize the life chances of the poor (1976: 335).

The study of both deviance and stratification in recent American sociology, therefore, has been dominated by an emphasis on individual motivation at the expense of structural issues.

This emphasis has been further reinforced by

the para-ideology of science and technology [that] makes the exercise of governmental power acceptable by seemingly depoliticizing politics. Scientific and technological knowledge conceal class-specific interests, value systems, and the nature of domination. Because scientific methodologies do indeed develop independently from group or class interests, it is easy to convey implicitly the idea that decision-making based on science and technology is just as detached from special interests. This innovation of scientific methods seriously and deleteriously obscures the political process (Mueller, 1973: 111).

This para-ideology appears to allocate resources independently of values that, in fact, are the actual bases of political decisions (cf. Habermas, 1975). The technocratic para-ideology cuts across class lines "since efficiency, rational administration, and technical rules appear to be at first glance disassociated from any class interests" (Mueller, 1973: 145).[5] The roles of the professional expert and scientist serve to turn decision making into an "objective" exercise of technical competence and administrative expertise.

In the field of deviance this process appears in the form of welfare and psychiatric professional approaches to social problems. The definition of what constitutes a social problem is made by trained experts who may depart quite substantially from public perception of social problems. For example, Lauer (1976) presents data to indicate that, although the public views war and peace as the problem of greatest concern, the most significant problem among sociologists is crime and delinquency, with war and peace listed as the least significant. In addition, the impact of the para-ideology is frequently felt by investigators who find research questions defined by their employer. As Kohn recently revealed in a footnote:

> I also want to acknowledge certain limitations of perspective built into the task force effort and carried over to this paper. It hardly takes much expertise in the sociology of knowledge to be aware that a review undertaken for a government agency by its employees is likely to deal gingerly with fundamental questions about the social structure, economic, and political organization of the society. Furthermore, NIMH being the governmental agency in question, there was (and there remains) an over-emphasis on social problems that fall outside. Thus, for example, I talk about schizophrenia and discrimination but not about war or imperialism (1976: 94).

Even where the social scientist studying deviance has not performed the role of hired hand to social control agencies (see Quinney [1975] for extensive documentation of such practices in American sociology) the investigator is led away from asking political questions about deviance by psychologism, professionalism (Furner, 1976), and scientism (Skura, 1976). Until recently this has meant the dominance of concerns with etiology and corrections (Matza, 1969). For a variety of historical reasons sociological investigators of deviance were trained in social psychology rather than political economy. It was a relatively short step from social psychology to behavior modification, group therapy, parole prediction, and other forms of correctional praxis. More recently, the emphasis has shifted to a rebirth of concern with deterrence (cf. Gibbs and Erikson, 1975); however, both the corrections and deterrence orientations, regardless of their fundamental differences, have a common perspective. Both orientations take deviance for granted; what is problematic for the investigator are the determinants of individual acts.

NASCENT POLITICAL ORIENTATIONS

The field of deviance underwent a major revolution in the 1960s. Although this revolution took a variety of forms, new orientations had a common concern with political processes in the social construction of deviance. Pearson has succinctly characterized these trends in his observation that

> in traditional social thought and social practice deviance has placed itself outside politics, secured a neat division between "welfare matters" on one side, and "political science" on the other. . . . The 1960's announced a par-

tial surrender of these firm boundaries. The misfit paradigm exploited a number of the thinning spots in this division of politics and welfare and argued the essentially moral and political character of deviance control. Anti-psychiatry pointed to the need for an engagement with the political undergirdings of psychiatry and the ideology of humane, liberal social-welfare programmes. Social work itself underwent a crisis of some magnitude . . . the benign face of social welfare emerged as a candidate for political dissection: it was seen, that is, as a political agent (1975: 143).

Several different routes were taken to arrive at the notion that political processes were inherent in deviance (i.e., that politics and deviance could not be divorced). The absence of a single theory of social structure—or even a clearly articulated set of alternative theories of social structure—resulted in a consensus on the significance of political processes but a conflict over approaches, theories, and paradigms from which to view the phenomenon. The approaches were essentially the following.[6]

1. Atheoretical case studies of definitional change. This category includes Hall (1935) on theft, Becker (1963) on the Marihuana Tax Act, Chambliss (1964) on vagrancy, and Rothman (1971) on asylums. These studies document changes in definitions of deviance in specific historical periods. No theories are articulated or tested empirically. In most cases theoretical concepts are introduced in an ad hoc fashion (e.g., Becker's notion of "moral entrepreneurs," the idea that deviance definitions can be adequately explained in terms of the activities of professional stigmatizers pursuing their own material or ideal interests).

2. Theoretical case studies of definitional change. Gusfield (1963) on the temperance movement and Erikson (1966) on Puritan crimes exemplify this category of investigations, which seeks to illustrate, if not test, some general theory of society by examining instances of deviance transformation (Weber's status group conflict in the case of Gusfield, Durkheim's ritual punishment thesis in the case of Erikson).

3. Commentary on the New Left. Horowitz and Liebowitz (1968) make use of the peculiarities of the New Left in blurring boundaries between political activism and deviant activity. They examine the general relationship between politics and deviance to extrapolate trends toward an increasing merger of the two.

4. Antipsychiatry. The writing of Laing (1967) and Szasz (1975) is directly concerned with criticizing the role psychiatrists play as agents of the state. Their critiques, however, raise fundamental ques-

tions about the process of deviance definition and the role that political power plays in determining what categories of behavior require "medical treatment" (cf. Scheff, 1966 and 1974).

5. Conflict theory.[7] The proliferation of studies of definitional change led several writers (e.g., Chambliss, 1976; Quinney, 1977; Turk, 1977) to develop a synthesis, "conflict theory," that attempts to spell out political processes underlying the creation of deviance. As Lemert points out:

> Radical critics and those who write on the politicization of deviance properly have noted the superficiality of the moral crusader formulation, as well as faulting labeling theory generally for its neglect of conflict and power. But the alternative theory of so-called radical sociology I find very generalized as well as doctrinaire. Neither the Marxian concept of class, the power elites of Mills, nor the new left "urban alliance" of blacks and students have much immediate or practical use for research into the dynamics of societal reaction. . . .
>
> (Empirical materials [Hall, 1935; Chambliss, 1964; Taylor and Taylor, 1973; Lemert, 1970]) make it doubtful that the emergence of new morality and procedures for defining deviance can be laid to the creations of any one group, class or elite. Rather, they are the products of the interaction of groups. . . . To understand the interplay of many groups out of which materialize new categories of moral and legal control requires a model of interaction quite different from those fathered by the psychologically oriented thought of Mead or from those of the class conflict theorists (Lemert, 1974: 462-63).

Chapter 6 undertakes an extensive review and critique of the conflict approach. We need to note here, however, that the approach has typically used case study evidence in a polemical fashion to attack the opposing "functionalist" perspective. Consequently, conflict theory has not adequately examined the political processes underlying the creation of deviance (see Gurr [1977], especially pp. 750-66).

AN ALTERNATIVE PERSPECTIVE
ON THE SOCIAL DEFINITION OF DEVIANCE

The conflict/consensus debate rests primarily on differences in terminology or in emphasis. In the former case, the two positions say the same thing but in terms with different connotations. The connotations may have polemical import, but they lack empirical consequences. The problem is not so much the absolute polarity of these approaches but their different emphases at particular levels of analysis. In 1880 Engels diagnosed the problem of the investigators who study objects and processes in "irreconcilable antitheses":

> Positive and negative absolutely exclude one another; cause and effect stand in a rigid antithesis one to the other. At first sight this mode of thinking seems to us very luminous, because it is that of so-called common sense. But sound common sense, respectable fellow that he is in the homely realm of his own four walls, has very wonderful adventures as soon as he ventures out into the wide world of research. . . . In the contemplation of individual things, it forgets the connection between them; in the contemplation of their existence, it forgets the beginning and end of that existence; of their repose, it forgets their motion. It cannot see the wood for the trees (1961: 58–59).

Alternatively, conflict and consensus positions may be saying different things, but when they do, it usually turns out to be a difference in emphasis. A few moments of reflection will show that the alleged polarity is continually violated by the real world. Take, for example, the notion that conflict is incompatible with consensus. Consensus over common goals quite often produces conflict, *not* integration. If everyone agrees to withdraw his or her money from the bank at the same time, this consensus produces all manner of conflict and strain (cf. Merton, 1968: 476-77; Mann, 1970; Olson, 1965). Simmel (1955) gave extensive attention to situations in which conflict at one level of social organization produced integration at another level. For example, role conflict such as political cross pressures in voters may produce great strain and disequilibrium at the level of personality, but the societal consequence is integration since the cross-pressured individuals are likely to become political moderates who typically react in apolitical fashion. Similarly, conflict at the intergroup levels (war between nation-states) may produce greater integration within the conflicting groups, so that the overall level of conflict might even decrease. Lest Simmel be cast into the fire as a functionalist, it is worth recalling that Marx made a very similar argument about the conditions under which classes would be formed. It is not enough, Marx pointed out, to have an aggregate of individuals who share an objective circumstance of oppression. To become a class, these individuals must come to share some consciousness of their common situation. Such a consciousness, Marx points out, often evolves only out of a period of protracted conflict with some opposition group. In short, conflict and integration are not opposed to each other universally, and thus opposition provides a weak foundation for the construction of alternative sociological theories or paradigms.[8]

Despite the claims of various advocates, no coherent theory at the present time integrates the disparate data on deviance definition. One could hope that out of a greater accumulation of case studies of definitional change a coherent theoretical perspective would grow. Past experience, however, provides no basis for believing that more abstracted empiricism will generate a systematic framework and sense of direction. Kuhn (1970: 15) characterizes such a state of affairs as random fact gathering and points out that in most disciplines practitioners have continued to spin their wheels collecting interesting facts that add up to virtually nothing. Only when a coherent perspective has been articulated (even when that perspective has later proven to be wrong) does the field advance beyond hallucinatory appreciation of the phenomenon.

One step in developing a coherent perspective on deviance definitions is to find an alternative to the standard classification of studies into conflict and consensus categories. We propose to examine how the study of political processes in the creation of deviance may be (and has been) undertaken at various degrees of abstraction and various levels of analysis.

Degree of Abstraction

The first dimension is degree of abstraction. By degree of abstraction we refer to the extent to which simplifying assumptions are introduced into the analysis. Many studies seek to cover the waterfront, be true to the phenomenon, reproduce the phenomenon in its full detail, place the reader in the role of the actors, and so on. Typically, these studies are historicist, their generalizations being bound by specific space and time coordinates. Indeed, to generalize beyond the arbitrarily drawn space and time coordinates is held by such writers to be illegitimate, scientistic, or antihumanistic.

In studies using low degrees of abstraction, attention revolves around accounting for some specific unique event. All events having nonreplicable features (e.g., the passage of the Marihuana Tax Act of 1937 and the police riots in Chicago in the fall of 1968) are unique. To account for single events embedded in a matrix of social circumstances requires a very broad consideration of processes. The most satisfactory form such an analysis can take is narrative (recounting a sequence of events). When several narratives are combined, we move to a slightly higher degree of abstraction. Specific details of the process fall away or are deemphasized and we have a natural history. Sutherland's (1950) pioneer empirical study in the sociology of law on the sexual psychopath is representative of this genre. The narrative and the natural history, however, are still at a fairly low level of abstraction, far removed from general theory. The most difficult stage of abstraction is to transcend the sequence-of-events perspective to one that places the phenomenon in a more *general theory*. The following discussion briefly illustrates how degrees of abstraction yield different perspectives on the same phenomenon.

Narrative

We begin with the specific question of how gay activists got the American Psychiatric Association (APA) to remove the medical stigma attached to homosexuality. A narrative account simply relates the major events. Thus, Ron Gold, publicity director of the Gay Activist Alliance of New York, met with Columbia University clinical psychiatrist Robert Spitzer. Gold requested a meeting with the APA's Committee on Nomenclature and Statistics. Subsequently, on May 9, 1973, at the APA convention in Honolulu, a session was held entitled "Should Homosexuality Be in the APA Nomenclature?" (see Stoller et al., 1973). As a consequence of this meeting involving Gold and five psychiatrists, the Committee on Nomenclature proposed reclassification of homosexual preference. In April 1974 at the annual meeting, a plurality of the 21,000 members of the APA voted to remove homosexuality from the list of "sexual orientation disturbances." This vote made homosexuality a matter of individual choice that became a medical problem only when the individual became troubled over his or her inclination. This decision was seen by gay activists as a major civil rights victory since it removed one of the major bases of discrimination against homosexuals. Labeled as psychopaths, for example, homosexuals could be deported under immigration laws and legitimately (on moral or legal grounds) be prevented from entering certain occupations and professions or from living in certain residential areas. Opposition to this redefinition was strong, one critic calling it the "medical hoax of the century" ("An instant cure," 1974: 45). The change was made in large measure because of the lobbying efforts of gay rights activist groups such as the Gay Task Force (McCaghy, 1976: 381). Although gay rights organizations like the Mattachine Society and the Daughters of Bilitis were organized in the early fifties, it was only after the success of the civil rights movement that these organizations adopted a successful militant strategy (Lee, 1977: 50). Gay rights organizations had since the early sixties proliferated. More than 200 campus homosexual groups had attained official recognition by the mid-seventies. Gay rights activists challenged discriminatory laws in the courts and sought to pressure television stations from broadcasting offensive stereotypes about homosexuals. Further legitimation was gained through annual mass public demonstrations. All of these efforts parallel the strategies and tactics evolved over the years by civil rights activists. Both the changed public climate and the skillful lobbying in the APA were instrumental in changing the medical definition of homosexuality in 1974 (cf. Spector, 1977).

The narrative thus explains a change in the definition of deviance by recounting in a schematic form the sequence of major events that lead up to the change in a particular instance.

Natural History

At the second level of abstraction, one or more additional cases that are analogous to the first case are considered and common denominators are explicated. For example, labor unions have been stigmatized with various labels. In the early part of the nineteenth century, unions were defined by the courts as criminal associations conspiring to restrain trade. Although space limitations prevent us from examining in detail the transformation from criminal association to legitimate interest group (but see, for example, Gregory [1958]), we can find several similarities between this definitional transformation and the one outlined above. The natural history that underlies both transformations includes the organization of the stigmatized, the use of public demonstrations of their positions and demands, the creation of a committee vanguard, and the lobbying of selected organizations within the establishment most likely to be receptive to claims of the stigmatized (see Blumrosen [1962] for an account of the use of state legislatures to overcome the more conservative judiciary in expanding the rights of unions).

The natural history, then, spells out common elements in the destigmatization of both labor organizations and homosexuals; in so doing, it ignores many of the particular features of the events, actors, and context in the two cases. The construction of such natural histories, though often useful, ought to be viewed as preliminary to the next level of abstraction, theory.

Theory

At this third level we seek a general theory that not only accounts for the transformation in definition of homosexuality and of labor organization but also allows us to see these transformations as a special instance of an even more general process that includes events outside the areas of law or deviance. As Collins has suggested:

> The next step clearly must be to abolish the field of deviance entirely, to link its materials with what is known of general explanations of stratification and politics (1975: 17).

To illustrate this approach, the two cases discussed above can be viewed as special instances of the process of *group mobility*. Group mobility is a relatively unexplored area in the sociology of stratification, but our present body of knowledge does suggest that patterns and regularities do occur in widely disparate settings. The advantage of viewing the transformation of deviance as a group mobility process is that we now can see relationships between "deviance" and social phenomena that might not otherwise be considered by investigators of this substantive area. We will consider two such areas— Sanskritization in India and professionalization in Western society— and suggest how a model of group mobility could be developed.

Sanskritization. In the classical Hindu conception of society there are four major castes—Brahmins (priests), Kshatriyas (warriors), Vaisyas (merchants), and Sundras (laborers). Below these castes are the untouchables, so defined because mere contact or presence of an untouchable is perceived as polluting. An individual's caste membership is fixed at birth, determined by the quality of her or his performance in previous incarnations. For example, a shiftless laborer is likely to be reborn as an untouchable; a successful warrior can anticipate rebirth as a Brahmin. An individual who seeks upward mobility in this life violates caste obligations and will be reborn at a lower position. Despite the rigidity of the hierarchy, mobility does take place, but most of the mobility is group rather than individual.[9] Within the four major castes are some two thousand subcastes for whom movement is possible, especially in the middle regions of the hierarchy (Srinivas, 1955). Such movement is accomplished by the adoption of life-style characteristics (e.g., occupation, diet, and customs) of upper castes. The Brahmins engage in high-status nonmanual occupations, refrain from consuming alcoholic beverages and meat, and sacrifice fruit and flowers rather than blood in their religious rituals. Their sexual relations are subject to strict regulation; for example, widows are expected to remain chaste. To move upward in the system, therefore, the subcaste must change its occupation and adopt the customs and ritual of the higher caste. For example, an aspiring subcaste may give up meat, switch from alcohol to cannabis, restrict sexual activity, and alter its ceremonial practices. These pretensions may produce hostility from the subcaste's neighbors, which may be countered by moving to a new village where its past is unknown or gaining the political support of a local power holder or the religious benediction of the local Brahmins. Ironically, the new, higher-status position the subcaste finally achieves is not perceived as the result of a mobility process but as a permanent caste position that had been obscured by circumstantial adversity visited on past generations. Thus, group mobility is possible without undermining the legitimation of a fixed caste system (an adaptation that should be kept in mind in considering the revolutionary character of other forms of group mobility).

We see in subcaste mobility how resources—religious symbols, political power, material advantage, and cultural standards—can be mobilized to increase the social position of an entire group. An analogous process occurs in Western society in the form of professionalization of occupational groups.

Professionalization. To the layman, a profession is an occupation that requires some extraordinary competence based on a body of technical knowledge. Medicine is, for the modern Westerner, the archetype of a profession. Wonder drugs, kidney transplants, polio vaccine, and other seemingly miraculous treatments testify to the charismatic powers of the occupation of physician. A historical view of medicine, however, reveals that the professionalization of the occupation long preceded its competence. When the AMA was founded in 1847, the major distinction between "real doctors" and "quacks" was social class background; in terms of technical competence and valid theories of disease, there was no discernible difference (Larson, 1977). Only through a concerted effort to upgrade the profession in the latter part of the nineteenth century did medicine attain its present status.

In general, the process of professionalization appears to obey the same basic laws as the process of group mobility for subcastes. In place of flower sacrifices, there are more secular rituals that an occupation must adopt if it is to become a profession. These typically include: (1) association with a university, certifying that the profession does in fact possess a special technical knowledge base; (2) a service, rather than profit, ideology; (3) autonomy (the possession of a charter that grants control over practitioners); (4) monopoly (the ability to exclude nonprofessionals from marketing the same service).

The rising occupation, like the rising subcaste, seeks to adopt the values of the established professions (e.g., service and educational credentials). It may eschew advertising, increase the degree requirements for practitioners, introduce recognized (and possibly irrelevant) technology, or move the professional school from independent status to affiliation with a university. Apart from the manipulation of symbols, the occupation may rely upon benedictions or endorsements of the established professions, as well as the use of state power in the form of licensing to restrict the market of competitors.

Level of Analysis

The second dimension in developing an alternative perspective on the social definition of deviance is level of analysis. This is most commonly discussed in terms of a distinction between micro and macro levels such as personality and organization. A variety of distinctions can be made along this dimension (cf. Lazarsfeld and Menzel, 1961), but a case can be made for initially keeping the discussion simple. A simple micro/macro distinction in types of variables being analyzed yields the typology in table 2.

Studies that employ micro independent variables focus on the role specific individuals or groups play in the creation of deviance. Typical micro independent variables are charismatic leaders, interest groups, and social movements. Studies that employ macro independent variables, on the other hand, emphasize characteristics of the society as a whole in accounting for social definitions of deviance. Typical macro independent variables are labor market requirements of a nation-state, collective solidarity of a community, and changes in the dominant mode of production. Dependent variables can be similarly classified. Studies that have a micro dependent variable examine the definition of a particular individual as a deviant. For example, the moral career of a mental patient or the role of social welfare agencies in increasing the recidivism of a delinquent are typical micro level problems. Studies that have macro dependent variables as their focus, however, are concerned with categories of deviance, such as mental illness or delinquency, rather than how particular individuals come to be identified as instances of the deviant category. The macro dependent variable, then, can be seen as a property of the collective.

Table 2. Typology of Definitional Studies in Terms of Levels of Analysis
in Independent and Dependent Variables

| | | Independent Variable | |
		Micro Definition	Macro Definition
	Micro definition	"The social integration of queers and peers" (Albert J. Reiss, Jr.)	*Crime and the Community* (Frank Tannenbaum)
Dependent Variable	Macro definition	"Being sane in insane places" (D. L. Rosenhan)	*Being Mentally Ill* (Thomas Scheff)
		The Child Savers (Anthony Platt)	"The triumph of benevolence: The origins of the juvenile justice system in the United States" (Anthony Platt)
		Symbolic Crusade (Joseph Gusfield)	*Wayward Puritans* (Kai Erikson)

This system of categorizing studies does not automatically lead to a preference order of modes of analysis. Tastes for micro analysis or macro analysis differ among researchers, and this scheme provides no basis for adjudicating between such tastes. Table 2 does, however, provide us with one basis for considering the relationships among the variety of diverse studies that have been conducted on the social creation of deviance. Such a comparison does suggest that it may in the future be more fruitful to recognize explicitly multiple levels of organization in studying the definition of deviance.

The following cases illustrate the utility of multiple-level explanations. The first case examines the role of moral entrepreneurs and associated groups. The next case, child abuse definitions, involves definitional changes created by a variety of professional organizations. Finally, in the third case, opiate laws, we examine the one-sided political process in which opiate use is redefined as a by-product of status groups pursuing their own economic interests.

Noninstitutionalized Actors: Redefinition by Moral Entrepreneurs and Associated Collective Agents

The general role of collective agents in the political process of altering definitions of deviance is exemplified by the gay activists in the case we examined in the previous section. We now consider, more specifically, the part played by moral entrepreneurs. Becker (1963), for example, attributes to Bureau of Narcotics chief Harry Anslinger the primary role in orchestrating passage of legislation that criminalized marihuana smoking. Recently, however, Galliher and Walker have suggested that "Anslinger's documented behavior is usual enough, and not that of a zealous, moral crusader or a power hungry bureaucrat . . . Blaming a government official for what many, including liberals, see as a ridiculous law is not unexpected, except in sociologists trained to analyze structural conditions rather than individual characteristics" (1977: 374). Although it appears now that the moral entrepreneur interpretation of the passage of the Marihuana Tax Act of 1937 is primarily mythical, careful investigation may reveal such entrepreneurial basis for other instances of criminalization. Such entrepreneurs can be viewed as agents of charismatic law giving "that constitutes the primeval revolutionary element which undermines the stability of tradition" (Weber, 1968: 761). Perhaps the clearest example of the role of moral entrepreneurs in creating social definitions of deviance is the anticommunist crusade of Joseph McCarthy, senator from Wisconsin from 1947 to 1957. Considerable debate has developed over the social and political bases of McCarthy's purge of suspected communists in the federal government. It seems clear, however, that

> one can scarcely discount his personal effectiveness as an imaginative political entrepreneur who exploited the mass media by accommodating his "exposes" to the exigencies of deadlines, and who employed the bulging briefcase, the non-existent "document," garbled figures, and so on, with stunning effect (Polsby, 1960: 263).

The social movement supporting this senator's actions is similarly important. His ability to transform definitions was based in a more general movement called McCarthyism. Parsons (1965) outlines the basic ingredients of McCarthyism by delineating its support among certain interest groups and examining the structural conduciveness in the fifties for a popular revolt against the upper classes. Although it is beyond the scope of this work to lay out the more extensive set of factors affecting the emergence and success of a typical social movement (e.g., structural conduciveness surrounding the movement, the function of public events, the ideology of the movement, its impact on movement organization, and a variety of organizational and institutional linkages), it has become readily apparent that these dimensions are essential to explaining how some social movements become institutionalized. The role of social movements in transforming social and legal definitions of deviance has been detailed by writers like Gross (1977) and Gamson (1975).

Institutionalized Actors: Redefinition by Professional Organizations

The role of professional organizations in altering definitions of deviance is exemplified by a brief synopsis of Pfohl's (1977) account of societal reaction to child abuse and of the social forces that contributed to a definition of child beating as deviant. In the interest of disciplining their children, many parents and caretakers employ forms of physical punishment such as occasional spanking, which to a certain degree is perceived as permissible. But limits are understood. Severely beating a child for troublesome toilet training, for example, is defined as deviant. Inflicting a child with bruises, welts, abrasions, lacerations, or burns goes far beyond what is deemed as proper discipline.

For centuries the intentional beating of children has been a legitimate method for achieving disciplinary, educational, or religious obedience. A tradition of legitimized violence toward children (spare the rod, spoil the child) grew out of the common-law heritage of America. Legal guardians were believed to have the right "to impose any punishment deemed necessary for the child's upbringing" (Pfohl, 1977: 311). Beaten, neglected, and delinquent children first received attention from a series of three reform movements beginning in the early nineteenth century. The House of Refuge movement, based on the concept of preventive penology rather than child protection, removed children from homes where they had been subjected to urban disorganization and poverty. They were then placed in institutions where they received a normative upbringing. The nineteenth-century movement toward institutionalization failed to differentiate between abuse and poverty and therefore inspired no social reaction against beating as a form of deviance.

Similarly, the Societies for the Prevention of Cruelty to Children and the juvenile court system as it developed in the early twentieth century failed to attach a label of deviance to abusive parents and guardians. The elements of preventive penology and institutionalization were retained as the child, rather than the caretaker, remained an object of reform. Both reform movements continued to identify child abuse with poverty and social disorganization.

The labeling of child abuse as deviance and its subsequent criminalization are recent phenomena. State legislatures did not pass statutes prohibiting the caretaker's abuse of children until 1962. As Pfohl (1977) points out, without an organized application of a label of deviance, the definition of child abuse as deviant was not due to any increase in abuse itself but was initiated by pediatric radiology.[10] John Caffey's investigation of bone injuries, skeletal trauma, and multiple fractures in young children prompted a shift in medical diagnosis away from unspecific trauma toward a diagnosis specified as misconduct and deliberate injury. Concern for beaten children dramatically increased.

> The symbolic focal point for the acceptable labeling of abuse was the 1962 publication of an article entitled "The Battered Child Syndrome" in the *Journal of the American Medical Association*. . . . It defined the deviance of its "psychopathic" perpetrators as a product of "psychiatric factors" representing "some defect in character structure" . . . evidenced by the AMA editorial, the discovery of abuse as a new "illness" reduced drastically the intraorganizational constraints on doctors' "seeing" abuse. A diagnostic category had been invented and publicized. Problems associated with perceiving parents as patients whose confidentiality must be protected were reconstructed by typifying them as patients who needed help . . . . This last statement is testimony to the power of medical nomenclature. It was evidenced by the fact that (prior to its publication) the report which coined the label "battered child syndrome" was endorsed by a Children's Bureau conference which included social workers and law enforcement officials as well as doctors. . . . The discovery of the "battered child syndrome" was facilitated by the opportunities for various pediatric radiologists to advance in medical prestige, form coalitions with other interests, and invent a professionally acceptable deviant label. The application of this label has been called the child abuse reporting movement (Pfohl, 1977: 319).

Social welfare agencies recognized abuse as an illness, and, although various law enforcement agents argued that the abuse of children was a crime and should be prosecuted, most legal scholars endorsed treatment rather than punishment of abusers (Wolkenstein, 1976).

The impact of defining child abuse as an illness is evident in two findings. Prosecution of offenders is low, having not increased since the "discovery" of child abuse, and reporting statutes have been modified so as to channel reporting toward welfare rather than law enforcement agencies.

Abuse was labeled an illness, and "the opportunity of generating a medical, rather than socio-legal label for abuse provided the radiologists and their allies with a situation in which they could both reap the rewards associated with the diagnosis and avoid the infringement of extra-medical controls" (Pfohl, 1977: 319). Thus, an opportunity for more intraorganizational prestige led pediatric radiologists (whose specialty had been devoid of most risk taking and had little involvement in life-or-death decisions) to define child abuse as deviance. They also were able to ally with the more prestigious pediatrics and psychodynamically oriented psychiatry by creating deviance from abuse. These two subfields, however, also experienced some degree of marginality in the medical profession. Their interests were advanced by joining the efforts of pediatric radiologists against the problem of child abuse. Thus, three groups within organized medicine benefited from the definition of child abuse as "sick."

Redefinition by the State

According to Matza:

> By pursuing evil and producing the appearance of good, the state reveals its abiding method — the perpetuation of its good name in the face of its own propensities for violence, conquest, and destruction. Guarded by a collective representation in which theft and violence reside in a dangerous class, morally elevated by its correctional quest, the state achieves the legitimacy of pacific intention and the appearance of legality — even if it goes to war and massively perpetrates activities it has allegedly banned from the world. But that, the reader may say, is a different matter altogether (1969: 197).

Although many statutes were enacted to control drug usage in twentieth-century America, two particular laws, the San Francisco Ordinance of 1875 and the Harrison Act of 1914, significantly contributed to the definition of the opiate user as deviant. The San Francisco Ordinance of 1875 is significant because it was the first law to legislate opium use in America. Its enactment inspired similar ordinances and laws across the country. In addition, the San Francisco Ordinance illustrates how political and economic ambitions frequently replaced concern for social welfare as the motivation for the enactment of drug laws.

The San Francisco Ordinance, prohibiting the smoking of opium in dens, was directed more against Chinese users than against the drug itself. Chinese immigrants, primarily peasants, joined the gold rush to California (see Hamilton, 1978). By the 1860s, surface gold mining had declined and successful mining soon required deeper excavation and expensive equipment. Many immigrants, unable to invest in the necessary equipment, were financially pressured to return to China. In 1867, a second wave of Chinese immigrants arrived in California, drawn primarily by railroad construction.

The period of rapid growth, labor shortages, and high wages ended with the depression of 1873. The Caucasian labor force attributed the slump to Chinese competition (see Courtney [1956] for an extensive treatment of the crises leading to a variety of anti-Chinese ordinances), and exclusion of the Chinese became the rallying cry throughout the white working class. Initially, recreational smoking of opium had aroused no public concern. Labor contractors had even offered an allowance of one-half pound of opium per month in addition to regular earnings so as to specifically attract the reputedly industrious Chinese laborers. But now the smoking of opium by the Chinese became a convenient focus for moral indignation. In 1875, the city of San Francisco adopted an ordinance prohibiting the smoking of opium in dens. Following this enactment, many Chinese were heavily fined or imprisoned as a result of unrestrained and arbitrary police raids and searches. Although the ordinance reduced the Chinese labor force in San Francisco as a result of extensive imprisonment and arrest, the labor unions who had pressed for enactment were not satisfied. At the first meeting of the Federation of Organized Trades and Labor Unions (later called the American Federation of Labor) in 1881, the Chinese Cigarmakers of California were formally condemned and a boycott of nonunion cigars was launched. Largely as a result of the American Federation of Labor's lobbying efforts, Congress enacted the Chinese Exclusion Act in 1889, barring any further Chinese immigration into the United States and effectively reducing labor competition.

The San Francisco Ordinance precipitated a nationwide trend in drug control. In 1883, Congress ratified the tariff on opium prepared for smoking; in 1887, Congress prohibited the importation of opium by Chinese persons entering America; 1890 marked the passage of a law that limited the manufacture of smoking opium to American citizens; in 1909, following the Shanghai Conference, the importation and manufacture of opium was severely restricted; by 1914, 27 states had enacted laws similar to the San Francisco Ordinance to control the use of opium.

In sum, the first opium laws were motivated by economic and political concerns rather than by a commitment to social welfare. The application of a negative label to Chinese opium smokers was the precursor of modern attitudes about opiates.

CONCLUSION

The political character of deviance is most clearly manifested when new categories of deviance are being created or old categories are being transformed. The overt political conflict between economic groups, status groups, interest groups, and professions has received much attention in the form of empirical studies of discrete historical episodes of conflict. The difficulty has been that overt conflict appears only in certain areas, most of which involve victimless crimes. An attempt to develop a theory of deviance definition by simply extrapolating from these studies is apt to be a lopsided theory of social definition of victimless crime. The attraction of victimless crimes for a political analysis—their overt political character—has the hidden consequence of obscuring the political nature of forms of deviance for which no clear historical episodes of political conflict over definitions can be found (e.g., assault, homicide).

The alternative conception of political deviance developed in this chapter and pursued in the subsequent chapters in this volume takes politicality as inherent in all forms of deviance. Briefly, deviance is socially defined and as such is created, maintained, and changed through political processes. It is essential to recognize this political character of deviance in order to understand and explain the definitional transformations that are a recurrent feature of deviance.

This position represents a change from apolitical conceptions of deviance. Early studies concentrated on explaining why particular actors engaged in certain forms of action. In recent years the major problem has become how a form of action comes to be defined as deviant or conversely redefined as normal. This change is in large measure based on a broader historical and comparative view of deviance that recognizes the variability in social definitions of deviance.[11] Such recognition comes mainly in the form of historical case studies that in themselves are mere curiosities.

1. Under the Fugitive Slave Laws of the 1850s, aiding and abetting an escaped slave was a crime. With the passage of the Fourteenth Amendment less than a decade later, slavery was itself the crime.

2. In 1800, the organization of a labor union was a crime, a conspiracy in restraint of trade. By 1940, not only were unions legal, but employers were required by law to engage in collective bargaining.

Taken together, these episodes underline the basic idea in our notion of political deviance. At one time, child abuse was normal, part of the natural rights of parents, and quite distinct from child molesting. Through a political process this conventional form of socialization became delegitimized. Inherent in the deviance, however, is a latent structure of politicality which makes possible the redefinition of the action as conventional. Just as blacks, by making certain appeals, could transform looting into political protest, child molesters or abusers have the political potential of manipulating the definitions of their behavior. The task for a sociology of deviance, then, is to examine the political processes that maintain, create, and change the definition of certain behaviors as deviant.

NOTES

1. A number of works treat the history of theories of crime and deviance. For example, Ettinger (1932) lays out the preclassical school beginning with the Egyptian utilitarian view of the individual, where deviance was seen as the result of ignorance, and progressing to the theological stand developed in the Code of Hammurabi in 1927 B.C. and then the classical Greek belief that deviance was a product of free will or conscious choice, which was capable of being misdirected by lack of harmony in the character of the individual. These stages of "development" are also elaborated in the work of Barnes and Teeters (1951) and similar work by historians of crime. For example, the influence of the English criminal justice system is carefully described by Samaha (1973). Pike in *A History of Crime in England* generally concluded from his data on migration that "the Irish incomers into our towns and countries, if not the English, Scotch, and foreign incomers also, possess, therefore, a natural disposition which leads them into a prison more frequently than the native inhabitants" (1876: 517).

2. A vivid example of this general conception is Lombroso's statement that pictures the deviant as

an atavistic being who reproduces in his person the ferocious instincts of primitive humanity and the inferior animals . . . the irresistible craving for evil for its own sake, the desire not only to extinguish life in the victim, but to mutilate the corpse, tear its flesh, and drink its blood" (1911: xiv-xv).

3. There were a few exceptions to this general apolitical development. One major departure was Bonger's work (especially Bonger, 1916 and 1936). Beginning with utopian socialists such as Fourier who argued that private property led to the emergence of the penal code because some of the masses resented the state of affairs, Bonger looked at the relationship between crime and economic conditions.

4. Many of the factors that may contribute to changes in the definition of acts or actors have been touched upon by a variety of labeling theorists. For example, Rubington and Weinberg (1978) and Cullen and Cullen (1978) discuss the methods used by the deviants, the status of the definers (labelers) and the defined, etc.; however, this paper suggests that the focus of the labeling approach has been misdirected. It has spent most of its energy on explaining the effects of a deviant label once the die has been cast, that is, on the impact of the label on the individual rather than the social creation of labels (the initial definition of deviance).

5. According to Mueller:

Books written from widely differing perspectives affirmed the stability of the socio-political arrangements. For Herbert Marcuse, society and man had become one-dimensional. In his view, coercion and repression were no longer explanations for political domination, and he argued that large segments of the population had become integrated since their language and consciousness were such that they no longer conceived of ideas and values that contradicted the established political order. For Daniel Bell, the "end of ideology" had come and, implicitly, the end of major societal conflicts. Pluralism appeared to many as a working feature of the political system which allowed for at least minimal fulfillment of the needs of all groups in society. Arnold Rose tried to demonstrate that there were indeed countervailing powers and institutions which offset the influence of the power elite described by C. Wright Mills. Others proposed that attitudes and values supportive of political institutions had been successfully transmitted in the socialization process.

From both Marcusian and [pluralist] perspectives, similarities between the interpretations of political reality by those in power and by those subjected to it could be extrapolated. Politics, as the ongoing discussion of means and ends, seemed to subside since what was meaningful for the rulers appeared meaningful for the ruled as well (1973: 150).

Mueller maintains that the politicality of the late 1960s "shattered" these perspectives. His work emphasized the emergence of political processes underlying social arrangements, and he stressed the processes of delegitimation that were becoming apparent in academic and nonacademic circles. Yet, only a few years later, the impact of the turbulent sixties is much less certain and the shattered perspectives appear to be glued together once again.

6. Concern with the moral and political character of deviance control has been pursued in various conflict and critical forms that are not included in our brief outline (cf. Taylor and Taylor, 1973; Platt, 1974; Taylor et al., 1973 and 1975; Pearson, 1978). A well-known argument contained within most of these works contends that the top-priority item in the study of deviance and crime should not be the deviations of lower-class individuals but, instead, should include broader problems of economic advantage and disadvantage, civil rights and race, etc. It should be noted that essentially this position was presented more than 35 years ago in a penetrating article by C. Wright Mills (1942). As Mill's political analyses became overshadowed by the apolitical emphasis, so may the recent surge toward a "new" political economy (cf. Miller, 1976) or conflict approach to deviance.

7. According to Bierstedt:

[One] consequence of an excessive emphasis on empiricism in contemporary sociology is that. . . . the construction of systematic sociological theory has been relegated to the writers of textbooks intended for use by introductory students . . . A similar observation can be made of no other science. (1949: 591).

Although less true of the field as a whole 30 years later, Bierstedt's observation certainly holds for contemporary literature in the sociology of law, crime, and deviance. Austin Turk's experience is not unusual.

Embarrassment provided much of the initial push that led to the writing of this book. I was embarrassed at my lack of good answers when confronted by students who wondered, somewhat irreverently, why criminology is "such a confused mishmash". . . . Some of these students were especially bothered by the "unreality" of criminological studies, by which they meant the lack of sustained attention to connections between the theories and statistics on crime, and *what they heard every day about relations among social conflicts, political maneuvers, and law violation and enforcement* (1969: vii). [Emphasis added.]

8. Chambliss (1976) has suggested that work in the area of law and social structure is now engaged in a paradigmatic struggle between advocates of the dominant functional approach and advocates of the "new" conflict school. His thoughts can be traced to Dahrendorf's (1959) contrast between the functional approach view of society as a relatively integrated whole versus the conflict school view of society as experiencing inconsistency and pervasive conflict. Following Dahrendorf and Chambliss, Hagan et al. (1977) suggest that the issue is really one of determining which acts defined as deviant emerge from consensus versus conflict. For example, Hagan et al. maintain that homosexuality has been defined as deviant via conflict (i.e., dominant groups in society have succeeded in designating homosexual acts and actors as deviant). On the other hand, they claim that assault is defined as a deviant act via consensus. Although the simplicity of this view seems compelling, it ignores the fact that these definitions change over time, the actual diversity of supposedly homogeneous acts such as homosexuality or assault, and the bases of consensus or conflict over definitions of deviance.

9. The analogy to gays is straightforward: through psychotherapy an individual homosexual may in certain instances be transformed into a "normal" heterosexual. Similarly, laborers could move up in the firm or out to the frontier.

10. The term "pediatric radiology" is something of a misnomer. Although John Caffey coined the term, the group of physicians who discovered child abuse might be more properly referred to as radiological pediatricians.

11. This variability is evidenced in a number of relatively isolated but important sets of studies tracing the development (i.e., enactment and/or enforcement) of particular laws (cf. Currie, 1968; Platt, 1969; Marx, 1974; Reasons, 1974; Conrad, 1975 and 1977; Erikson, 1976; Balbus, 1977; Scull, 1977). The more subtle role of political power and its relationship to rule making is presented at other levels of analysis by Garfinkel (1956) and Goffman (1956).

REFERENCES

"An instant cure." 1974. *Time.* April 1: 45.

Balbus, Isaac D. 1977. *The Dialectics of Legal Repression.* New Brunswick, N. J.: Transaction Books.

Barnes, Harry Elmer, and Negley K. Teeters. 1951. New Horizons in Criminology. 2nd ed. Englewood Cliffs, N.J.: Prentice-Hall.

Becker, Howard S. 1963. *Outsiders: Studies in the Sociology of Deviance.* New York: Free Press.

——. 1973. *Outsiders: Studies in the Sociology of Deviance.* 2nd ed. New York: Free Press.

Bell, Daniel. 1962. "Crime as an American way of life." In Daniel Bell. *End of Idology.* New York: Free Press.

Bergesen, Albert James. 1977. "Political witch hunts: The sacred and the subversive in cross-national perspective." *American Sociological Review* 42: 220-33.

Berk, Richard A., Harold Brackman, and Selma Lesser. 1977. *A Measure of Justice: An Empirical Study of Changes in the California Penal Code, 1955-1971.* New York: Academic Press.

Bierstedt, Robert. 1949. "A critique of empiricism in sociology." *American Sociological Review* 14: 584-92.

Black, Donald. 1976. *The Behavior of Law.* New York: Academic Press.

Blumrosen, Alfred W., 1962. "Legal process and labor law: Some observations in the relations between law and sociology." In William M. Evan (ed.). *Law and Sociology*. New York: Free Press.

Bonger, William A. 1916. *Criminality and Economic Conditions*. Boston: Little, Brown.

———. 1936. *An Introduction to Criminology*. London: Methuen.

Brecher, Edward M., and the Editors of Consumer Reports. 1972. *Licit and Illicit Drugs*. Boston: Little, Brown.

Chambliss, William. 1964. "A sociological analysis of the law of vagrancy." *Social Problems* 12: 67-77.

———. 1976. "Functional and conflict theories of crime: The heritage of Emile Durkheim and Karl Marx." In William Chambliss and Milton Mankoff (eds.). *Whose Law? What Order? A Conflict Approach to Criminology*. New York: John Wiley.

Cohen, Yehudi A. 1969. "Ends and means in political control: State organization and the punishment of adultery, incest, and violation of celibacy." *American Anthropologist* 71: 658-81.

Collins, Randall. 1975. *Conflict Sociology: Toward an Explanatory Science*. New York: Academic Press.

Conrad, Peter. 1975. "The discovery of hyperkinesis: Notes on the medicalization of deviant behavior." *Social Problems* 23: 12-21.

———. 1977. "Medicalization, etiology and hyperactivity: A reply to Whalen and Henker." *Social Problems* 24: 596-98.

Coser, Lewis. 1976. "Two methods in search of a substance." In Lewis Coser and Otto Larson (eds.). *The Uses of Controversy in Sociology*. New York: Free Press.

Courtney, William J. 1956. "San Francisco anti-Chinese ordinances, 1850-1900." Ph.D. dissertation. San Francisco: R and E Research Associates.

Cullen, Francis T., and John B. Cullen. 1978. *Toward a Paradigm of Labeling Theory*. Lincoln: University of Nebraska Studies 58.

Currie, Elliot P. 1968. "Crimes without criminals: Witchcraft and its control in Renaissance Europe." *Law and Society Review* 3: 7-32.

Dahrendorf, Ralf. 1959. *Class and Class Conflict in Industrial Society*. Stanford, Calif.: Stanford University Press.

Douglas, Mary. 1973. *Natural Symbols: Explorations in Cosmology*. New York: Vintage Books.

Durkheim, Emile. 1947. *The Elementary Forms of the Religious Life*. Glencoe, Ill.: Free Press.

———. 1964. *The Division of Labor in Society*. New York: Free Press.

Engels, Friedrich. 1961. "Socialism: Utopian and scientific." In Arthur P. Mendel (ed.). *Essential Works of Marxism*. New York: Bantam Books.

Erikson, Kai T. 1962. "Notes on the sociology of deviance." *Social Problems* 9: 307-14.

———. 1966. *Wayward Puritans: A Study in the Sociology of Deviance*. New York: John Wiley.

———. 1976. *Everything in Its Path*. New York: Simon and Schuster.

Ettinger, Clayton. 1932. *The Problem of Crime*. New York: Long and Smith.

Furner, Mary O. 1976. *On Advocacy and Objectivity*. Lexington, Ky.: University of Kentucky Press.

Galliher, John F., and Allynn Walker. 1977. "The puzzle of the social origins of the Marihuana Tax Act of 1937." *Social Problems* 24: 367-76.

Galtung, Johan. 1967. *Theory and Methods of Social Research*. New York: Columbia University Press.

Gamson, William A. 1975. *The Strategy of Social Protest*. Homewood, Ill.: Dorsey Press.

Garfinkel, Harold. 1956. "Conditions of successful degradation ceremonies." *American Journal of Sociology* 61: 420-24.

Gibbs, Jack P., and Maynard L. Erickson. 1975. "Major developments in the sociological study of deviance." In Alex Inkeles (ed.). *Annual Review of Sociology*. Vol. 1. Palo Alto, Calif.: Annual Reviews.

Giddens, Anthony. 1976. "Classical social theory and the origins of modern sociology." *American Journal of Sociology* 81: 703-29.

Goffman, Erving. 1956. "The nature of deference and demeanor." *American Anthropologist* 58: 473-502.

———. 1963. *Stigma*. Englewood Cliffs, N. J.: Prentice-Hall.

Gold, David, Clarence Lo, and Erik Wright. 1976. "Recent developments in Marxist theories." *Monthly Review* 5: 29-43 and 6: 36-41.

Gouldner, Alvin. 1973. *For Sociology: Renewal and Critique in Sociology Today*. New York: Basic Books.

Gregory, Charles O. 1958. *Labor and the Law*. New York: W. W. Norton.

Gross, Harriet Engel. 1977. "Micro and macro level implication of a sociology of virtue: The case of draft protestors to the Vietnam War." *Sociology Quarterly* 18: 319-39.

Gurr, Ted Robert. 1977. *The Politics of Crime and Conflict*. Beverly Hills Calif.: Sage.

Gusfield, Jospeh R. 1963. *Symbolic Crusade: Status Politics and the American Temperance Movement*. Urbana, Ill.: University of Illinois Press.

Habermas, Jurgen. 1975. *Legitimation Crisis*. Boston: Beacon Press.

Hagan, John, Edward T. Silva, and John H. Simpson. 1977. "Conflict and consensus in the designation of deviance." *Social Forces* 56: 320-40.

Hall, Jerome. 1935. *Theft, Law and Society*. Indianapolis: Bobbs Merrill.

Hamilton, Gary G. 1978. "Adventurism and the California gold rush." *American Journal of Sociology* 83: 1,466-90.

Hawkins, Richard, and Gary Tiedeman. 1975. *The Creation of Deviance*. Columbus, Ohio: Charles E. Merrill.

Helmer, John. 1975. *Drugs and Minority Oppression*. New York: Seabury Press.

Henslin, James M., and Paul M. Roesti. 1976. "Trends and topics in social problems 1953-1975: A content analysis and a critique." *Social Problems* 24: 54-65.

Horowitz, Irving Louis, and Martin Liebowitz. 1968. "Social deviance and political marginality: Toward a redefinition of the relation between sociology and politics." *Social Problems* 15: 280-96.

Humphreys, Laud. 1972. *Out of the Closets: The Sociology of Homosexual Liberation*. Englewood Cliffs, N. J.: Prentice-Hall.

Inverarity, James M. 1976. "Populism and lynching in the South: A test of Erikson's theory of the relationship between boundary crisis and repressive justice." *American Sociological Review* 41: 262-80.

Kaplan, John. 1978. *Criminal Justice*. Mineola, N. Y.: Foundation Press.

Kirchheimer, Otto. 1961. *Political Justice: The Use of Legal Procedure for Political Ends*. Princeton, N. J.: Princeton University Press.

Kitsuse, John I., and Aaron V. Cicourel. 1963. "A note on the uses of official statistics." *Social Problems* 11: 131-39.

Kohn, Melvin L. 1976. "Looking back: A 25-year review and appraisal of social problems research." *Social Problems* 24: 94-108.

Kuhn, Thomas S. 1970. *The Structure of Scientific Revolutions*. Chicago: University of Chicago Press.

Laing, R. D. 1967. *The Politics of Experience*. Middlesex: Penguin Books.

Larson, Magali S. 1977. *The Rise of Professionalism: A Sociological Analysis*. Berkeley, Calif.: University of California Press.

Lauderdale, Pat. 1976. "Deviance and moral boundaries." *American Sociological Review* 41: 660-76.

——, Harold Grasmick, and John P. Clark. 1978. "Corporate environments, corporate crime and deterrence." In Marvin D. Krohn and Ronald Akers (eds.). *Theories of Crime, Law, and Sanctions.* Beverly Hills, Calif.: Sage.

——, and Gerald Larson. 1978. "Marxist and 'organizational' approaches to delinquency and the sociology of law: Crucial problems in 'testing' the perspectives." (Comment on Hagan and Leon, *ASR,* August 1977.) *American Sociological Review* 43: 922-25.

——, and Steve McLaughlin. 1978. "Levels of analysis, theoretical orientations and levels of abstraction." Paper presented at the annual meeting of the American Sociological Association, Session 179, San Francisco.

Lauer, Robert H. 1976. "Defining social problems: Public and professional perspectives." *Social Problems* 24: 122-29.

Lazarsfeld, Paul, and Herbert Menzel. 1961. "On the relation between individual and collective properties." In Amitai Etzioni (ed.). *Complex Organizations.* New York: Holt, Rinehart and Winston.

Lee, John A. 1977. "Going public: A study in the sociology of homosexual liberation." *Journal of Homosexuality* 3: 49-79.

Lemert, Edwin. 1970. *Legal Action and Social Change.* Chicago: Aldine.

——. 1974. "Beyond Mead: The societal reaction to deviance." *Social Problems* 21: 457-68.

Lieberson, Stanley. 1971. "An empirical study of military-industrial linkages." *American Journal of Sociology* 77: 562-84.

Lombroso, Cesare. 1911. *Criminal Man According to the Classification of Cesare Lombroso.* New York: G. P. Putnam.

McCaghy, Charles H. 1976. *Deviant Behavior.* New York: Macmillan.

Mann, Michael. 1970. "The social cohesion of liberal democracy." *American Sociological Review* 35: 423-39.

Marx, Gary. 1974. "Thoughts on a neglected category of social movement participant: The *agent provocateur* and the informant." *American Journal of Sociology* 80: 402-42.

Marx, Karl. nd. *Capital.* Vol. 1. New York: Modern Library. (Originally published in 1867.)

——. 1950. *Marx-Engels Selected Works.* Vol. 1. London: Lawrence and Wishart.

——. 1971. *A Contribution to the Critique of Political Economy.* London: Lawrence and Wishart.

Matza, David. 1969. *Becoming Deviant.* Englewood Cliffs, N. J.: Prentice-Hall.

Merton, Robert K. 1938. "Social structure and anomie." *American Sociological Review* 3: 672-82.

——. 1968. *Social Theory and Social Structure.* New York: Free Press.

Miller, S. M. 1976. "The political economy of social problems: From the sixties to the seventies." *Social Problems* 24: 131-41.

Mills, C. Wright. 1942. "The professional ideology of social pathologists." *American Journal of Sociology* 49: 165-80.

Mintz, Beth, et al. 1976. "Problems of proof in elite research." *Social Problems* 23: 314-24.

Mueller, Claus. 1973. *The Politics of Communication.* Oxford: Oxford University Press.

Musto, David. 1973. *The American Dream: Origins of Narcotics Control.* New Haven, Conn.: Yale University Press.

Nagel, Jack H. 1975. *The Descriptive Analysis of Power.* New Haven, Conn.: Yale University Press.

Olson, Mancur. 1965. *The Logic of Collective Action.* Cambridge, Mass.: Harvard University Press.

Packer, Herbert L. 1962. "Offenses against the state." *Annals of the American Academy of Political and Social Science* 339: 77-110.

Parsons, Talcott. 1965. "Youth in the context of American society." In Eric H. Erickson (ed.). *The Challenge of Youth.* Garden City, N. Y.: Doubleday.

Pearson, Geoffrey. 1975. *The Deviant Imagination*. New York: Homes and Meier.

———. 1978. "Goths and vandals: Crime in history." *Contemporary Crises* 2: 119-39.

Pfohl, Stephen J. 1977. "The 'discovery' of child abuse." *Social Problems* 24: 310-23.

Pike, Luke O. 1876. *A History of Crime in England*. London: Smith, Elder.

Platt, Anthony. 1969. *The Child Savers*. Chicago: University of Chicago Press.

———. 1974. "The triumph of benevolence: The origins of the juvenile justice system in the United States." In Richard Quinney (ed.). *Criminal Justice in America*. Boston: Little, Brown.

Polsby, Nelson W. 1960. "Toward an explanation of McCarthyism." *Political Studies* 8: 250-64.

Quinney, Richard P. 1973. *Critique of Legal Order: Crime Control in Capitalist Society*. Boston: Little, Brown.

———. 1975. *Criminology: Analysis and Critique of Crime in America*. Boston: Little, Brown.

———. 1977. *Class, State and Crime: On the Theory and Practice of Criminal Justice*. New York: David McKay.

Reasons, Charles. 1973. "The politicizing of crime, the criminal and the criminologist." *Journal of Criminal Law and Criminology* 64: 471-77.

———. 1974. "The politics of drugs: An inquiry in the sociology of social problems." *The Sociological Quarterly* 15: 381-404.

Reiss, Albert J., Jr. 1961. "The social integration of queers and peers." *Social Problems* 9: 102-19.

Rock, Paul E. 1973. *Deviant Behavior*. London: Hutchinson University Library.

——— (ed.). 1977. *Drugs and Politics*. New Brunswick, N. J.: Transaction Books.

Rosenhan, D. L. 1973. "Being sane in insane places." *Science* 179: 150-58.

Rothman, David J. 1971. *The Discovery of the Asylum: Social Order and Disorder in the New Republic*. Boston: Little, Brown.

Rubington, Earl, and Martin S. Weinberg. 1978. *Deviance: The Interactionist Perspective*. New York: Macmillan.

Samaha, Joel. 1973. *Law and Order in Historical Perspective*. New York: Academic Press.

Schattschneider, E. E. 1960. *The Semisovereign People*. New York: Holt, Rinehart and Winston.

Scheff, Thomas J. 1966. *Being Mentally Ill: A Sociological Theory*. Chicago: Aldine.

———. 1974. "The labeling theory of mental illness." *American Sociological Review* 39: 444-52.

Scull, Andrew T. 1977. "Madness and segregative control: The rise of the insane asylum." *Social Problems* 24: 337-50.

Shepard, Jon M., and Harwin L. Voss. 1978. *Social Problems*. New York: Macmillan.

Simmel, George. 1955. *Conflict and the Web of Group-Affiliations*. Translated by Kurt H. Wolff and Reinhard Bendix. New York: Free Press.

Skura, Barry. 1976. "Constraints on a reform movement: Relationships between SSSP and ASA, 1951-1970." *Social Problems* 24: 15-32.

Spector, Malcolm. 1977. "Legitimizing homosexuality." *Society* 14: 52-56.

Srinivas, M. N. 1955. "A note on Sanskritization and Westernization." In Reinhard Bendix and Seymour M. Lipset (eds.). *Class, Status and Power*. New York: Free Press.

Stinchcombe, Arthur L. 1978. *Theoretical Methods in Social History*. New York: Academic Press.

Stoller, Robert J., et al. 1973. "A symposium: Should homosexuality be in the APA nomenclature?" *American Journal of Psychiatry* 130: 1,207-16.

Sutherland, Edwin. 1940. "White-collar criminality." *American Sociological Review* 5: 1-12.

———. 1948. "Crimes of corporations." In Albert K. Cohen, Alfred Lindesmith, and Karl

Schuessler (eds.). 1956. *The Sutherland Papers*. Bloomington, Ind.: Indiana University Press.

———. 1950. "The diffusion of sexual psychopath laws" *American Journal of Sociology* 56: 142-8.

———, and Donald R. Cressey. 1978. *Criminology*. 10th ed. Philadelphia: J. B. Lippincott. (First edition published in 1924.)

Szasz, Thomas. 1975. *Ceremonial Chemistry*. Garden City, N. Y.: Anchor Books.

Tannenbaum, Frank. 1938. *Crime and the Community*. Boston: Ginn.

Taylor, Ian, and Laurie Taylor (eds.). 1973. *Politics and Deviance*. Middlesex: Penguin Books.

Taylor, Ian, Paul Walton, and Jock Young. 1973. *The New Criminology: For a Social Theory of Deviance*. New York: Harper and Row.

———. 1975. *Critical Criminology*. London: Routledge and Kegan Paul.

Turk, Austin. 1969. *Criminality and Legal Order*. Chicago: Rand McNally.

———. 1977. "Class, conflict and criminalization." *Sociological Focus* 10: 209-20.

Weber, Max. 1958. *Protestant Ethic and the Spirit of Capitalism*. New York: Charles Scribner.

———. 1968. *Economy and Society*. Edited by Guenther Roth and Claus Wittich. New York: Bedminster Press.

Wolkenstein, Alan S. 1976. "Evolution of a program for the management of child abuse." *Social Casework* 57: 309-16.

Part I
*The Emergence of
the Politics of Deviance
in Collective Interaction
and Social Movements*

Chapter 2

Political Deviance in Courtroom Settings

Jerry Parker and *Pat Lauderdale*

INTRODUCTION

During the trial of the Chicago Seven, defense attorney Leonard Weinglass stated:

> "When Dave Dellinger and Tom Hayden and Rennie Davis, all men in the peace movement, stated shortly after the Convention, 'We have won, we have won,' Mr. Schultz attempts to indicate to you that what they were talking about is that they have won in their plans to have violence."
>
> "I submit to you that the more reasonable interpretation of that is that people in the United States have won and the peace movement has won because people stood up for a principle, they stood up for what they thought was right" (Clavir and Spitzer, 1970: 561-62).

As Weinglass's statement illustrates, varying definitions of behavior emerge in courtroom settings. This paper explores factors that affect the definition of behavior as political deviance rather than as criminal. It is primarily concerned with one element of political analysis

---

Note: Parts of this paper were prepared while the senior author was a deviance fellow supported by NIMH Training Grant #07410-16.

discussed by Lauderdale and Inverarity in the preceding chapter: how definitions of behavior as political are removed or established. We suggest that an analysis of courtroom interactions is useful in understanding change in the definition of political deviance. Our analysis of how definitions change is interactionist; it views the definition of political deviance as: (1) the problematic and negotiated outcome of a definitional process, (2) affected not only by historical conditions and location but also by the actions of participants, and (3) distinct from the hegemonic definition offered by the state and/or popular opinion.

With the emergence of the "new" criminology, a great deal of attention has been given to the political nature of deviance and renewed attention has been given to a number of well-known political trials.[1] These accounts, however, fail to explain systematically how definitions of political deviance emerge and are maintained or removed because they focus on trials that are a priori defined as political. Thus, although the trials of Angela Davis, Julius and Ethel Rosenberg, Aleksandr Solzhenitsyn, and other *cause célèbres* are now generally seen as political, the extent to which these trials have been defined as political has varied both over time and by location. If we are to understand the emergence and change of the definition of trials as political, it will be necessary to consider the generic features of the definitional process not only for those cases where the definition has been crystallized but also for those cases where no such hegemonic consensus exists.[2] For the most part, the existing literature on political trials is inadequate for this purpose.

A similar observation can be made about recent sociological attempts to deal with political deviance in terms of the motivation or behavior of supposed deviants. For example, Sternberg (1972) notes that political deviants often announce their intentions, publicly, challenging the very legitimacy of the laws and/or their application in specific situations, attempt to change the norms they are denying, lack personal gain as a goal and appeal to a higher morality, pointing out the void between professed beliefs and actual practices. (Also, see Hawkins and Tiedeman [1975].) Similarily, Barkan (1977) argues that political trials can be distinguished from "mere" criminal cases by the nature of the defendants' goals and the degree of their participation. However, these analyses move little beyond the statement that "political" goals and activist "political" participation are what make particular trials political. Though these works, as well as the literature on political trials, help lay the groundwork for an interactionist view of political deviance, they neither treat the interactions and strategies involved in the emergence of definitions of behavior as political deviance nor integrate the concept with traditional treatments of deviance. To gain a more useful conception of political deviance, we will need, as Gross (1977: 338) suggests, "to know more about how historical circumstances intertwine with subjective processes and cultural responses."[3] One step toward such a conception can be gained by an interactionist analysis of political trials as status degradation ceremonies.

TRIALS AS STATUS DEGRADATION CEREMONIES

Since a criminal trial is one of the most institutionalized and routinized settings in which competing definitions of behavior are offered, we begin by looking at those processes that structure interactions in these trials.[4] In particular, we examine criminal trials as a species of status degradation ceremony (Garfinkel, 1956).[5] Status degradation ceremony refers to "any communicative work between persons, whereby the public identity of an actor is transformed into something looked on as lower in the local scheme of social types" (Garfinkel, 1956: 421). Two of the procedural aspects of criminal trials are of interest in our consideration of trials as status degradation ceremonies. These are the adversary nature of such trials and the operation of social control mechanisms in such trials. In this country, criminal trials are defined as adversary proceedings. Two competing and variously antagonistic positions are presented, within a fixed procedural scheme, to a supposedly impartial third party (either a judge or a jury). In interactionist terms, two definitions of an antecedent situation (the crime) are developed and presented by the prosecution and the defense respectively. The jury bases its decision on the definition it believes to be more reasonable. This is, of course, an oversimplification: numerous definitions of situations are developed by both sides and the jury must operate on an amalgam of these definitions. Still, the conception of courtroom settings as arenas in which definitions of a situation are presented is useful in that it allows us to envision the process in which competing arguments are presented. Additionally, it allows us to relate definitions of the courtroom situation (i.e., remarks, gestures, or appearances made by either the prosecution or the defense) to definitions of the antecedent situation (i.e., the crime). The use of this relational ability will become apparent when we consider the second aspect of courtroom settings, the operation of social control mechanisms in such trials.

We are not concerned with the legal sanctions mobilized by the verdict of guilty (i.e., imprisonment, fines, exile, etc.) but rather with the more intangible mechanisms of social control that result from degradation. Garfinkel is quite clear that it is not simply the defendants' guilt or innocence but rather their total identities that are at stake in a status degradation ceremony. By "total identity" Garfinkel means not only persons' overt actions but also their motivational or intentional aspects. Therefore, we would suggest that the prosecution will advocate a definition of the defendant's actions that transcends one particular situation. The prosecution will attempt to prove that the accused is now, was at the time of the crime, and has always been motivated in a way that should be stigmatized. Such a strategy, which involves both act and actor, is well advised. As Lindesmith and Strauss (1949: 159) note, "Knowledge of the motivation of other people and of ourselves is needed . . . a constant necessity in social intercourse. Through such insight we are able to acquire insight into the actions of others, to identify with them and to put ourselves in their places imaginatively or to 'take their role.'" Many legal questions such as insanity defenses (Scheff, 1966) and distinctions between varying degrees of murder, hinge upon this concept of criminal intent (*mens rea*). Likewise, issues such as severity of sentence and type of treatment recommended are decided, at least partially, on the basis of imputed motivation. As Scott and Lyman (1968: 47) state, "In law a person's actions are usually distinguished according to their intent." What better way to discredit the total identity of the accused than to define his or her behavior in a number of prior situations as having been motivated by discreditable intent?

This retroactive nature of identity transformation involved in status degradation ceremonies is of considerable importance. Garfinkel reasons that it is only through this retroactive consideration that justification can be found for ritually segregating the accused from society. If it can be shown that the denounced person has, in a sense, deceived society (i.e., has portrayed his or her motivation as being other than it has always been), the full power of moral indignation may be brought to bear on the denounced. This idea of moral indignation is important because of its relationship to Erikson's (1966) concept of moral boundary. By defining situations so that the preexisting discredited intention is highlighted, the prosecution defines the accused as not merely one who has transgressed a moral boundary but rather as one who has always been outside a moral boundary. Such an argument, if believed, is a compelling basis for the idea that the accused should now be both physically and symbolically segregated.

Two definitions of political deviance could be formulated from the above considerations. Briefly stated, they are: (1) deviance is political when the intentions of the accused are *presented,* either by the prosecution or by the accused, as being political (i.e., the locus of the political nature of deviance is in the actor); and (2) deviance is political when an audience *perceives* an actor as having intentions that transgress some moral boundary for purposes of altering the political structure (i.e., the locus of political deviance is in the reaction it provokes).

Both definitions, by focusing on the defendant, fail to consider the complex processes of interaction that occur. Specifically, neither gives adequate attention to the development of conflicting definitions of situations, either at one point in time or over a period of time. Both ignore the adversary nature of courtroom proceedings as well as the retroactive identity transformation involved in status degradations. The development and interplay of a variety of definitions of situations are simply not fully treated by either of these definitions.

To treat this development and interplay of definitions adequately, as well as to give proper attention to the interactions involved, it will be necessary to consider another aspect of the trial as status degradation ceremony. This aspect is the relationship to legitimate authority that the denouncer must develop and maintain with the audience to whom the denunciation is made. Garfinkel devotes considerable attention to this aspect, and, although it is not necessary to repeat his entire argument, a brief summary may be helpful. Using a dramaturgical model, because the success of the ceremony is dependent upon presentation and perception, Garfinkel states that a successful status degradation ceremony will contain these elements:

1. Both event and perpetrator must be removed from the realm of their everyday character and be . . . placed within a scheme of preferences which show the following properties:

A. The preferences must not be for event A over event B but for event of *type* A over event of *type* B . . . .

B. The witness must appreciate the characteristics of the typed person and event by referring the type to a dialectical counterpart. . . .

2. The denouncer must so identify himself to the witnesses that during the denunciation they regard him not as a private but as a publicly known person [who makes] the dignity of the suprapersonal values of the tribe salient and accessible to views. . . .

3. The denouncer must arrange to be invested with the right to speak in the name of these ultimate values . . . [and] . . . must get himself so defined by the witnesses that they locate him as a supporter of these values. . . .
4. The denouncer [must] fix his distance from the person being denounced, . . . the witnesses must be made to experience this distance, [and] . . . the denounced person must be ritually separated from a place in the legitimate order . . . (1956: 422-23).

Notice that these conditions are essentially accomplishments of the denouncer. The denouncer must persuasively present himself or herself as being motivated by commonly accepted and legitimated values that the audience regards as its own. The denouncer must structure and define situations such that he or she is seen by the audience as one of their own, who by virtue of position has legitimate authority to speak for them. The need to establish legitimate authority to speak for an audience defines the political nature of the role of denouncer or prosecutor. The denouncer must: (1) remove both event and perpetrator from their everyday setting, (2) define situations in such a way that the total identity of the accused is transformed into a lower social type, (3) invoke widely held suprapersonal values as the motivation for the denunciation, and (4) ritually separate the denounced person from a place in the legitimate social order. But this is not sufficient: the process of status degradation and denunciation is complete only when the denouncer has established legitimate authority to speak for an audience. In law it is assumed, of course, that the prosecutor speaks for the public and the state. However, as Garfinkel's treatment of status degradation ceremonies points out, the prosecution cannot treat this as an assumption. Rather, the prosecutor's right and authority to speak for the particular audience to whom the denunciation is made *must be established* by the manner in which the courtroom situation is defined and structured. The prosecutor must establish himself or herself as a "public" person, acting as the legitimate representative of the audience.

We have stressed this need to establish legitimate authority by virtue of careful definition and presentation of situations because it is in the successful disputation of the prosecution's authority that counterdenunciations find their effectiveness. It is a fact that not all status degradation ceremonies are successful. Garfinkel's article suggests that one reason for the failure of such ceremonies is that the prosecution/denouncer fails to achieve the requisite conditions previously outlined. *However, it appears equally likely that such ceremon-*

ies might fail not owing to some error of omission on the part of the prosecution but rather because aggressive countermeasures are successfully undertaken by the defendant. What we are suggesting is that these countermeasures are themselves denunciations and that they operate upon the same principles (i.e., have the same requisite conditions) as the prosecution's denunciations. Further, since denunciations are political by virtue of the prosecution's need to establish legitimate authority to speak for a particular audience, we suggest that counterdenunciations made by the defense are political by virtue of their challenge to the legitimacy of the prosecution's authority, and the attempt of the defendant to legitimate his or her own authority to speak for the particular audience.

THEORETICAL ARGUMENT

We suggest that the definition of behavior as political deviance is a product of the counterdenunciations instituted by defendants during courtroom proceedings, not simply of the defendants' intentions and motivations. Since counterdenunciations are processes, the locus of political deviance is to be found in the interactions associated with counterdenunciations. In order to better understand these interactions, let us now turn out attention to two further questions. How have counterdenunciations traditionally been understood, and what are the requisite steps in the making of a political counterdenunciation?

With regard to the first question, we note that the process of counterdenunciation is not a new one to the field of sociology. McCorkle and Korn (1964: 520), in analyzing defensive reactions to imprisonment, speak of a strategy that they call "rejection of the rejectors." Likewise, Matza and Sykes (1957: 668), in their article on techniques of neutralization, explain the process of "condemnation of the condemners" as being one in which "the delinquent shifts the focus of attention from his own deviant acts to the motives and behaviors of those who disapprove his violations." Emerson (1969: 138), when he discusses the interactions involved in a juvenile court, defines counterdenunciation as a defensive strategy that "seeks to undermine the discrediting implications of the accusation by attacking the actions, motives and/or character of one's accuser." Although such examples are useful, they do not provide the specificity necessary either to generalize about the conditions of the communicative work or, as we are interested in, to analyze the political nature of counterdenunciation. Hence we turn to the second question, that of outlining the conditions of a political counterdenunciation. We suggest the following conditions:

1. The person making the counterdenunciation (usually either the accused or the defense attorney) must remove both the event (the denunciation) and perpetrator (the prosecution) from their everyday setting.

2. The accused must then define situations in such a way that the total identity of the prosecutor is transformed into something looked upon as lower in the local scheme of social types.

3. In transforming the total identity of the prosecutor, the accused must show that the prosecutor's motivation is private rather than public and that the prosecutor has misrepresented this motivation to the audience.

4. The accused must present situations showing that the private nature of the prosecution's motivation undermines the legitimation of the prosecution's authority.

5. Just as the prosecutor will make a denunciation in the name of widely held suprapersonal values, so must the accused make a counterdenunciation in the name of equally basic suprapersonal values.

6. The accused must make salient the fact that his or her own appeal to basic suprapersonal values confers a more legitimate authority than the prosecutor's to speak for a public audience.

It is through the fulfillment of the above conditions that the locus of political deviance is to be found. It is in the interactions involved in the accused's attempt to meet the above conditions that the political nature of supposed deviance is defined.[6]

PRESENTATION OF CASES

Having suggested that political deviance is a consequence of the interactive process of counterdenunciation and having outlined the conditions of counterdenunciation, let us now turn our attention to the application of our analytical scheme to substantive cases. The cases with which we will be concerned are those of David Henry Mitchell III; The Fort Hood Three (David Samos, James Johnson, and Dennis Mora); the Cantonsville Nine; and the Chicago Seven.[7] Material has been drawn primarily from the work of Bannan and Bannan (1974), Berrigan (1970), Clavir and Spitzer (1970), and Becker (1971).

These cases exhibit, to a greater or lesser degree, the strategies, vocabularies, and interactions involved in counterdenunciations.

They merit study as cases of political deviance because the defendants attempted, with varying degrees of effort and success, to denounce those who brought them to trial. They are presented in the hope that they will demonstrate concretely the process of counterdenunciation, clarify the conditions of counterdenunciation, and give substantive examples of the strategies and vocabularies used in cases of political deviance.

Although the defendants in these cases were tried on a variety of charges, the issue addressed in each case was the morality and/or legality of the Vietnam War. Since each case received considerable media attention (although the amount and type of coverage varied from case to case), it might be argued that it was this media coverage rather than any process of counterdenunciation that contributed to the political nature of the trials. Certainly the media brought the political nature of the trials to the attention of the public. However, we would argue that the type of media coverage these cases received was more a product of the process of political counterdenunciation.

The first case we shall consider is that of David Henry Mitchell III, who was indicted in May of 1965 for willful failure to report for induction into the armed forces in violation of the Universal Military Training and Service Act. He was subsequently arrested and came to trial before the United States District Court for the District of Connecticut in September. During both his initial and his appellate trials, Mitchell attempted to use many of the strategies implied by our conditions of political counterdenunciation.

From the prosecutor's viewpoint, Mitchell's trial hinged on a question of fact: either Mitchell had refused induction or he had not. Mitchell, on the other hand, attempted to show that he did not consider his trial to be a commonplace question of fact. Initially, he attempted to remove both event and perpetrator from their everyday setting. The following interaction between Mitchell and Judge William Timbers is demonstrative.

Judge Timbers: "You see the case, Mr. Mitchell, as far as the law is concerned, is a relatively simple case. . . ."

Mitchell: "I do not agree that the issues of my defense are clearcut and simple. . . . I think they involve many things— Nuremburg trials, international law, conventions of war crimes and torture and genocide . . ." (Bannan and Bannan, 1974: 23, 25, 26).

Notice that in making reference to the Nuremburg trials Mitchell is not only removing the event of his trial and its perpetrator from their everyday setting but also attempting to define the total identity of the prosecution as similar, by implication, to that of the defendants in the Nuremburg trials. This use of the Nuremburg principle as both a legal and a moral weapon was a common tactic of peace protesters. Mitchell's condemnation of the government (his prosecutor) is quite clear: "'I non-cooperate with my government, not because I am a pacifist or occupy a position somehow uninvolved with the world, but on the contrary because I am very involved and specifically condemn the United States for crimes against peace and humanity'" (Bannan and Bannan, 1974: 25).

Besides stating that the United States was guilty of crimes against peace and humanity, Mitchell also attempted to show that the government's motivation in bringing draft resisters to trial was other than that presented by the prosecution. It was Mitchell's position throughout his trials, as the following quotation indicates, that the government's motivation in prosecuting draft resisters was to cover up its own crimes:

> "The government helps increase the interest in the issues by prosecuting draft refusers. Our job is to utilize every threat, FBI visit, court fight, or jailing as a means of following through on our prosecution of militarism and the real criminal. When the government acts and creates publicity on the issue, we must use every means to make sure that they end up with burnt fingers and a kick in the behind" (Bannan and Bannan, 1974: 27).

Having attempted to fulfill the first three conditions of a political counterdenunciation (i.e., removing the trial from its everyday setting, transforming the identity of the prosecution, and impugning the motivation of the prosecution), Mitchell attempted, in his second trial, to invoke the suprapersonal value of responsibility to an individual moral code (see Gross [1977: 333] for further elaboration of the origins of this individualistic moral code):

> "I was obliged and had a duty and responsibility, not just morally, but also legally, because of the Nuremburg judgment, which laid down principles of individual responsibility and guilt, which transcend those of a nation, to refuse to cooperate with the draft which was engaged in, as the major instrument for securing manpower for various criminal activities around the world, notably Vietnam, where we were stepping up activity there in behalf of Diem at that time" (Bannan and Bannan, 1974: 32).

Mitchell's view of his motivation contrasts sharply with his view of the motivation of the "real criminal" illustrated in the previous quotation. This was, however, the only significant attempt made to present situations in such a way that the private nature of the government's motivation would undermine the prosecution's legitimacy. Mitchell did not attempt to develop fully his own legitimate authority to speak for a public by his appeal to suprapersonal values. Still, certain elements of a political counterdenunciation were present in the Mitchell case.

Such elements are also present in the case of the Fort Hood Three. The Fort Hood Three (David Samos, James Johnson, and Dennis Mora) were ordered to duty in Vietnam in June 1966. The three men were, at that time, privates in the United States Army and were accorded a customary month's leave. In late June 1966 the three soldiers held a news conference at which they stated their opposition to the war in Vietnam. Since Mora was tried first and every argument used in his trial was later used in the trials of Samos and Johnson, we concentrate our attention on his trial.

That Mora's attorney, Stanley Faulkner, attempted to remove the trial from its everyday setting is quite evident. Faulkner attempted to have the case tried in a civilian court and, failing that, attempted to introduce into the criminal trial the question of the legality of the Vietnam War and to challenge the impartiality of the trial officer (the judge). While none of these attempts was successful, they illustrate actions to remove both event (a court-martial) and prosecutor (the army) from their everyday settings.

Certain attempts were also made by the defense to transform the identity of the prosecution. This was partially attempted in the defense's questioning of the legality of the Vietnam War. The more crucial attempt at redefinition of the prosecution's identity came in the argument that the army had ordered Mora to Vietnam as a means of entrapment. The entrapment defense rested upon a peculiar military procedural rule that states: "'Disobedience of an order, ... which is given for the sole purpose of increasing the penalty for an offense which it is expected that the accused may commit, is not punishable under this article'" (Bannan and Bannan, 1974: 70). It was the defense's argument that, based on previous statements made by Private Mora, the army knew he would disobey any order to be transferred to Vietnam. The defense maintained that if Private Mora were to be charged at all it should be with violation of Article 134 of the Uniform Code of Military Justice, which forbids "'uttering disloyal statements with intent to cause disaffection and disloyalty among the civilian population and members of the military forces'" (Bannan and Bannan, 1974: 71). But in fact Private Mora was charged with willfully disobeying an order to travel to a site to embark for Vietnam. The defense contended that this order was given only to ensure that Private Mora would receive harsher punishment and therefore constituted a scheme of entrapment. As Faulkner stated, "'The Department of the Army proceeded to invoke the order to go to Vietnam, knowing that it would not be obeyed, only for the purpose of imposing the greatest penalty that could have been imposed'" (Bannan and Bannan, 1974: 67). Although the judge ruled that issuance of the order did not constitute entrapment, the depiction of the army as a vindictive force attempting to entrap a soldier represents one tactic intended to transform the identity of the prosecution.

It is interesting that the defense did not call into question the private nature of the prosecution's motivation. Two reasons for this can be suggested. First, to impugn the motivation of army personnel in an army court-martial may have been thought an unprofitable courtroom tactic. Second, and perhaps more likely, it may not have been the case that the prosecution's motivation was seen as private, in the typical sense of that word. That the army's motivation was the protection of its system of discipline, and hence its own self-interest, was assumed from the beginning of the trial. The private motivation in this case, then, was that of a corporate body rather than that of an individual or small group of persons. This, coupled with the fact that the trial took place within the peculiar legal system of that group, may have made the question of private motivation a moot one. Hence, it is not surprising that no attempt was made to undermine the legitimate authority of the prosecution by reference to this private corporate motivation. Still, in applying our analytical scheme, we must note that in this particular trial no such attempt was made to meet the fourth condition.

Turning to our fifth condition, that of the accused's use of suprapersonal values, the record indicates that the defendant's actions both prior to arrest and during the trial provide examples of this. At the time of their well-publicized statement regarding their intentions about going to Vietnam the defendants appealed to the suprapersonal values of justice and morality: "'We have made our decision. We will not be part of this unjust, immoral, and illegal war. We want no part of a war of extermination. We oppose the criminal waste of American lives and resources. We refuse to go to Vietnam!!!'" (Bannan and Bannan, 1974: 64). In the case of Private Mora, an additional suprapersonal value, that of individual responsibility, was introduced during the trial. Speaking of his moral commitment against the war, Private Mora stated, "'I believe to act contrary to what you know is right is to die a little. . . . If a man is without a moral code he is like the sea without water. That is the only way I know how to act'" (Bannan and Bannan, 1974: 74).

It is interesting to note that with this statement of suprapersonal values Mora's use of the strategies outlined in our conditions comes to an end. Little attempt seems to have been made to undermine the legitimation of the prosecution. Additionally, there was no attempt to amplify the legitimation of the accused suprapersonal values. In the initial trial this may have been due to the context, which was that of a military court-martial rather than a civilian criminal trial. In appellate courts such issues were never raised because they did not constitute grounds upon which an appeal could be made.

The next case with which we will be concerned is that of the Cantonsville Nine. This case has been discussed by both Berrigan (1970) and Bannan and Bannan (1974), and it is from their discussions that our material will be drawn. The Cantonsville Nine (Daniel Berrigan, Philip Berrigan, Thomas Lewis, David Darst, Marjorie and Thomas Melville, John Hoga, George Mische, and Mary Moylan) were charged on four federal felony counts. The charges were: (1) damaging the property of the United States, (2) unlawfully obliterating records of the Selective Service System, (3) interfering with the administration of the Selective Service System, and (4) conspiring to commit the infractions in the first three counts. The charges resulted from actions taken by the defendants on May 17, 1968, at Local Draft Board Number 33, Cantonsville, Maryland. The actions involved the taking, by force and without authorization, and burning, with a crude form of napalm, of 378 draft files. The defendants were arrested at the time of their actions and brought to trial before Judge Roszel C. Thomsen, chief judge in the United States District Court for the District of Maryland, on October 4, 1968. The defendants were represented by attorneys William Kunstler, Harold Buchman, Harrop Freeman, and William C. Cunningham. The prosecution was headed by Arthur Murphy and Barnet Skolnik, assistant United States attorneys for the district.

Even before the trial began, it appeared that neither the defense nor the prosecution would consider this an ordinary trial. The prosecuting attorneys, Murphy and Skolnik, were selected because of their minority status. In a trial in which the role of the state as a mechanism of social control was certain to be a key issue, who better to represent the state than a black and a Jew, the historic victims of state repression? Although the previous cases exhibited dramaturgical presentations on the part of the defense, in this case both sides appear to have made symbolic attempts to redefine the courtroom situation. The defense began their pretrial definition by inviting a large number of prominent supporters such as Bishop James Pike, Noam Chomsky, Harvey Cox, and Gordon Zahn, who participated in demonstrations and street theater shows outside the court building.

In the opening portions of the trial it became increasingly clear that neither the defense nor the prosecution would opt for a "normal" trial. The prosecution's case was opened by Murphy, who clearly stated that this was not the usual type of criminal case because of its ramifications (Bannan and Bannan, 1974: 129). For the defense's part, three actions best represent its view of the trial as atypical. First, the defense refused both to participate in jury selection and to challenge any members of the jury. Although the *stated* reasons for this were a lack of faith in the jury selection process and a desire for a speedy trial, the *symbolic* aspect of this attempt to define the trial as a nonevent cannot be overlooked. Second, the defense asserted that not only had the defendants committed the acts of which they stood accused but "they are proud of it, and they think it is one of the shining moments in their personal lives" (Bannan and Bannan, 1974: 129). The implication here was that the facts of the case were not in question but rather that the authority of the court to construe those facts as criminal was the crucial issue of the trial. Third, Kunstler's reply to Murphy's statement about the usual trial is instructive. Murphy, while he had said this was not a usual trial, later showed that he intended to try it as if it were. Kunstler's analogy of the trials of Socrates and Jesus as other trials that had been treated as normal by prosecutors further illustrates the defense's attempt to remove the trial and prosecution from their everyday setting.

Having to a degree redefined the trial situation as somehow out of the ordinary (much more so than the previous cases that have been presented), the defense then began to transform the identity of the prosecution, in this case the state. This was primarily done by citing instances of atrocities. David Darst, speaking of the reasons for his protest, is an example of this: "'First of all to raise a cry, an outcry at what was clearly a crime, an unnecessary suffering, a clear and wanton slaughter'" (Berrigan, 1970: 34). Thomas Lewis's statement is equally an attempt to transform the identity of the state: "'We have representatives in Vietnam who are doing terrible things in our name. We were saying to the military, this is wrong. This is immoral. This is illegal.'" (Berrigan, 1970: 42). Intermingled with these at-

tempts to redefine the identity of the prosecution were other attempts to show that the motivation for the war, and hence the motivation for the prosecution of those who opposed it, was private rather than public. That is, the defendants attempted to show that it was
not the American public who supported the war and their persecu-
tion but rather a small group of persons who held a private profit
motive. Thomas Lewis's response to a question about those who
opposed his view of the war is instructive: "'What do these people
represent? Such people are defending their personal interests. They
are gaining from the war. They are an elite minority who are very
wealthy'" (Berrigan, 1970: 46). While defendant Lewis was perhaps
the most vocal on this issue, the positions of the other defendants
were essentially similar to his. A small private elite sought both the
continuation of the war and the defendants' prosecution.

An ancillary strategy was to undermine the legitimacy of the
state's authority by pointing out the inaccessibility of certain leaders.
Summarizing the defendants' attempts to contact certain national
leaders, Philip Berrigan stated: "'The military were immune from
any citizen influence. They were a law unto themselves'" (Berrigan,
1970: 26).

This is not, it should be pointed out, strictly the strategy that our
analytical scheme would suggest. That is, the defendants did not
directly suggest that the private motivation of the prosecution undermined the legitimation of their authority. In fact, the defense seems
to have regarded the prosecutors and others directly involved in the
trial as little more than puppets. They identified their adversary not
as those in the court but rather those "in whose manicured hands the
power of the land lies" (Berrigan, 1970: 30). Hence, it was their
strategy not to attack the prosecutors or the judge but rather to pro-
selytize them. Philip Berrigan's statement at the close of his direct
examination is typical: "'To the prosecution we say, "Refuse to in-
dict opponents of the war, prefer to resign, practice in private." To
federal judges we say, "Give anti-war people suspended sentences to
work for justice and peace or resign your posts"'" (Berrigan, 1970:
31).

It is, of course, impossible to predict how the outcome of the
trial would have changed if a direct attack had been made on the
prosecution's motivation. We note only that it is with regard to the
fourth condition that the trial of the Cantonsville Nine least con-
forms to our analytical scheme.

Having examined how the defense attempted to redefine the
courtroom situation from one of criminal court to one of moral

court and attempted to transform the identity and motivation of the state as prosecutor, we may also see that attempts were made by the defendants to speak to an alternative set of suprapersonal values. Foremost among these, perhaps due to the visible Catholic association of the defendants, was an emphasis on Christian suprapersonal values. Almost to a person the defendants cited some Christian ethic in explanation of their motives. Thomas Lewis's statement is indicative: "'I came to the conclusion that the war is totally outrageous from the Christian point of view'" (Berrigan, 1970: 40). Similar are the statements of Daniel Berrigan: "'If my religious belief is not accepted as a substantial part of my action, then the action is eviscerated of all meaning...'" (Berrigan, 1970: 83) and David Darst: "'My thinking is part of an ethic found in the New Testament. You could say that Jesus too was guilty of assault and battery when he cast the money changers out of the temple...'" (Berrigan, 1970: 36).

Another suprapersonal value, closely related to strictly Christian ethics, was a concern for the poor and the disadvantaged. All the defendants deplored the waste of resources on warfare when certain basic needs were not met for a share of the world's people. As David Darst states in describing his intention:

> [Our act was] "an outcry against the fact that our country can spend eighty billions a year chasing imaginary enemies around the world. .... I saw many little children who did not have enough to eat. This is an astonishing thing that our country cannot command the energy to give bread and milk to children. Yet it can rain fire and death on people ten thousand miles away" (Berrigan, 1970: 36).

In stating their belief in certain widely held suprapersonal values, the defendants were clearly seeking to establish their authority to speak for a larger segment of the population, to demonstrate that it is they, not the elected and appointed leaders, who have a legitimate authority to speak for the American people.

Philip Berrigan's appeal to the "American democratic tradition" can be seen as an attempt to fulfill our final condition—that of making salient the defendants' appeal to suprapersonal values that legitimate their authority to speak for a public audience:

> "I came to the conclusion that I was in direct line with American democratic tradition in choosing civil disobedience in a serious fashion. There have been times in our history when in order to get redress, in order to get a voice vox populi arising from the roots people have so acted ... we have a rich tradition of civil disobedience" (Berrigan, 1970: 28-29).

The statements of Thomas Lewis can be taken in the same vein: "'We were speaking as Americans. We were proud to be Americans'" (Berrigan, 1970: 42) and "'I then moved into civil disobedience. This is a legitimate form of social protest. It is well documented in Christianity. Civil disobedience was practiced by the early Christians'" (Berrigan, 1970: 43).

Similar statements were made by other defendants, but these need not be repeated here. We suggest that such statements are intended, by their appeal to American and Christian traditions, to legitimate the authority of the accused. They are verbal behaviors intended to define situations so that the defendants are viewed not as variants from certain traditions but as adherents to basic suprapersonal values already legitimated.

In the cases reviewed to this point, none of the defendants used all of the conditions of political counterdenunciation. In our final case, however, that of the Chicago Seven, each of the conditions is met.

Little attention needs to be given to the background of this case, it being one of the most publicized "political" trials of the era. However, let us recall a few pertinent facts to better understand the context of the trial. The conspiracy trial of the Chicago Seven (David Dellinger, Bobby Seale, Jerry Rubin, Rennie Davis, Abbie Hoffman, Tom Hayden, and Lee Weiner) was marked by several unusual features and is of special significance because of the presence of these special features. The defendants were some of the best-known protesters and antiwar activists in the country. The supporting witnesses for the defense were well-known intellectuals. The trial was a conspiracy trial, implying a difficult prosecution on a law of questionable constitutional virtue. The prosecution witnesses were almost exclusively police officers on the Chicago force or appointed officials of the city of Chicago. The presiding judge was considered one of the most reactionary on the federal bench. Aside from these concrete features, several more symbolic features were embodied in the trial. For the ideologies represented by both the prosecution and the defense, the trial was something of a last stand. It was the last major antiwar trial and the culmination of a decade of protest. Additionally this trial was the first that revolved around events integrally related to the electoral political process (the 1968 Democratic National Convention).

The defendants and their agents took several measures to further remove both the event and prosecution from the everyday setting of a criminal trial. First among these, and setting the hostile tone of the relationship between the judge and the defendants at the very outset of the trial, was an attempt to remove the assigned judge before the proceedings even began. Second, the conduct of the defendants during the opening statements of prosecutor Schultz (Tom Hayden raised a clenched fist, and Abbie Hoffman threw kisses at the jury) was intended to convey a definition of the trial as quite at odds with the accepted order of a judicial event. Numerous instances later in the trial—the use of costumes (black robes and Santa Claus suits), guerilla theater performances in the streets, press conferences held during the trial proceedings, open refusal to abide by court procedural rules—further demonstrate a serious strategy of removing the trial and the act of prosecution from their everyday setting.

In removing the trial and the prosecution from its everyday setting the defendants intended to show that they considered the trial and prosecution not only unusual but also unjust and illegitimate, lower in a scheme of social types. This they did by attacking the identity and motivation of the prosecution, suggesting that it was they (or their superiors) who were in fact the criminals. Defense attorney William Kunstler's opening statement to the jury is most eloquent on this point.

Mr. Kunstler:	"We hope to prove before you that the prosecution which you are hearing is the result of two motives on the part of the Government. . . ."
Mr. Schultz:	"Objection as to any motives of the prosecution, if the Court please."
Judge Hoffman:	"I sustain the objection. You may speak of the guilt or innocence of your clients, not to the motive of the Government" (Clavir and Spitzer, 1970: 15).

Having been overruled on this point, Kunstler continued with a somewhat veiled attack on the government's (prosecution's) identity and motivation.

"The evidence will show that there were forces in this city and in the national government who were absolutely determined to prevent this type of protest, who had reached a conclusion that such a protest had to be stopped by all means necessary, including the physical violence perpetrated on demonstrators. . . . The defense will show that the real conspiracy in this case is the conspiracy to curtail and prevent the demonstrations against the war in Vietnam and related issues. The real conspiracy was against these defendants" (Clavir and Spitzer, 1970: 16).

Having at least covertly introduced the idea that the prosecution's identity was not that of a servant of the public but that of a conspiratorial agent engaged in the suppression of accepted rights of protest, the defense attorneys proceeded to question the source of that identity. The defense strategy here was to show that the motivation (and hence the identity) of the prosecution was not public (i.e., not for the people of Chicago or the nation) but private (i.e., for selected officials who controlled the futures of many of the prosecution agents). This aspect of the defense strategy comes across most clearly in the cross-examinations of prosecution witnesses made by attorneys Kunstler and Weinglass.

Mr. Kunstler: "And would it be a fair statement to say that you are sort of a protege of the mayor?"

Mr. Raymond Simon, Corporation Counsel of the City of Chicago: ". . . I worked under the mayor's tutelage, sure. I think I would be proud to be considered that, Mr. Counselor, if that is the point you are making, yes."

Mr. Kunstler: "That is exactly the point I am making, Mr. Simon. You are very fond of the mayor, is that correct?"

Mr. Simon: "Yes, that is correct,"

Mr. Foran, Prosecuting Attorney: "Your Honor, I object. I don't know why I should have to keep getting up to object."

Judge Hoffman: "I think it is inappropriate since there is an objection. I am not here to determine a witness' affection for the mayor of the city. What has that got to do with the charges here?"

Mr. Kunstler: "Your Honor, it goes to his credibility. The mayor is, in our opinion, a party here, and that goes to his credibility" (Clavir and Spitzer, 1970: 31).

Similar statements were asked of David Stahl, the mayor's administrative assistant, by defense attorney Weinglass. Complete questioning along this line was in all cases overruled by the court. Nevertheless, in questioning city administrators, police officers, and undercover agents of the FBI, the defense made progress in showing that the motivation of the prosecution (and the events that led to the prosecution) were part of a somewhat systematic effort to find something, at times almost anything, on which to prosecute specific defendants.

One important point brought out by such lines of questioning was the extensive surveillance of the defendants and the extent to which both local and national agencies had been mobilized against the demonstrators at Chicago. This was perhaps the first antiwar trial at which the use of paid informants and *agents provocateurs* was so freely admitted by the government. Such tactics, when used so extensively and with such apparent lack of control, had a definite effect on the legitimate authority of the government and the prosecution. Not only was this effect felt generally in the media, but more important it was felt by members of the jury. Remembering these events, one juror, at the conclusion of the trial, stated, "For the first time in my life I was afraid of my government" (Clavir and Spitzer, 1970: xi). The hidden and private nature of the testimony given by prosecution witnesses certainly undermined the legitimate authority of the prosecution, as did the courtroom demeanor of Judge Hoffman. The defense actually had to do very little to meet the fourth condition.

While the work of transforming the nature of the trial and prosecution and undermining the legitimate authority of the prosecution (and the state) was largely done for the defendants, they did go to some lengths to legitimate their own authority by appealing to suprapersonal values. Most notable were their appeals to constitutional guarantees of right of assemblage, speech, and dissent. In his opening remarks to the jury, Kunstler noted that the defendants and the unindicted demonstrators "came to Chicago in the summer of 1968 to protest in the finest American tradition the National Convention of the party in power. They organized to do so. They were conscious of their rights as citizens to so demonstrate . . ." (Clavir and Spitzer, 1970: 96).

Similarly, the testimony of defendant Abbie Hoffman describing his speech at the Coliseum during the week of the convention reveals an appeal to basic suprapersonal values.

". . . 'that we were a new generation that was growing in a free society in America. We are the vision of the founding fathers of this country,' I said. 'When you march to the amphitheater tomorrow, you should keep in mind a quote from a two-thousand year old Yippie with long hair named Jesus who said that when you march into the den of the wolves you should be as harmless as doves and as cunning as snakes'" (Clavir and Spitzer, 1970: 359).

Such appeals to suprapersonal values were certainly intended to portray the defendants as persons who, by virtue of their allegiance to principles already legitimated (and in contrast to the prosecution's use of questionable surveillance and entrapment tactics), had a basic right to speak for the audience. This is most clearly pointed out by attorney Weinglass's summation to the jury:

"This was the time when Americans in large numbers had a moral permit, and they were exercising their moral permit, but that does not mean a violent permit. Civil disobedience can be nonviolent. It can be people who, because of their feeling of the law, without wanting violence, wanting to exercise their higher right of exercising their moral indignation, but not wanting to attack the police" (Clavir and Spitzer, 1970: 560).

Later in the summation Weinglass again returned to the idea that adherence to certain suprapersonal values gives a legitimated authority to speak for an audience. In relating Clarrence Darrow's remark about President Lincoln's opposition to the Mexican American War, Weinglass stated:

"It seems to me that if the lesson of the country teaches anything, it is that the true patriots are the people who take a position on principle and hold to it, and if there are people in this country who feel that the people in Vietnam are not our enemies, but another part of the humanity of this planet against whom this country is transgressing, and they take action, peaceful action, to protest this feeling, like Abe Lincoln did 120 years ago, there is nothing terribly unpatriotic about it, and rather to derive from hatred of their country, it seems to me to derive from love of country. . . ."

"When Dave Dellinger and Tom Hayden and Rennie Davis, all men in the peace movement, stated shortly after the Convention, 'We have won, we have won,' Mr. Schultz attempts to indicate to you that what they were talking about is that they have won in their plans to have violence.

"I submit to you that the more reasonable interpretation of that is that people in the United States have won and the peace movement has won because people stood up for a principle, they stood up for what they thought was right" (Clavir and Spitzer, 1970: 561-62).

We see that, in this trial, all of the elements of the analytical scheme were brought into play. Both event and prosecutor were removed from their everyday setting. The identity of the prosecution was transformed and the private and almost conspiratorial nature of the prosecution's motivation was shown. These attempts were the basis of the defense's challenge to the prosecution's authority as well as a convenient device to establish the accused's moral authority. Further, the accused made great use of certain suprapersonal values as the basis for their appeal for legitimate authority to speak for the American public.

CONCLUSION

Gross (1977: 337) suggests that we need to understand "how the type of deviance and historical circumstances interact to alter response to deviants." Conceptualizing the interactions between antiwar defendants and prosecutorial others as one determinant of the type of deviance, we have suggested that one alteration in response to deviants is a change in the definition of their behavior from that of being simply criminal to that of being politically deviant. The change in this response is dependent both upon the facility with which actors are able to engage in counterdenunciations and the presence or emergence of a broader context of social movements that facilitates counterdenunciations by supplying legitimation for actors.

In dealing with antiwar trials during a particular historical period we have dealt only with situations in which the context for counterdenunciations is somewhat crystallized and the efficacy of defendants in facilitating such interactions is well developed. A remaining question is the responses that may be made to virtuous deviance when collective action is more diffuse and social movement support for such action less crystallized. Analysis of such situations suggests interesting possibilities for further integration of research in social movements, political sociology, and media sociology with the area of deviance.[8]

NOTES

1. While the political situation of the 1960s greatly increased the number of accounts of political trials, numerous works existed prior to that time. Among these are Ginger (1958), Grebstein (1960), Halasz (1955), and Kirchheimer (1961). Later works relevant to political trials include Aptheker (1975), Davis (1974), and Major (1973) concerning the trial of Angela Davis; Berrigan (1970), Bannan and Bannan (1974), Casey (1971), Clavir and Spitzer (1970), Epstein (1970), Freed (1973), Lukas (1970), Mitford (1969), and Schrag (1974) concerning various antiwar trials; as well as the diffuse works on other political trials, Becker (1971), Brumbaugh (1969), Carter (1969), Davies (1970), Ehrmann (1969), Feuerlicht (1977), Morris (1967), Nizer (1973), Raines (1974), Russell (1971), Solzhenitsyn (1973), and Zimroth (1974). In addition, the political nature of deviance was being pursued in a variety of sociological works, including Horowitz and Liebowitz (1968), Rock (1973), Taylor and Taylor (1973), and Taylor et al. (1973).

2. We note that consensus about whether or not a particular trial is political is almost never complete and varies considerably with historical conditions and location. For example, the trial of Julius and Ethel Rosenberg was probably not seen as political by the majority of persons in this country at the time of its ajudication. However, in other countries the trial was defined as being political. Similar observations can be made for a number of trials that have only recently been popularly defined as political (e.g., Scottsboro, Sacco and Vanzetti, etc.). Likewise, a number of trials that have to some extent been seen as political in this country (e.g., Solzhenitsyn, Biko, and Schransky) have not been defined as political elsewhere.

3. While Gross (1977) is primarily interested in developing a "sociology of virtuous deviance," her emphasis upon both micro and macro level implications and her suggestion that differing degrees of virtue (as exhibited by draft refusers versus resisters) may have an effect on the permeability of moral boundaries suggests a potential interface between interactionist social psychology and a political consideration of deviance.

4. This approach differs somewhat from the majority of previous works on both American and other political trials. Previous research on political trials has tended to be concerned with factors that affect the disposition of cases commonsensically defined as political. We are primarily concerned with the processes and interactions that lead to the definition of a trial as political.

5. Garfinkel notes that the types of interactions in which he is interested occur in a variety of settings. However, he further notes that in our society "the court and its officers have something like a fair monopoly over such [status degradation] ceremonies, and there they have become an occupational routine" (1956: 424).

6. Lauderdale (1976) suggests that political deviance may occur independently of the actions of actors in status degradation ceremonies. That is, he suggests that the inability of the actors to recognize and/or articulate the political nature of their actions does not necessarily exclude them and their acts from the political arena. He maintains that "traditional" forms of deviance such as theft, homicide, or juvenile delinquency should not necessarily be isolated from the prevailing view of political deviance. The process of creating the definition of deviance and its routinization are the key elements in Lauderdale's analysis. In addition, his analysis illustrates the power of elites or the state in defining actors or actions as politically deviant (cf. Thio [1978] for a similar view of deviance).

7. The cases selected do not represent an attempt to verify the analytical scheme presented. Rather, they have been chosen because they show that all elements of the analytic scheme were not present in early resistance trials, hence allowing at least a suggestion that the strategy of resistance trials (and its attendant consequences for the definition of political deviance) developed over time. While cases that dealt with issues other than the Vietnam War could just as well be used as examples, we have omitted consideration of these here.

8. The authors would like to thank James Inverarity, Rhoda Estep, Kai Erikson, Harold Finestone, and Howard Becker for their comments and suggestions on earlier versions of this paper.

REFERENCES

Antonio, Robert J. 1972. "The processual dimension of degradation ceremonies: The Chicago conspiracy trial: Success or failure?" *British Journal of Sociology* 34: 287-97.

Aptheker, Bettina. 1975. *The Morning Breaks: The Trial of Angela Davis.* New York: International.

Bannan, John F., and Rosemary S. Bannan. 1974. *Law, Morality and Vietnam.* Bloomington, Ind.: Indiana University Press.

Barkan, Steven E. 1977. "Political trials and the pro se defendant in the adversary system."

Becker, Theodore L. (ed.). 1971. *Political Trials.* New York: Bobbs-Merrill.

Berrigan, Daniel. 1970. *The Trial of the Cantonsville Nine.* Boston: Beacon Press.

Brumbaugh, Robert S. (ed.). 1969. *Six Trials.* New York: Thomas Y. Crowell.

Carter, Dan T. 1969. *Scottsboro: A Tragedy of the American South.* Baton Rouge, La.: Louisiana State University Press.

Casey, William Van Etten. 1971. *The Berrigans.* New York: Avon Books.

Clavir, Judy, and John Spitzer (eds.). 1970. *The Conspiracy Trial.* New York: Bobbs-Merrill.

Davies, Rosemary Reeves. 1970. *The Rosenbluth Case: Federal Justice on Trial.* Ames, Iowa: Iowa State University Press.

Davis, Angela. 1974. *An Autobiography.* New York: Random House.

Davis, Nanette J. 1975. *Sociological Constructions of Deviance.* Dubuque, Iowa; William C. Brown.

Ehrmann, Herbert B. 1969. *The Case That Will Not Die:* Commonwealth *vs.* Sacco and Vanzetti. Boston: Little, Brown.

Emerson, Robert M. 1969. *Judging Delinquents.* Chicago: Aldine.

Epstein, Jason. 1970. *The Great Conspiracy Trial.* New York: Random House.

Erikson, Kai T. 1966. *Wayward Puritans: A Study in the Sociology of Deviance.* New York: John Wiley.

Feuerlicht, Roberta Strauss. 1977. *Justice Crucified: The Story of Sacco and Vanzetti.* New York: McGraw-Hill.

Freed, Donald. 1973. *Agony in New Haven.* New York: Simon and Schuster.

Garfinkel, Harold. 1956. "Conditions of successful degradation ceremonies." *American Journal of Sociology* 61: 420-24.

Ginger, Raymond. 1958. *Six Days or Forever?* Tennessee *v.* John Thomas Scopes. Boston: Beacon Press.

Grebstein, Sheldon N. (ed.). 1960. *Monkey Trial:* The State of Tennessee *vs.* John Thomas Scopes. Boston: Houghton Mifflin.

Gross, Harriet Engel. 1977. "Micro and macro level implications of a sociology of virtue: The case of draft protestors to the Vietnam War." *Sociological Quarterly* 18: 319-39.

Halasz, Nicholas. 1955. *Captain Dreyfus.* New York: Simon and Schuster.

Hawkins, Richard, and Gary Tiedeman. 1975. *The Creation of Deviance.* Columbus, Ohio: Charles E. Merrill.

Horowitz, Irving Louis, and Martin Liebowitz. 1968. "Social deviance and political marginality: Toward a redefinition of the relation between sociology and politics." *Social Problems* 15: 280-96.

Kirchheimer, Otto. 1961. *Political Justice: The Use of Legal Procedure for Political Ends.* Princeton, N.J.: Princeton University Press.

Lauderdale, Pat. 1976. "Political deviance: A reconsideration of standard approaches to deviance." Unpublished paper. Minneapolis: University of Minnesota.

Lindesmith, Alfred, and Anselm Strauss. 1949. *Social Psychology.* New York: Holt, Rinehart and Winston.

Lukas, Anthony. 1970. *The Barnyard Epithet and Other Obsenities: Notes on the Chicago Conspiracy Trial.* New York: Harper and Row.

McCorkle, Lloyd W., and Richard Korn. 1964. "Resocialization within Walls." In David Dressler (ed.). *Readings in Criminology and Penology.* New York: Columbia University Press.

Major, Reginald. 1973. *Justice in the Round: The Trial of Angela Davis.* New York: Third Press.

Marx, Gary. 1974. "Thoughts on a neglected category of social movement participant: The *agent provocateur* and the informant." *American Journal of Sociology* 80: 402-42.

Matza, David, and Gresham M. Sykes. 1957. "Techniques of neutralization: A theory of delinquency." *American Sociological Review* 22: 664-70.

Merton, Robert K. 1968. *Social Theory and Social Structure.* New York: Free Press.

Mitford, Jessica. 1969. *The Trial of Dr. Spock.* New York: Alfred A. Knopf.

Morris, Richard B. 1967. *Fair Trial: Fourteen Who Stood Accused from Anne Hutchinson to Alger Hiss.* New York: Harper and Row.

Nizer, Louis. 1973. *The Implosion Conspiracy.* Garden City, N.Y.; Doubleday.

O'Brien, Francis W. 1971. *Was Justice Done?* Rockford, Ill.: Rockford College Press.

Raines, John C. 1974. *Conspiracy: The Implications of the Harrisburg Trial for the Democratic Tradition.* New York: Harper and Row.

Rock, Paul E. 1973. *Deviant Behavior.* London: Hutchinson University Library.

Russell, Francis. 1971. *Tragedy in Dedham: The Story of the Sacco-Vanzetti Case.* New York: McGraw-Hill.

Scheff, Thomas J. 1966. *Being Mentally Ill: A Sociological Theory.* Chicago: Aldine.

Schrag, Peter. 1974. *Test of Loyalty: Daniel Ellsberg and the Rituals of Secret Government.* New York: Simon and Schuster.

Scott, Marvin B., and Stanford Lyman. 1968. "Accounts." *American Sociological Review* 33: 46-62.

Solzhenitsyn, Aleksandr. 1973. *The Gulag Archipelago, 1918-1956.* New York: Harper and Row.

Sternberg, David. 1972. "The new radical-criminal trials: A step toward a class-for-itself in the American proletariat?" *Science and Society* 36: 274-301.

Taylor, Ian, and Laurie Taylor. 1973. *Politics and Deviance.* Middlesex: Penguin Books.

Taylor, Ian, Paul Walton, and Jock Young. 1973. *The New Criminology: For a Social Theory of Deviance.* New York: Harper and Row.

Thio, Alex. 1978. *Deviant Behavior.* New York: Houghton Mifflin.

Zimroth, Peter L. 1974. *Perversion of Justice: The Prosecution and Acquittal of the Panther 21.* New York: Viking Press.

Chapter 3

The Bicentennial Protest: An Examination of Hegemony in the Definition of Deviant Political Activity

Pat Lauderdale and **Rhoda E. Estep**

INTRODUCTION

Thirty years ago George Orwell conceived of a world where the existence or nonexistence of events would be directly manipulated by the agents of social control.

> "Some years ago you had a very serious delusion indeed. You believed that three men, three one-time Party members named Jones, Aaronson, and Rutherford—men who were executed for treachery and sabotage after making the fullest possible confession—were not guilty of the crimes they were charged with. You believed that you had seen unmistakable documentary evidence proving that their confessions were false. There was a certain photograph about which you had a hallucination. You believed that you had actually held it in your hands. It was a photograph something like this."
>
> An oblong slip of newspaper had appeared between O'Brien's fingers. For perhaps five seconds it was within the angle of Winston's vision. It was a photograph, and there was no question of its identity. It was *the* photograph. It was another copy of the photograph of Jones, Aaronson, and Rutherford at the Party function in New York, which he had chanced upon eleven years ago and promptly destroyed. For only an instant it was before his eyes, then it was out of sight again. But he had seen it, unquestionably

he had seen it. He made a desperate, agonizing effort to wrench the top half of his body free. It was impossible to move so much as a centimeter in any direction. For the moment he had even forgotten the dial. All he wanted was to hold the photograph in his fingers again, or at least to see it.

"It exists!" he cried.

"No," said O'Brien.

He stepped across the room. There was a memory hole in the opposite wall. O'Brien lifted the grating. Unseen, the frail slip of paper was whirling away on the current of warm air; it was vanishing in a flash of flame. O'Brien turned away from the wall.

"Ashes," he said. "Not even identifiable ashes. Dust. It does not exist. It never existed."

"But it did exist! It does exist! It exists in memory. I remember it. You remember it."

"I do not remember it," said O'Brien (Orwell, 1949: 203-4).

The power of the American media institutions has become more widely recognized since McLuhan's proclamation that "the media is the message." But most of our knowledge about the media and their influence on mass protest is still fragmentary and discursive. Since the mass media make decisions or nondecisions regarding what the population sees, hears, and reads, they can play a major role in creating cultural hegemony (cf. Goldenberg, 1975; Gitlin, 1977). Mass media are the primary means of communicating common interests or goals at the mass level, the central mechanisms that let people in Long Island know what people in Long Beach are thinking and doing. Media are capable of denying the existence of acts and movements of protest through selective inattention. Or, through selective emphasis, they can derogate the significance of protest by caricature or bias. Can mass media, then, turn an event attended by tens of thousands of people gathered from all corners of the United States into a nonevent through their own actions or inactions?

This paper examines one such incident, the July Fourth Coalition March. We focus upon how the march was reported, misrepresented, and/or unreported in 18 major newspapers across the United States. In order to interpret the newspaper coverage, portions of works from several areas of sociological inquiry are integrated. The areas include social movements, deviance, political sociology, and media sociology.

On July 4, 1976, Americans engaged in a massive celebration of the greatest "protest" in the history of the country, the secession of the emerging "states" from the British Empire. Yet, in the midst of this Bicentennial celebration, acts and movements of immediate protest occurred. The largest, the July Fourth Coalition March, took place in Philadelphia with approximately thirty-five to forty thousand participants.[1] This march was planned and executed by a group of people who called themselves the July Fourth Coalition. Groups represented in the coalition included the Puerto Rican Socialist Party, the American Indian Movement, gay activists, and various women's groups. The coalition agreed that the march would celebrate a Bicentennial without colonies, with employment, with democracy and equality for all. The problem for this paper is to explore the factors affecting the coverage of this march in the midst of the national rite.

There are two principal indicators of the extent of media distortion or manipulation in reporting an event, the amount of coverage given the event and the characterization of the event. The amount and type of news coverage of an event in turn affects not only the perception of protest but the probability of success of many social movements.[2] Information is crucial to the reality perceived by the public, as well as to the success achieved by the participants. In general, the types of coverage or communication sponsored by news media may reveal the extent to which "distorted" communication is used by social control agencies of the society (cf. Mueller, 1973).

One factor influencing media distortion is the routine or nonroutine nature of the event. The July Fourth Coalition March was a nonroutine, or irregularly occurring, event. Such events are generally subject to a broader range of interpretation by the public and media than regularly or frequently occurring events. In other words, a nonroutine event is typically more ambiguous in terms of meaning or definition than a recurrent routine event. Nonroutine events are more easily misinterpreted by news assemblers (Molotch and Lester, 1975).

TURNER'S MODEL OF THE
SOCIAL DEFINITION OF PROTEST

Turner (1969) develops a model to characterize the syntax of public definitions of protest. He argues that we should "avoid assuming that there are objectifiable phenomena that must be classified as deviant, as protest, or as rebellion" (1969: 817). Five conditions must be present for a disturbance to be defined as social protest or a political act rather than as rebellion or deviance.

1. The activity should meet the folk conception of protest. This

stereotype of "genuine" political acts involves the actors being identified as belonging to an acknowledged oppressed group, being seen as unable to ameliorate the situation alone, and showing indications of merit through moral virtue.

2. There should be a balance between appeal and threat.

3. There should be a conciliation with a target group.

4. There should be an invitation from a third party to form a coalition.

5. There should be a bargaining relationship (e.g., with public officials).

Participants in a demonstration need to convey that they are acting collectively rather than individually and legitimately rather than illegitimately. Although protest may be a resource for the demonstrating group, definition is a resource for the dominant group. In exchange for legitimacy the minority group gives up certain aspects of its protest via conciliation, coalition, and bargaining.

Turner's approach is extended by Gary Marx (1970). Marx claims that for an activity to be perceived as protest additional characteristics are necessary. They include "the development of the disorders out of prolonged community conflict and out of a focused context, an overlap in roles between conventional political activists and riot participants, the presence of riot spokesmen, the presentation of demands, selectivity in attack, and a link between the source of the trouble as identified in the generalized belief and those targets actually attacked" (1970: 27). For Marx, generalized belief linking the trouble, the targets, and the instrumentality of the collective action is crucial to the recognition of protest.

For Turner and Marx the characterization of the event is a critical factor in determining how the event is evaluated. However, such a view has two shortcomings. First, Turner and Marx confine their analyses to the immediate causes of perception of protest. That is, they propose that a disturbance will be perceived as protest when a collective activity demonstrates the characteristics of protest. Second, Turner, in particular, concentrates on how protest can be distinguished from rebellion, or deviance, perhaps because that dimension was more problematic with respect to the Watts riot. However, he did not address the crucial distinction between a nonroutine and a routine event.

While Turner spells out the necessary conditions for the emergence of protest definitions, he does not indicate the independent variables that affect his five model variables. In arguing that the objective features of the protest are not necessarily important, he implies that there are structural factors at work but then fails to indicate what those might be.

A MODEL OF THE POLITICS OF DEFINITIONS

The behavior of the participants and the form of the participation influence the definitional process. For example, if the demonstrators want to be viewed as protesters, they should attempt to portray their actions as collective rather than individual and legitimate rather than illegitimate. In addition, the collective action appears more legitimate if the actors are committed to the goals of the group even at the expense of their individual interests (cf. Swanson, 1971). Yet even broader identification of characteristics is desirable.[3] The components of a conceptual framework that precede the definitions and labeling of an event are preconditions for studying collective demonstrations (Burke, 1954).

Turner's explanation of the recognition and definition of protest in terms of the actors involved implies that the actors must be acknowledged as part of an oppressed group in order for the public to perceive their actions as protest. On the other hand, Molotch and Lester's (1975) analysis of news coverage of the Santa Barbara oil spill suggests that the greater the power discrepancy is between two parties competing for coverage of an event, the less likely the weaker party is to gain access to the media. In short, the positions of the key actors influence not only the definition of the event but also whether or not the event will be reported. Another striking example is the well-documented absence of coverage of the women's movement, partly attributable to the lower social status of women in society (cf. Morris, 1973).

The message of the demonstrators and the perception or intent of the news media interact to determine the coverage of the purpose or activity image of the collective action. The clarity of the messages and the goals of the demonstration, as well as the congruence of these goals with dominant cultural values, are clearly significant in the reporting of a nonroutine event. Beyond the overriding values of society, the government may also have a vested interest in promoting a policy that highlights certain types of news and neglects other features. The impact of these various components in promoting cultural hegemony is succinctly characterized in the observation that governmental constraints on political communication, the mobilization of bias by powerful interests, and the commercial character of the media create a situation where news items that would invite challenges of the status quo are either omitted or embedded in interpretations which depreciate them. If members of the audience have no counterinterpretations or alternative sources of information, they may mistake for the real world the selected messages presented by the media (Mueller, 1973: 100).

More specifically, however, we suggest that three primary factors affect the likelihood of coverage. First, studies on variation in the volume and definition of deviance find that the volume of perceived deviance is inversely proportional to the solidarity of the social system (Erikson, 1966; Inverarity, 1976; Lauderdale, 1976). This suggests that the greater the solidarity of a social system, the fewer the disturbances reported by the news media. Second, ties between news media and other social institutions, especially governmental social control agencies, increase the likelihood that news events representing values antithetical to the institutional structure of the society will be suppressed. Third, unless the participants in the event offer the media a reason to notice the demonstration and thereby demand coverage (e.g., through violence or overwhelming participation), it is relatively easy for the news media to overlook the political participation of groups seldom given the automatic recognition granted to routine events.[4]

Given that an event is reported, what influences the manner in which it is reported? We contend that, in a nonroutine event, the more responsive the news media is to the definitions expressed by participants, the more likely is a definition of protest rather than of deviance (assuming, of course, that the participants want to be characterized as legitimate, political actors). Further, we note that the tone of newspaper coverage depends on media responsiveness, or willingness to report newsworthy events "objectively." Finally, following Turner's scheme, we argue that the participants, once identified as part of an oppressed group and as nonviolent, encourage a media definition of the event as protest rather than as deviance or rebellion.

METHODS

We have adopted Molotch and Lester's (1975) strategy of contrasting two available samples of news reports—one created for the Philadelphia local public and one created by newspapers in the rest of the country. In order to examine national newspaper coverage of the July Fourth Coalition March in Philadelphia, we survey a cross-section of 18 newspapers in major United States cities. Of these, 3 are Philadelphia papers, reviewed to determine whether local coverage differs substantially from national coverage. The remaining 15 newspapers have been selected according to the scheme suggested by Molotch and Lester, which strives for geographic diversity while attempting to tap any existing geographic bias.[5]

The data collected for the study are articles appearing in the newspapers between June 27 and July 11, one week before and one week after the march. These articles provide information on both the amount and type of coverage given the event. Articles are analyzed in four ways, according to: (1) the absence or presence of coverage; (2) the amount of coverage, if any (i.e., the number of entire articles devoted to the march or the number of paragraphs of coverage given; (3) the timing of the coverage (i.e., whether it occurred before or after the actual event; and (4) the kind of coverage (i.e., whether the report describes the event in an "objective" fashion or portrays it in either a subjectively positive or subjectively negative manner (Lauderdale, 1976: 673-74). The first two criteria provide an indication of the volume of coverage; the last two provide an indication of the definition given to the event.

The system of coding the information identified from each newspaper story is as follows: (1) the number of paragraphs devoted to the actual Philadelphia march;[6] (2) the location of the story in the newspaper (lead versus nonlead story; front page versus other); (3) the placement of the actual report of the march within the article when the article is not devoted entirely to the march; and (4) keywords inviting a conception of the participants as legitimate and organized protesters as opposed to illegitimate and unorganized deviants or rebels.

DATA ANALYSIS

Amount of Coverage

The lack of coverage by prominent newspapers of the July Fourth Coalition March in Philadelphia is strikingly illustrated in table 3. The lack of variance in the coverage, with the exception of Philadelphia, is even more noticeable. Such uniformity among the papers suggests that, for this particular event, amount of coverage should *not* be associated with characteristics of newspapers themselves, or with their geographical location or political persuasion (Tuchman, 1973; Molotch and Lester, 1975), the social-psychological processes of the persons working for them, their interorganizational network, or their individual links with other social control agencies. More specifically, we think the data suggest that the relative absence of coverage of the march is directly related to the high solidarity exhibited on July 4, 1976, through the elaborate rituals of the nation's anniversary. This will be explored further in the interrelated section on context of the coverage.

Table 3. Amount of Coverage of the July Fourth Coalition March:
Number of Total and Partial Articles in Each Newspaper
Before and After the March

| | June 27-July 4 | | July 5-July 11 | |
| | Full | Partial | Full | Partial |
Newspapers	Articles	Articles	Articles	Articles
Philadelphia Evening Bulletin (local)	0	4	1	3
Philadelphia Inquirer (local)	0	2	0	0
Philadelphia Daily News (local)	1	4	0	1
New York Times (East)	1	1	1	1
Boston Globe (East)	1	0	1	0
Washington Post (East)	0	2	0	2
Atlanta Constitution (South)	0	0	0	0
Dallas Morning News (South)	0	1	0	0
New Orleans Time-Picayune (South)	0	1	0	1
St. Louis Post-Dispatch (Midwest)	0	1	0	1
Detroit News (Midwest)	0	0	0	1
Minneapolis Tribune (Midwest)	0	0	1	0
Chicago Tribune (Midwest)	0	2	0	2
Milwaukee Journal (Midwest)	0	1	0	0
San Francisco Chronicle (West)	0	0	0	1
Seattle Daily Times (West)	0	0	0	1
Denver Post (West)	0	0	0	1
Los Angleles Times (West)	0	2	0	1

The second factor in accounting for the lack of coverage is media-government relations. Local Philadelphia television stations did, as a matter of policy, bar coalition advertisements. Although we have no data on the decision-making processes in the newspaper offices, the *Philadelphia Evening Bulletin* revealed the following:

> The July Fourth Coalition, another dissident group that has been upstaged by the Rich Off Our Backs group, held a press conference yesterday to discuss its plans for tomorrow. Alan Howard, a spokesman, . . . said that the coalition plans to file a complaint with the Federal Communications Com-

mission against television stations in New York, Boston and Washington for refusing to sell it time for spot announcements. He said Philadelphia Channels 10, 17, and 48 also refused to sell the Coalition time, but allowed the group to air its views on public affairs and news programs (July 3, 1976, section A, pp. 1-2.).

We have no data on the reasons for this ban; however, both the mayor's office and the police perceived a threat from the march. There is little question about the extent of police preparation and concern.

Since last January, Fencl and other officers in state and federal departments had begun gathering intelligence on the potential for violence with the various protest groups which promised to come to Philadelphia on the fourth of July (*Philadelphia Evening Bulletin,* July 11, 1976, section D, pp. 1-2).

Similarly, two major elected officials in Philadelphia portrayed the march as threatening and actually worked to prevent its occurrence; they were Councilman Moore and Mayor Rizzo. Although Moore and Rizzo perceived the event as threatening, such a view was adopted neither by the governor of Pennsylvania nor by the Department of Justice, as evidenced by the refusal of both authorities to provide the National Guard troops requested by the mayor.

Reactions to troop denial ranged from jubilation to distress yesterday. "I am distressed (by the federal response)," Mayor Rizzo said in a statement. "I feel that the Federal Government is playing politics with people's lives and, if there are disturbances in Philadelphia on July 4th, the blood is on their hands."

"The potential for disruptions, confrontations, and possible violence during the Bicentennial ceremony at Independence Hall is very real, indeed," Rizzo said (*Philadelphia Evening Bulletin,* June 22, 1976, section A, pp. 1, 5).

The third factor affecting amount of coverage is the nature of the event. Compare the newspaper coverage of a separate, much smaller march organized by the Rich Off Our Backs (ROOB) Coalition in Philadelphia, with the coverage of the July Fourth Coalition March. In the Philadelphia newspapers, the ROOB parade received far more coverage than the July Fourth Coalition March despite participation by only about one-tenth as many marchers. For instance, in a Philadelphia newspaper published on June 30, 11 paragraphs of information were devoted to discussion of ROOB activities. Another paragraph of the article mentioned briefly the July Fourth Coalition, as "a second and unrelated group planning to demonstrate July 4" (*Philadelphia Evening Bulletin,* June 30, 1976, section A, p. 21). The total coverage from the designated two-week period appearing in the *Philadelphia Evening Bulletin* accorded 171 paragraphs to ROOB Coalition activities in contrast with 28 paragraphs concerning July Fourth Coalition activities. Similarly, the *Philadelphia Daily News* devoted 72 paragraphs exclusively to ROOB activities and 44 paragraphs to July Fourth Coalition activities. The *Philadelphia Inquirer* mentioned the July Fourth Coalition in a single paragraph as compared with 41 paragraphs in which it mentioned the ROOB. This column space differential is significant as an indicator of the absolute and relative importance of various topics within a newspaper (Rock, 1973).

The participants in the ROOB parade were frequently associated by the newspapers with the Revolutionary Student Brigade and Vietnam Veterans, two organizations with a history of "militant" tactics. An illustrative passage follows:

> Earlier in the morning, the Rich Off Our Backs groups, which included a contingent of Vietnam veterans in their old fatigues, marching to radical slogans set to military cadence, held their demonstration. Their thrust was an economic analysis (*New York Times,* July 5, 1976, section C, p. 18).

The ROOB, then, received more attention due to the potential of violence associated with their parade in contrast to the anticipated pas- -sivity of the July Fourth Coalition March. Such an explanation coincides with a great deal of sociological theory viewing violence as a necessary catalyst for social response, including news coverage and public interest (Sorel, 1950; Waskow, 1966; Coser, 1967; Gamson, 1975).

In general, the explanations for the lack of coverage of the July Fourth Coalition March involve different levels of analysis. First, nationwide celebration and resultant solidarity could have reduced attention to actual dissidence occurring on July 4, 1976. Second, government censorship and influence of news media could be held at least partially responsible for lack of coverage.[7] Third, failure to report the event can be traced to the perception by the media of the July Fourth Coalition March as relatively quiet and nonviolent and therefore easy to neglect. Given the lack of variation in independent variables in case studies such as this one, we can not pursue the relative impact of these three factors on coverage. Our in-depth analysis of this case, however, does reveal suggestive information about how the media react to collective disturbances.

Context of Coverage

Apart from scanty coverage, the page placement of full articles about the July Fourth Coalition March and placement of those paragraphs "sandwiched" between other lead or headline articles yield further insight into the type of social control exercised over the report of the protest march.

Table 4 summarizes the placements of all full articles concerning the July Fourth Coalition March in Philadelphia. Of immediate interest is the fact that there were no front-page stories about the march. Further documentation of newspaper portrayal of the event as unimportant is found in the small number of paragraphs that discuss the march in those articles that mention it at all. The one exception was a full-length story, accompanied by photographs, featuring the July Fourth Coalition March in the July 29 edition of the *Philadelphia Inquirer*.

Table 4. Context of Coverage of the July Fourth Coalition March: Placement of Full Articles on Philadelphia March

Newspaper	Date	Number of Paragraphs in Article	Placement of Article
Philadelphia Evening Bulletin	July 5	14	Section A, p. 27
Philadelphia Daily News	June 29	43*	Section A, pp. 5, 23
New York Times	June 30	5	Editorial page (letter to the editor)
New York Times	July 5	13	Section C, p. 18
Boston Globe	July 2	15	Editorial page (column)
Boston Globe	July 5	13	Section A, p. 2
Minneapolis Tribune	July 5	8	Section A, p. 2

*Also, the equivalent of 12 paragraphs was devoted to pictures of radical persons involved in the July Fourth Coalition and to symbols of the forthcoming march.

The actual context of mention of the march within various articles is examined in table 5. In no instance did the report of the protest march receive headline status. In many cases (12 of 31), the march was mentioned after several paragraphs about the official governmental parade. A second prominent context for the story was its use as a contrast to the harmony existing elsewhere in the country on the Bicentennial (6 of 31). A third context associated the march with such negative occurrences (Mueller, 1973) as traffic fatalities and drownings during the July Fourth holiday weekend in cities as different as New Orleans and Detroit.[8] In sum, the newspapers used a minimum of space reporting the July Fourth Coalition March and uniformly placed the coverage in a context where the march could easily be overlooked or viewed in a negative manner.

Table 5. Context of Coverage of the July Fourth Coalition March:
Material Surrounding Mention of Philadelphia March
in Articles with Partial Coverage

Newspaper	Date	Number of Paragraphs on March	Context of Mention of March
Philadelphia Evening Bulletin	June 30	1	After announcement of other parades in Philadelphia
Philadelphia Evening Bulletin	July 1	4	After 11 paragraphs on ROOB*
Philadelphia Evening Bulletin	July 2	5	After 14 paragraphs on ROOB*
Philadelphia Evening Bulletin	July 3	1	On third of 5 pages listing local events
Philadelphia Evening Bulletin	July 7	1	After many paragraphs on ROOB*
Philadelphia Evening Bulletin	July 11	2	In editorial as support for condemning Mayor Rizzo
Philadelphia Evening Bulletin	July 11	2	After discussion of police chief's handling of ROOB*
Philadelphia Inquirer	June 29	1	After 7 paragraphs on ROOB*
Philadelphia Inquirer	July 2	1	In connection with police preparation for the dissenting group subsection, billed as "Radicals"
Philadelphia Daily News	June 30	13	Within article on ROOB*
Philadelphia Daily News	June 30	2	About nonappearance of bands due to Rizzo's prediction of terrorism
Philadelphia Daily News	July 2	1	After 9 paragraphs on ROOB*
Philadelphia Daily News	July 7	14	In editorial comment on failures of the Bicentennial
New York Times	July 4	2	After report on President Ford's speech
New York Times	July 5	1	After report on President Ford's speech
Washington Post	June 29	2	In contrast to official and small-town celebrations
Washington Post	July 4	2	In context of protests used to say that democracy survives in the United States

*ROOB — refers to the Rich Off Our Backs Coalition March, also transpiring in Philadelphia on July 4, 1976.

Table 5. (Continued)

Newspaper	Date	Number of Paragraphs on March	Context of Mention of March
Washington Post	July 5	2	In connection with Rizzo's request for troops
Washington Post	July 5	2	In contrast to peaceful observance of Bicentennial
Dallas Morning News	July 4	4	After report of President Ford's speech
New Orleans Times-Picayune	July 3	2	With report of traffic fatalities, drownings, etc.
New Orleans Times-Picayune	July 5	1	With report of traffic fatalities, drownings, etc.
St. Louis Post-Dispatch	July 4	1	After report of official events
St. Louis Post-Dispatch	July 6	1	After discussion of President Ford's speech
Detroit News	July 5	1	With report of traffic deaths
Chicago Tribune	July 2	1	In contrast to great Bicentennial
Chicago Tribune	July 4	3	After discussion of major parades
Chicago Tribune	July 5	8	After discussion of ROOB* group
Chicago Tribune	July 7	1	In contrast to great Bicentennial
Milwaukee Journal	July 3	2	In contrast to Ford; under subheading "Radical Observations"
San Francisco Chronicle	July 5	1	To support idea that protest was insignificant
Seattle Daily Times	July 5	1	In contrast to a safe Bicentennial
Denver Post	July 5	1	To support argument of harmony in country
Lost Angeles Times	July 2	1	In contrast to official and small-town observances
Los Angeles Times	July 4	1	In contrast to overall unity of country
Los Angeles Times	July 5	1	In contrast to expected violence

Content of Coverage

For the most part, among those newspapers which reported the event, the July Fourth Coalition March was viewed as a disturbance rather than as rebellion or deviance, as evidenced by table 6. The exceptions (see the fourth column of table 6) were a *Chicago Tribune* columnist who depicted the protesters as confused deviants and five other newspapers that implied that no demonstrations had occured since violence did not erupt.[9] In other words, only portions of Turner's characteristics of a protest were acknowledged by the press. For example, the following lead article appearing in the *Philadelphia Evening Bulletin* after the march shows how the perception of the event did fit some of Turner's description of what a protest would be, although not all parts of his scheme are present in this instance:

> There were a lot of soapboxes yesterday in Fairmont Park where the July 4th Coalition celebrated the Bicentennial.
>
> The marchers touched dozens of causes and points of view on banners and placards and in their shouts and chants. And at the park, about 30 speakers expounded for nearly three hours until they were driven away by torrents of rain.
>
> Typical was a large display of pamphlets and books in one area of the clearing. "The Gay Question" was squeezed between "China: The Trouble Within" and "Lenin: On the Emancipation of Women."
>
> Thousands of people marched behind banners demanding, "Free Puerto Rico Right Now."
>
> And the parade, which stretched a dozen city blocks at a time, was led by a group of American Indians carrying a banner, "Wounded Knee 1973" to the sound of drum beats.
>
> Blacks spoke of hundreds of years of enslavement. The Socialist Workers Party distributed "A Bill of Rights for Working People." Several banners demanded, "Remember Attica!"
>
> There were supporters for "Iranian People's Struggle." And still another group distributed flyers calling for turning over the Panama Canal to Panama.
>
> Karen DeCrow, president of the National Organization for Women, blamed the "oppression" of women on "ruling classes of this country."
>
> "Recall Rizzo, Save PGH," chanted one group, referring to the planned closing of Philadelphia General Hospital by the Rizzo Administration.
>
> Estimates of the crowd varied from about 17,000 by the police to 50,000 by Coalition spokesmen.
>
> They came from all over the country (*Philadelphia Evening Bulletin*, July 5, 1976, section A, p. 27).

For the most part, the newspapers viewed the march as both innocuous and amorphous. Although there is some evidence that the

Table 6. Content of Coverage of the July Fourth Coalition March:
Representation of Philadelphia March

	Full Articles		Partial Articles	
Newspaper	Number Seeing March as Protest	Number Not Seeing March as Protest	Number Seeing March as Protest	Number Not Seeing March as Protest
Philadelphia Evening Bulletin	1	0	7	0
Philadelphia Inquirer	0	0	2	0
Philadelphia Daily News	1	0	4	1
New York Times	2	0	2	0
Boston Globe	2	0	0	0
Washington Post	0	0	3	1
Atlanta Constitution	0	0	0	0
Dallas Morning News	0	0	1	0
New Orleans Times-Picayune	0	0	2	0
St. Louis Post-Dispatch	0	0	1	1
Detroit News	0	0	1	0
Minneapolis Tribune	1	0	0	0
Chicago Tribune	0	0	3	1
Milwaukee Journal	0	0	1	0
San Francisco Chronicle	0	0	1	0
Seattle Daily Times	0	0	0	1
Denver Post	0	0	0	1
Los Angeles Times	0	0	3	1

papers also perceived the demonstration to be legitimate and organized as well as having a generalized belief, the march paled in comparison to Turner's imagery of a protest. This outcome, however, does
not appear to have resulted from only social-psychological factors
but, instead, is largely attributable to the structural characteristics
surrounding the "event" (Smelser, 1963; Portes, 1971; Freeman,
1973; House and Mason, 1975).

CONCLUSION

A theory of protest that concentrates solely on the nature of the
event is inadequate to explain or predict a wider range of protest
events (cf. Zald and Ash, 1966). First, national attention accorded
major riots (such as those in Detroit and Watts) has led many observers (e.g., Turner, 1969) to believe that achievement of recognition is not problematic. Second, working from commonsense classifications of collective events (e.g., riots) retards adequate theoretical

development. Indeed, Gary Marx berates early theorists in the collective behavior field for regarding the actions of actors and crowds as substantially different from other more rational actions of individuals. Third, viewing only publicized protests or riots as a useful categorization of "events" upon which to build a theory of collective action is problematic. Such a strategy of theoretical development has long been decried by deviance theorists. Primary targets of such vehement criticism are those labeling theorists who attempt to understand the process of acquiring a deviant label by studying only those already stigmatized with the label (Gibbs, 1966).

Instead, we propose that a more adequate theory of collective action would begin by dividing collective behavior into routine and nonroutine events. A sample of nonroutine collective events and their processing by a range of social control agencies, including the press, would provide one basis for building a theory. Such a study would address the issue as involving two problematic accomplishments: (1) receiving news coverage, and (2) obtaining the kind of coverage desired. In the current study, the issue of discrepant realities was discovered by investigating alternative sources of media, like *The Guardian*.[10] Following the course of a movement further reveals differing realities and can be accomplished by using alternative sources of media.

We further conclude that more than one level of analysis should be incorporated in an explanation of protest. Turner emphasizes the social-psychological dimension of public evaluations of events. The theoretical inadequacy lies in Turner's failure to consider the structural constraints on perception. To be sure, follow-up studies on the Turner article have focused on positional or structural characteristics of the perceivers or audience (Jeffries et al., 1971; Altheide and Gilmore, 1972; Ransford, 1972). Still lacking, however, are studies combining an emphasis on audience perception of collective events with the various levels of structural constraints surrounding the event. As discussed earlier, perceptions are influenced by the amount and type of information readily available to the public (Lewis, 1976). The amount and type of information about collective events can be contingent on structure at several different levels: (1) societal constraints as a context for the operation of the news media; (2) network alliances between the press and other legitimized institutions in the society (Roscho, 1972); and (3) market constraints on the news organization itself.[11]

Finally, we have seen that a particular, focused protest involving tens of thousands of people was largely ignored by major newspapers in the United States. These papers did not appear to go out of their way to derogate the event or its participants. Rather, it was simply defined and treated as a nonevent. In other words, for the majority of people in the United States, it is an event that never occurred. Although some theorists will conclude from the investigation here that the protest was simply a one-shot expressive affair, it may well be that it was but one instrumental appendage of a more diffuse social movement. The protest on July 4, 1976, was not a social movement in and of itself; yet we wonder how many incipient social movements wither because of lack of media attention. This point is intrinsically important in that nonevents have not received systematic exploration in the sociological interface between social movements and deviance. In delineating the manner in which society can respond to a collective event or social movement, inattention has not been considered a crucial factor. Yet, in a large, mass, geographically dispersed society, this may be an effective means of social and political control.[12]

NOTES

1. Similar marches took place in Washington, D.C., and in San Francisco, although these marches had fewer participants than the Philadelphia march. All these marches were ignored by the news media, as was the Philadelphia march examined herein. It is therefore inferred that a complete analysis of the smaller marches would yield findings similar to those obtained from the primary march. Rhoda Estep provided detailed analysis for this paper as a participant-observer in the July Fourth Coalition Philadelphia March.

2. Since the success of many social movements depends on their ability to attract participants from the general public, the recognition or nonrecognition of a national demonstration may decidedly influence the extent to which the movement will flourish (cf. Freeman, 1973; Morris, 1973). In the incipient phases of social movements, the presentation of collective events as legitimate protest rather than deviance may be especially crucial to the success of the movement. This is particularly pertinent for movements that have mass support as a primary goal (Turner and Killian, 1957).

3. The mass media are more likely to find a particular political activity newsworthy if that activity has high-status members at the core of the action. If this assumption is correct, then (all else being equal, *especially violent behavior*) political activities with low-status members at the forefront are less likely to be part of mass social reality.

4. In a recent study, Snyder and Kelley (1977) convincingly demonstrate that event intensity and media sensitivity influence the frequency of reports of collective events.

5. Additionally, all else being equal, it was reasoned that, if the urban newspapers failed to report the march, coverage of this kind of event would be even less likely in rural papers.

6. The number of paragraphs is highly correlated with the number of column inches.

7. It is also possible that the lack of coverage can be traced to a solidification of social control that has occurred in the United States as a result of anti-Vietnam War protests.

As a society comes to feel increasingly threatened by dissenting groups, perhaps aided by police cries of alarm, it may expand its social control apparatus. . . . As the authorities in their handling of political activities blur the distinction between crime and politics, police who are already experienced with the use of informants, infiltration, and occasionally entrapment, in the area of traditional crimes may simply shift their resources and bring their past experience and perspectives to bear on political groups, in spite of important differences between the two phenomena (Marx, 1974: 431-32).

8. This same technique was used by the three Phildelphia papers, the *Los Angeles Times*, the *Washington Post*, and the *Chicago Tribune* to link the July Fourth Coalition with violence, the ROOB group, or Mayor Rizzo's earlier request for troops.

9. Concerning a related demonstration sponsored by the People's Bicentennial Commission, the *Chicago Tribune* evidently changed from favorable to unfavorable reports following contact by a government "researcher" on the People's Bicentennial Commission (cf. United States Congress, 1976: 203-4).

10. A final source of data consulted was an alternative newspaper, *The Guardian*, which gave full, front-page coverage to the July Fourth Coalition March in its July 4, 1976, issue. Also, this alternative newspaper has continued to report activities of the July Fourth Coalition (cf. *The Guardian*, May 25, 1977, p. 7, and *The Guardian*, June 8, 1977, p. 7). The number of participants in these later activities has been negligible (150) compared to the number (40,000) participating in the Philadelphia march on July 4. The contrast between the coverage provided by the two types of papers (prominent mass media versus alternative) and the number of participants supports the idea that movements need widespread media coverage of their events in order for the movements to maintain or increase their size and probably also their strength.

11. Although we cannot develop a more complete theoretical foundation in this paper, it seems useful to suggest the relevance of Burke's (1954) presentation of the five elements of a social act. In his framework, one would analyze: (1) the agency emphasizing the importance of the flow of the event (in particular, the behavior of the participants and the form of participation are seen as important to the defining process); (2) the key actors' position, which influence not only the definition of the event but also whether or not the event will be reported; (3) the role of the reporting agent, noting the structure of the news organization and its effect on the reporting or nonreporting of events; (4) the message of the actors including the clarity of the demonstration's goals and its coincidence with the dominant cultural values; and (5) the setting surrounding the event (which we have presented as the initial point of theoretical departure). Klapp's (1969) analysis of a public drama would be another relevant framework, especially in its relational dimensions.

12. We would like to thank Kai Erikson, Jana Hall, James Inverarity, Gerald Larson, Gary Marx, Jerry Parker, and Jeff Stitt for their comments on an earlier version of this paper.

REFERENCES

Alford, Robert R., and Roger Friedland. 1975. "Political participation and public policy." *Annual Review of Sociology* 8: 429-79.

Altheide, David L. 1976. *Creating Reality*. Beverly Hills, Calif.: Sage.

———, and Robert P. Gilmore. 1972. "The credibility of protest." *American Sociological Review* 37: 99-108.

Black, Donald. 1976. *The Behavior of Law*. New York: Academic Press.

Blumer, Herbert. 1971. "Social problems as collective behavior." *Social Problems* 18: 298-306.

Breed, Warren. 1958. "Mass communication and socio-cultural integration." *Social Forces* 37: 109-16.

Burke, Kenneth. 1954. *Permanence and Change*. 2nd ed. Los Altos, Calif.: Hermes Publications.

Coser, Lewis. 1967. *Continuities in the Study of Social Conflict*. New York: Free Press.

Erikson, Kai T. 1966. *Wayward Puritans: A Study in the Sociology of Deviance*. New York: John Wiley.

Fishman, Mark. 1977. "Manufacturing the news: The social organization of media news production." Ph.D. dissertation. Ann Arbor, Mich.: University Microfilms International.

Freeman, Jo. 1973. "The origins of the women's liberation movement." *American Journal of Sociology* 78: 792-811.

Gamson, William A. 1975. *The Strategy of Social Protest*. Homewood, Ill.: Dorsey Press.

Gibbs, Jack P. 1966. "Conceptions of deviant behavior: The old and the new." *Pacific Sociological Review* 9: 9-14.

Gitlin, Todd A. 1977. "The whole world is watching: Mass media and the new left, 1965-70." Ph.D. dissertation. Ann Arbor, Mich.: University Microfilms International.

Goldenberg, Edie N. 1975. *Making the Papers*. Lexington, Mass.: D. C. Heath.

Greisman, H. C. 1976. "Disenchantment of the world: Romanticism, aesthetics, and sociological theory." *The British Journal of Sociology* 27: 505.

House, James D., and William M. Mason. 1975. "Political alienation in America 1952-1968. *American Sociological Review* 40: 123-47.

Inverarity, James. 1976. "Populism and lynching in the South: A test of Erikson's theory of the relationship between boundary crisis and repressive justice." *American Sociological Review* 41: 262-80.

Jeffries, Vincent, Ralph H. Turner, and Richard R. Morris. 1971. "The public perception of the Watts riot as social protest." *American Sociological Review* 36: 443-51.

Klapp, Orrin E. 1969. *Collective Search for Identity*. New York: Holt, Rinehart and Winston.

Lauderdale, Pat. 1976. "Deviance and moral boundaries." *American Sociological Review* 41: 660-76.

Lewis, George H. 1976. "The structure of support in social movements: An analysis of organization and resource mobilization in the youth contra-culture." *British Journal of Sociology* 27: 184-90.

McCarthy, J. D., and Mayer Zald. 1973. *The Trends of Social Movements in America: Professionalization and Resource Mobilization*. Morristown, N.J.: General Learning Press.

Maravall, J. M. 1976. "Subjective conditions and revolutionary conflict." *British Journal of Sociology* 27: 31-33.

Marx, Gary T. 1970. "Issueless riots." *The Annals for the American Academy of Political and Social Sciences* 391: 21-33.

———. 1974. "Thoughts on a neglected category of social movement participant: The *agent provocateur* and the informant." *American Journal of Sociology* 80: 402-42.

Molotch, Harvey, and Marilyn Lester. 1975. "Accidental news: The great oil spill as local occurrence and national event." *American Journal of Sociology* 81: 235-60.

Morris, Monica. 1973. "The public definition of a social movement: Women's liberation." *Sociology and Social Research* 57: 526-43.

Mueller, Claus. 1973. *The Politics of Communication*. Oxford: Oxford University Press.

Orwell, George. 1949. *Nineteen Eighty-four*. New York: Harcourt, Brace.

Portes, Alejandro. 1971. "On the interpretation of class consciousness." *American Journal of Sociology* 77: 228-44.

Ransford, H. Edward. 1972. "Blue collar anger: Reactions to student and black protest." *American Sociological Review* 37: 333-46.

Rock, Paul. 1973. "News as eternal occurrence." In Stanley Cohen and Jock Young (eds.). *The Manufacture of News: A Reader.* Beverly Hills, Calif.: Sage.

Roscho, Bernard. 1972. *Newsmaking.* Chicago: University of Chicago Press.

Smelser, Neil F. 1963. *Theory of Collective Behavior.* New York: Free Press.

Snyder, David, and W. R. Kelley. 1977. "Conflict intensity, media sensitivity and the validity of newspaper data." *American Sociological Review* 42: 105-23.

Sorel, Georges. 1950. *Reflections on Violence.* London: Collier-Macmillan.

Swanson, Guy E. 1971. "An organizational analysis of collectivities." *American Sociological Review* 36: 607-23.

Tuchman, Gaye. 1973. "Making news by doing work: Routinizing the unexpected." *American Journal of Sociology* 79: 110-31.

———. 1978. *Making News: A Study in the Social Construction of Reality.* New York: Free Press.

Turner, Ralph. 1969. "The public perception of protest." *American Sociological Review* 34: 815-31.

———; and Lewis Killian. 1957. *Collective Behavior.* Englewood Cliffs, N.J.: Prentice-Hall.

United States Congress. 1976. "The attempt to steal the Bicentennial: The People's Bicentennial Commission." Hearings before the subcommittee to investigate the administration of the Internal Security Act and other internal security laws, 94th Congress, 2nd session, March 17-18.

Waskow, Arthur L. 1966. *From Race Riot to Sit-in, 1919 and the 1960s.* Garden City, N.Y.: Doubleday.

Zald, Mayer N., and Roberta Ash. 1966. "Social movement organizations: Growth, decay and change." *Social Forces* 44: 327-40.

Part II
The Institutionalization of Political Deviance

Chapter 4

The Politics
of Occupational Control
Hockey Violence
and the Criminal Law

Lyle A. Hallowell

INTRODUCTION

Despite insiders' claims that ice hockey is much less violent now than in its formative years, the sport is currently the subject of intense criticism and reform zeal over the nature, incidence, and consequences of aggressive play. Within the last few years, violence in ice hockey has generated provincial investigations in Canada, several criminal assault cases, numerous investigative analyses and editorial comments in the media, and an outpouring of indignant commentary. Although representatives of the hockey establishment and a few sports journalists contend that ice hockey has always involved aggressive behavior that could be labeled violent, the widely held conception is that legal action and reform demands are new. A careful look into the history of sport reveals earlier legal responses to hockey "roughness" without the widespread reform intensity of this decade. In that light, the task of this paper is to dissect the social conditions that contribute to changes in the legal status of violence in ice hockey.

Compared with other aggressive contact sports, hockey is not uniquely subject to public criticism and calls for reform. Earlier in this century, football, wrestling, and boxing faced public scrutiny and endured fundamental changes in playing style and rule structure. Football presents a particularly intriguing case since, despite current acceptance of aggressive play, three separate episodes of public indignation and reform action characterize the history of that sport (Dickinson, 1963). Charges of intentional brutality and widespread concern over fatalities led, in 1905, to a move to abolish the sport that was abated only by substantial changes in the game and a subsequent reduction in injury (Moore, 1967). A comparatively high number of fatalities—539 play-related deaths from 1931 to 1962—has plagued football, but public arousal has not been as great for football as it has for boxing. Proposals to outlaw boxing arise on occasion, usually in response to the more sensational instances of in-the-ring death, of which there have been 216 from 1945 to 1963. Political and religious leaders—including the Pope—have joined voices with less illustrious reform advocates to demand the abolishment of boxing as dangerous, corrupt, or simply immoral (Dickinson, 1963). Similarly, the high risk of injury and the public indignation about violence in sport in the early 1900s are considered factors in the transformation of professional wrestling from sport to drama (Stone, 1971).

Like the aforementioned sports, ice hockey involves the risk of serious physical injury (Wilson et al., 1977), but deaths attributed to play are rare. This lack of fatalities may have been a factor in the lack of organized and effective reform efforts in hockey's formative years in contrast to the reform zeal affecting other sports at that time. On the other hand, despite the low number of deaths, aggressive play in hockey *has* elicited police reactions, including arrest for assault. If legal reaction cannot be attributed to fatality rates alone, the social meaning of hockey violence and its social context must be explored.

To explore the discrepancy between incidence of aggressive play and police reaction I collected and tabulated reports of "abnormally aggressive incidents" and legal responses to them. "Legal response" was defined broadly to include warnings, complaints, and arrests, some of which advanced to later stages of criminal justice processing. Like many contact sports, hockey is full of aggressive action. The operational definition of "abnormally aggressive incident" assumes that only publicly known incidents influence public conceptions. Therefore, incidents that received press coverage are the data base. Reports of these incidents were drawn from sports journalists' histories of hockey and hockey violence and were supplemented by checks of newspaper files for several years. Figure 1 presents absolute frequency of abnormally aggressive incidents and legal responses in five-season increments from 1902 to the present. Absolute frequency was selected over per-game frequency because the public response is likely founded on the existence of an abnormal incident and a gut feeling of too much violence rather than any sense of the *rate* of aggressive play.

The graph allows us to reject several explanations for reactions to aggressive behavior in hockey. First, the hypothesis that legal or reform activity follows from an increase in the incidence of aggressive play is not supported. It is clear that the two periods during which legal action was taken—1907 to 1921 and 1967 to 1976—and the period of reform efforts—1967 to 1976—are characterized by increases in aggressive incidents. But the period from 1942 to 1956 also involved a substantial increase in aggression *without* legal or reform activity. Second, the hypothesis that legal responses follow from reform agitation is not supported, since legal action has been continual (albeit minimal) in the absence of a "moral crusade." Third, the possibility that reform movements are stimulated by legal action is not supported. Finally, any suggestion that reform action follows a secular increase in abnormally aggressive incidents is negated by the trimodal pattern obtained.

Media accounts from the early 1900s portray a higher incidence of very extreme types of attacks—primarily assaults with the hockey stick—including the stick-swinging death of Owen McCourt in 1907 (cf. Coleman, 1966). Another relevant observation is the focus of current reform efforts. In a series discussing violence in hockey, a reporter observed:

> Violence in all sports has escalated in the past few years. . . . Injuries have increased in nearly all games at all levels. More frightening is the increase in *intentional* injury.
> Because of the physical nature of hockey and the added dimension of court involvement, the current focus narrows to blood-letting on the ice (*Chicago Sun-Times*, May 2, 1976, p. 181).

In sum, the recent hockey violence reform movement cannot be explained as a direct reaction to the *presence of violence,* since other periods have involved hockey violence. It cannot be explained by *increased incidence of violence,* since other periods have displayed substantial increases in hockey violence. The *severity of violence* also fails to explain it, since other periods have involved more extreme attacks. Finally, *increased legal responses* do not necessarily lead to or follow from reform activity.

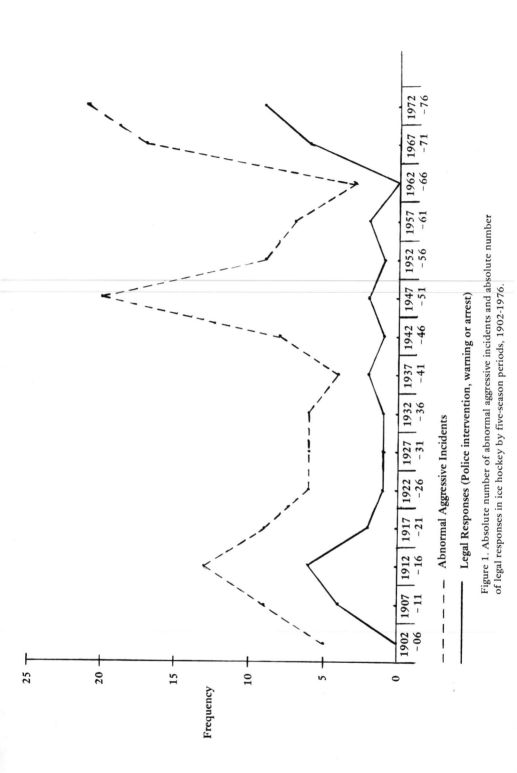

Figure 1. Absolute number of abnormal aggressive incidents and absolute number of legal responses in ice hockey by five-season periods, 1902-1976.

DEVIANCE DEFINING AND OCCUPATIONAL CONTROL

This study traces the creation of a new category of deviance—hockey violence—and a new type of deviant—the violent sportsman. Although defining aggressive behavior as a problem is not new (Fischler, 1974) or unique to ice hockey (Moore, 1967), current public and official reactions to hockey violence signal the onset of a "moral crusade" (Becker, 1963) aimed at redefining the moral status of aggressive behavior.[1] The social construction of a deviant type of violent sportsman is a political phenomenon. Recognition of the increasingly political nature of deviance (Horowitz and Liebowitz, 1968) and the increasingly political implications of deviance study (Cohen, 1974) is an important step in establishing a collective examination of the field.

For purposes of this analysis, the term "political" encompasses the struggle among *collectives* over the *resources* for survival (De Jouvenal, 1957). To the extent that deviance is political, it involves an organization of actors and the distribution of resources. The resource (in this study) is the criminal law or the police power of the state. As Turk says, "The empirical reality of law . . . seems, then, to be that it is a set of resources for which people contend and with which they are better able to promote their own ideas and interests against others . . ." (1976: 279-80). The capability of using criminal law against collective opponents (Gusfield, 1963) or to ward off opponents' attempts to apply criminal sanctions (Graham, 1972) is a political resource.

Taking the viewpoint of the organization and, consequently, the deviants reverses the usual emphasis of rule-making studies. Chambliss's (1976b) review of approaches to law creation reveals an emphasis on the forces in favor of legal change. This is particularly characteristic of cases in which public or moral indignation is the motive force behind rule-making endeavors. Thus, Gusfield's (1963) interpretation of the temperance crusade for prohibition laws and Duster's (1970) analysis of drug laws deal primarily with the power of organized moral entrepreneurs over unorganized deviants. However, focusing on legal regulation of a legitimate, *organized* enterprise such as professional ice hockey causes the problematic nature of defining deviance and of control to emerge. Here, resistance and negotiation characterize the control of deviance. In addition, the definition of deviance is no longer simply the outcome of the efforts of moral entrepreneurs. Both the *existence* and the *degree* of control are accomplishments of organizational leadership in interaction with organizations and individuals in the environment. Hence, the creation and maintenance of *non*control, exemplified by the consistent non-intervention of criminal law, is a viable topic for deviance study. In this sense, the present study parallels studies of white-collar crimes by emphasizing how occupational and organizational interests avoid, mitigate, co-opt, or divert the intervention of criminalizing interests, be they moral crusaders or criminal justice personnel.

Criminal justice intervention may not always be perceived by management as a threat to the organization. An organization might willingly enlist the forces of law to alleviate an internal control problem (Robin, 1967). However, the control of aggressive behavior in ice hockey by external organizations may pose an indirect or a direct threat. The indirect threat lies in the possibility that official reform action will lead to external control of aggressive play in hockey, substantially reducing organizational and occupational autonomy. The source of organizational problems and of pressures for organizational change lies increasingly in the external environment of other organizations. Accordingly, organizational effectiveness and survival necessitate increased responsiveness to and control over the external environment (Terryberry, 1968; Emery and Trist, 1965; Aldrich, 1971). The less autonomy the organization holds, the less potential it has for adapting to environmental changes that threaten its survival or effectiveness. One important facet of autonomy is the capability of the organization to define and control the conduct of its employees. Hughes (1971b) asserts that the mandate of an occupation to define proper thinking, belief, and conduct is an important feature of the occupation's relationship to the society. Further, he declares that the capability to define and control "mistakes" at work is an essential part of that mandate (1971a).

The indirect threat of reduced autonomy through increased legal control is surpassed by the direct threat of outside control of aggressive play. Aggressive play is part of the game, but legal sanction could reduce the spontaneity of play by introducing an element of caution disruptive to exciting, freewheeling styles. Also, if a certain portion of the public attends hockey games primarily to watch aggressive play, external controls on levels and types of aggression reduce the organization's responsiveness to that audience. Elias and Dunning, in their study of legal control of football in medieval England, state:

> The survival of the game evidently depended on a . . . balance between . . . a high control of the level of violence, because without it the game was no longer acceptable to most players and most spectators . . . and on the other hand, the preservation of a sufficiently high level of non-violent fight-

ing without which the interest of players and public alike would have flagged (1971: 73).

The autonomy of the organization in defining the appropriate level of aggressive play in contemporary ice hockey is considered necessary to ensure public interest and sustain income.

This study of collective rulemaking combines historical and structural approaches to explanation. Five generic factors are specified in the natural history of control over aggressive hockey. These factors produce seven distinct external control patterns,[2] each of which has characterized professional ice hockey at some time in its 70-year history. The control patterns are linked to exogenous structural and definitional aspects of society, the community, and hockey organizations. A change in one of these exogenous variables produces a change in one or more control pattern factors, leading to changes in external control patterns. Each control pattern has different consequences for the definition of aggressive behavior and occupational-organizational autonomy.

A THEORETICAL MODEL OF
EXTERNAL CONTROL PATTERNS

The model of external control patterns explains differences in public and official responses to aggressive play in ice hockey. It consists of five determinants arranged sequentially, following Smelser's (1963) "value-added model." Briefly, the value-added model proposes a distinct series of stages, each of which requires a certain "value" on previous stages before it can be activated as a determinant. In addition, the occurrence of each determinant follows no particular sequential order; only their activation as determinants in the value-added model requires this ordering.

Five Determinants of External Control Patterns

The dynamic pattern of stages and the underlying determinants of external control patterns include the following: (1) an awareness stage, based on the physical and social visibility of the sport and aggressive play; (2) an evaluation stage, hinging on the congruity or incongruity between normative evaluations of aggressive play by hockey interests and external publics; (3) a threat stage, based on the hockey organization's perceptions of the nature, probability, and impact of sanctions applied by the criminal justice system; (4) a responsibility stage, in which the degree of threat to the organization may be magnified through attribution of responsibility to a collective or organizational locus rather than an individual one; and (5) a response stage, determined by the legal action taken by the organization in either protecting its members or "disowning" them. A change in any determinant necessarily changes the control pattern, but a change in a determinant at the initial stages of the model has a more profound effect on the control pattern that results. In other words, as the model progresses through each stage, the outcome is increasingly determined and the possibilities are increasingly narrowed. A schematic diagram of the value-added model of external control patterns is presented in figure 2. A brief description of stages and determinants follows.

Awareness Stage

The awareness stage centers on the commonplace but crucial observation that behavior must be visible in order to be defined as problematic and sanctioned as deviant. Duster (1970) analyzed changes in drug laws in the United States and suggested that the physical visibility of the behavior—its arena of occurrence—affected the likelihood that deviant santions would be applied. Physical visibility is a crucial determinant of enforcement patterns (Chambliss and Seidman, 1971) and also underlies the observation that behavior is deviant according to some social audience (Erikson, 1966). However, physical visibility is not a sufficient condition for defining deviance. The behavior must be considered problematic by an audience and must be attributed a meaning; in short, it must have *social visibility* (Inciardi, 1972). Hence, this stage includes two necessary and distinct subparts. First physical visibility of hockey play is analyzed as it influences the likelihood that certain audiences will come into contact with the sport. This idea is based on studies that suggest that social groups differ in how they define, legitimate, and react to aggressive behavior (Blumenthal et al., 1972). Second, changes in social visibility follow changes in social conceptions of and public sensitization to aggressive behavior, changes in the style and incidence of aggressive play and in the specific characteristics of precipitating incidents.

Evaluation Stage

The evaluation stage refers to congruence or incongruence between definitions of and solutions to aggressive play by criminal jus-

Type of External
Control Pattern

INVISIBLE

TYPICAL

SYMBOLIC

SACRIFICIAL

PATERNAL

FARCICAL

POLITICAL

Individual

Collective

Individual—*RESPONSE*

Collective—*RESPONSE*

Not Threatened

Threatened—*RESPONSIBILITY*

Individual

Collective

Incongruent—*THREAT*

Invisible

Congruent

AWARENESS

Visible—*EVALUATION*

Figure 2. A value-added model of external control patterns.

tice representatives and hockey representatives. Robin (1967) provides some empirical support for this issue. He studied the differences in referral patterns of employee pilferers to criminal court. Since the corporation had control over referrals, these patterns differed depending on the internal requirements of the organization and the comparative advantages and disadvantages of prosecution. If aggressive play in hockey is perceived by management as a problem or as an unimportant aspect of the game, then the likelihood of organization opposition to legal intervention is decreased and, in some cases, might lead to active promotion. On the other hand, if aggressive behavior is viewed as a necessary part of the game, noncooperation or opposition to legal intervention is likely.

Threat Stage

Gusfield's study (1963) of the temperance crusade for prohibition laws, as well as analyses of white-collar and corporate crime (Stone, 1975; Aubert, 1952), indicate the importance of sanction threat to the organization of the deviant actor. Despite the existence of legal proscriptions, lack of enforcement reduces indignant protest to howling into the wind. In his study of the instrumental and expressive functions of regulatory agencies Edelman (1967: 39) concluded, "It is not uncommon to give the rhetoric to one side and the decision to the other." Legal statutes or common-law traditions are available for the prosecution of overly aggressive play in sport, but the nonexistence, episodic incidence, and nonsuccess of prosecution efforts pose little threat to the hockey organization.

Responsibility Stage

Even with a high probability of sanctions, the threat to the organization can be magnified or mitigated by the particular attribution of responsibility. As Cohen points out, "If deviant acts are attributed to collectivities, the consequences are different than if they are attributed to individuals" (1966: 22). If the public and law enforcers hold the individual responsible, the consequences for the hockey organization are less severe than if the organization is viewed as blameworthy. The prevailing conception of the source of hockey aggression has changed over the years. But, in addition to the specific problem of determining responsibility in ice hockey aggression, the issue of determining responsibility for acts undertaken by persons in institutionalized roles is widely disputed. Although some argue that legal individualism underlies the criminal law (Hallowell and Meshbesher, 1977; Cressey, 1969), there is a public split in the United States over the allocation of responsibility in occupational-organizational settings. Kelman and Lawrence (1972) studied public responses to the trial of Lieutenant William Calley and found that a majority disapproved of the trial per se, irrespective of its outcome. In their sample, 58% disapproved of criminal sanctioning if the individual followed what he believed to be the implicit orders of the authority for his legitimate role. The determination and legitimation of collective or individual responsibility for organizational-occupational behavior is an important matter for study. For our purposes, the determination of responsibility for aggressive behavior in ice hockey is crucial because: (1) a collective attribution might increase public indignation; (2) a collective attribution might activate other noncriminal sanctions or other legal activity; (3) a collective attribution might spawn other investigative activity; (4) a collective attribution might reduce the likelihood of individual convictions in assault cases; and (5) a collective attribution might increase the likelihood of ameliorative reforms by the hockey organization.

Response Stage

Regardless of attribution of responsibility, but often in conjunction with it, organizational management decides whether it will protect its members from legal prosecution. Group protection or nonprotection of the individual member is a long-standing theme of legal history. In earlier eras, collective responsibility, punishment, and protection characterized the response to harmful behavior (Kennedy, 1975). The decision to respond by protecting or banishing the deviant has been discussed (Coser, 1962). Consequences of these responses for particular social groups has been studied in groups and situations as divergent as guilds (Brentano, 1969), serf-lord relationships (Hay, 1975), corporation action in modern society (Stone, 1975), and employer-employee relationships in modern corporations (Robin, 1967). These studies show that, in addition to the pragmatic and direct consequence that the marshaling of group resources might abate the criminal sanction, the persistence of organizational authorities in either rejecting or protecting individual members influences both the solidarity of the group and the loyalty of members to authority. However, the decision to protect or reject the individual must also account for external relationships and definitions. The response stage is a strategic one since the organizational authority must choose between rejection in hopes of reducing public indignation through a well-timed "sacrifice" and protection in hopes of convincing the public of the propriety of the behavior or convincing the prosecutor of the difficulty of conviction. In the case of hockey players charged with assault, hockey officials display protection or rejection through public pronouncements, negotiations with prosecutorial officials, provision of legal fees, and testimony in cases brought to trial. Even if the reaction is ineffective in averting conviction, it still has potential impact on public definitions and the prevalence of solidarity or conflict in the hockey organization. This becomes especially crucial when players, teams, and levels of the hockey management hierarchy diverge on the definition and legitimation of aggressive play.

External Control Patterns and Organizational Outcomes

External control patterns vary in their consequences for the definition of harmful behavior and the autonomy of the organization. The value-added model produces seven types of external control patterns; each one exemplifies a particular configuration of determinants and a particular combination of consequences.

Alternative definitions of abnormally aggressive behavior can be classified as mistake, routine deviance, or political deviance. Each classification refers to the type of conflict (or lack of it) over definitions and the likelihood of routine sanctioning. If aggressive behavior is defined as a mistake, criminal justice intervention is absent. When this definition obtains, the organization is autonomous, retaining the power to define and control conduct. If aggressive behavior is defined as routine deviance, it is responded to with routine sanctions. Agents of the criminal justice system may intervene, consequently reducing the autonomy of the hockey organization. However, this effect may be minimized if the behavior is deemed unimportant by the league or the sanctioning has no implications for collective survival. Finally, aggressive behavior is defined as political deviance (for our analysis, "deviant" refers to the extent of criminal justice mobilization) when (1) conflict over the appropriate definition of the behavior occurs among organization officials, criminal justice representatives, and any public interest group members; (2) a dispute over who has the right to define the behavior—the question of mandate—occurs among criminal justice, organization, and interest group members; and (3) the league perceives the "definitional outcome" as a potential threat to its organization (as well as a threat to individual members). Thus, the autonomy of the organization is threatened by classifications of political deviance. Dispute over punishment between criminal justice representatives and the league guarantees that sanctions do not become routine.

The final consequence of external control patterns is the impact of evaluation and response for organizational solidarity and conflict. The importance of protection or rejection was discussed above, but this must be assessed in conjunction with possible disputes *within* the organization over the appropriateness of aggressive play. Hence, the effect of a particular response to outside sanction threats on certain subunits or individual members depends on the appropriateness of criminal justice assistance for deterring aggressive action. In other words, some interests in hockey may welcome outside intervention to reduce aggressive play and may oppose organizational efforts to avert prosecution. These individuals and groups conflict with those whose interests demand sustaining the pattern of aggressive play and raise a fundamental dilemma for management.

We now provide brief sketches of the external control patterns. The *invisible* pattern is characterized by low physical or social visibility. Aggressive behavior remains unproblematic to social audiences outside hockey. The *typical* control pattern refers to guaranteed visibility, congruent definitions between hockey and external interests, and routine sanctioning. The pattern is *symbolic* when visibility is joined by incongruent evaluations, but enforcement is not viewed as a threat. Whenever threat is added to visibility and incongruency, both responsibility and response stages become important. The *sacrificial* pattern refers to the situation in which an attribution of individual responsibility is followed by organizational rejection of the player and withdrawal of protection. The *paternal* pattern is characterized by organizational protection of individual players. Two patterns of control involve the attribution of responsibility to the collective but differ in organizational response. The *farcical* pattern is exemplified when the collective is threatened and legal maneuvers make it difficult or impossible for the organization to respond protectively. The *political* pattern involves all-out conflict between the organization and criminal justice representatives. The league intensifies its efforts to protect individual players and the image of the hockey organization.

The following section applies the general model of external control patterns to the history of the occurrence and control of aggressive behavior in professional ice hockey. The emphasis is on control from *external* agencies; the problems and programs of internal control are discussed only insofar as they affect external control patterns.

After a set of initial conditions (or independent variables) of society, community, and hockey organizations is determined, the pattern of control is described in terms of the configuration of control pattern determinants (or intervening variables). Finally, a discussion of the consequences of that control pattern follows. Changes in society, community, and hockey organizations will be included and analyzed as they produce changes in one or more determinants of new control patterns. The illustration of these seven control patterns relies heavily on the analysis of leading cases of aggressive incidents, and, admittedly, the quantity and quality of data vary across time. Therefore, the findings are to be considered suggestive. A more detailed analysis of the historical patterns of control in ice hockey is ongoing.

HOCKEY "VIOLENCE" AND EXTERNAL CONTROL

There are numerous factors that could be associated with changes in society's reaction to aggressive behavior. The following account attempts to highlight some aspects of society, community, and hockey organizations that change in a coincidental fashion with changes in control patterns. As such, these aspects cannot be taken as causes of control patterns, but, as an integrated scheme, they do organize the available data well. It goes without saying that a time period of more than 70 years aggravates analytical problems by its extent of social and organizational change. This problem has been alleviated somewhat by the reduction of variables to a core set that transcend historical eras (e.g., amount and style of aggressive play). Dates are tentative and approximate.

Typical Control and Hockey's Formative Years
(1890 to 1910)

Aggressive play, injury, and indignant protest arose in the first years of the game, and officials of amateur hockey responded with new rules and refereeing practices. Crowds were often rowdy and officials tended to leave the game when abusive language or aggressive behavior threatened their dignity. Although the guiding unit was the Amateur Hockey Association (AHA), by 1899 accusations that some players were playing for money appeared in the press. Reports of "rough" play increased with the expansion of leagues, teams, and games. Despite the lack of a Canadian organized professional league, this era involved the formation of initial public definitions of the sport. The typical control pattern features high visibility of aggressive play and congruent definitions by hockey organizations and the public, resulting in routine sanctioning of cases.

Awareness

The physical visibility of hockey was guaranteed by the newness of the sport and by active attempts of ice rink entrepreneurs to attract a large, paying clientele. Aggressive play continued and may have increased throughout this period (Coleman, 1966), one that featured many of ice hockey's more gruesome incidents. The death of Owen McCourt in 1907 focused public attention on aggression in hockey (Fischler, 1974) and led to denunciations of "the man-killing element" in the game. Neither the rule structure nor sanctions by referees and league officials deterred aggressive acts. Interleague competition for top players along with the financial necessity of keeping star players active diminished the effectiveness of internal sanctions. The patterns of aggressive play that resulted can best be described as individual-expressive: individual players acted on their own to settle a grudge or repay an opponent's blow but did not relate it to game-winning strategy or to the enhancement of their careers. Accounts of aggressive incidents were concentrated among a small group of players who tended to lead in penalty records.

Data on social visibility are sparse, but Gitler (1974) suggests that early audiences included many "genteel" spectators who were indignant about player and spectator aggression. In addition to a generalized dissatisfaction with "roughness," several key incidents channeled public indignation and led to arrest warnings and arrests. These incidents involved alleged attacks of one player on another with the hockey stick. The most frequent result was severe cuts on the head. The most serious result was the death of Owen McCourt. The coroner's inquest upon his death concluded

> that Owen McCourt came to his death by a blow from a hockey stick. . . . And, that in the opinion of this jury, there is no evidence of ill feeling previous to the assault, there was no justification by personal provocation for the blow. . . . After hearing the evidence, your jury further recommends that legislation be enacted whereby players or spectators encouraging or engaging in rough or foul play may be severely punished (Coleman, 1966: 140).

The defendant was acquitted, legislation was not enacted, and aggressive play continued—though with less extreme consequences. Three other players were arrested that same season and two received $20 fines.

Evaluation

Disputes over player sanctioning arose primarily to keep star players active. Arrests of players and subsequent trials were not considered threats to the fledgling sport except when a top player was involved. Even in these special cases, the league did not oppose court action. In fact, league officials made attempts to curb aggressive play through changes in rules but were unsuccessful. In short, hockey officials shared public opposition to extreme aggressive play, and, while not actively initiating legal response, they did not oppose it.

Outcome

The issue of external control of aggressive play served as an indirect threat to autonomy. Instead of focusing on the question of who defines appropriate conduct, hockey officials were concerned about the loss of star players through any form of sanctioning. The issue was one of many conflicts in the multi-league hockey world. One league president resigned in 1907 over a dispute concerning the internal control of aggressive players, but no evidence of similar arguments about external control exists. Regardless of disagreements about internal control, the basic legitimacy of the criminal justice system appears to have prevailed, and the "routine deviants" were sanctioned without protest.

**Symbolic Control and the Rise
of Professional Ice Hockey (1910 to 1922)**

A professional hockey league had existed in the United States since 1895, but the immediate precursor of the current National Hockey League (NHL), the National Hockey Association (NHA), was not formed until 1910. Competing professional leagues arose in 1911 and 1921 and lasted until 1925, leaving only the NHL (formed in 1917) out of remnants of the NHA (United States Congress, 1957). The threat of competition with amateur hockey for spectators was deepened by public response to the "evils of professionalism." In an article reprinted in a Toronto newspaper, a cynical Montreal editorial writer intoned:

> For years the work of professionalism was done in the dark, secret and underhanded: now it is in the light. But the work savors of a poisonous undercurrent which is gnawing at the vitals of our great Canadian summer

and winter sports, and sounding the death knell of both (*Toronto Globe,* December 5, 1912, p. 12).

Along with the opposition to professionalism came increased awareness of and opposition to aggressive play.

Awareness

The physical visibility of aggressive play remained high both in frequency of incidents and in introduction of new publics. In 1912, the NHA expanded to Toronto, and in the opening game a stick attack led to an arrest and a trial for assault. A prominent article in the *Toronto Globe* said:

> The sort of "sport" that permits a man to slash with a hockey stick an opponent who is down, and not looking at his assailant, is looked on too leniently by the authorities of the National Hockey Association, and the Toronto police mean to prevent a repetition, since the N.H.A. will not (December 25, 1912, p. 12).

The writer connected this case with another sport case and called for a jail term. He closed the article with a warning:

> The professional hockey promoters made a serious mistake when they practically condoned Cleghorn's offense. To a large extent their business is on trial here, and they have been the first to discredit it (p. 12).

What is significant about these statements is that in Toronto, contrary to the pattern in other cities, public indignation was continuous and was supported by continuous police activity. The social visibility of aggressive hockey was enhanced by the generation of a folk conception of aggressive play in ice hockey as a crime and of a folk prescription of police and court action as the appropriate solution. For a public to typify any concrete event or series of events requires that the event fit prevailing folk conceptions (Turner, 1969). In other words, aggressive play in ice hockey must look like crime before it can be typified as such and responded to with traditional folk prescriptions for similar "crimes." Although episodic reactions to disturbing events are common, once a particular incident is over and its emotionally charged atmosphere is diminished demands for charges or criminal complaints can be dropped, with no stable definition of the incident—folk conception—established and no continuous response—folk prescription—legitimated. Briefly, there are three possible definitions of an aggressive incident in ice hockey. First, the incident can be defined as normal, in which case it will be ignored.

Second, it can be defined as an exemplar of a preexisting folk conception, in which case it will be considered a crime or, more specifically, assault. Finally, it can be defined as something entirely new, in which case a unique folk conception will be developed to explain it (Cohen, 1972). All three outcomes involve public definitions of events and conditions but focus most readily on incidents of abnormal aggressive play. The process of defining a particular incident has important implications for the outcome. The establishment of a continuous rather than an episodic reaction to aggressive behavior requires that the folk conception precede the folk prescription, that the crucial "public" define the behavior as "very much like a crime of assault" and then activate the criminal sanction. It is suggested that some cases that do not lead to continuous legal attention or in which demands for arrest are dropped are characterized by an initial police reaction—folk prescription—that is not supported by the necessary folk conception and is consequently rescinded.

Data from hockey provide some support for these distinctions. Out of 30 total legal response incidents in professional ice hockey, 8 (or 26%) occurred in Toronto. The remaining 22 were scattered among 13 other communities. In terms of specific characteristics of incidents responded to, arrest incidents usually involved extreme injury, imputation of intent, use of the hockey stick, and spectator involvement. Table 7 demonstrates the importance of spectator involvement in eliciting a legal response. Of course, not all incidents including these elements generated a legal response. The implications are as follows: (1) certain characteristics of aggressive incidents tend to elicit a folk prescription; (2) these prescriptions—legal responses—are often fleeting; (3) one community has surpassed all others in legal responses. Taken in conjunction with other information, that Toronto had both public discussion of criminalization and that police issued pregame warnings in a proactive manner, these findings support the notion of the importance of a folk conception for continuity in definition of and reaction to aggressive play. I suggest an interaction of concrete features of incidents and community definitions as necessary for a continuing definition of aggressive play as deviant. These concrete features negate the dominant folk conception of the activity as "just in sport" and revoke the nonintervention definition that pervades sport activity as a "sacred" institution. Once this release has occurred, disturbed publics work to define reality and to draw on existing prescriptions of what to do about a problem. If this redefinition does not include a folk conception of aggressive play as a

Table 7. Percentage of Legal Responses to Abnormally Aggressive
Incidents in Ice Hocky from 1894 to 1976   (Arrest, Warning, Invervention)
by Role of Participants

Legal Response	Players, Officials	Players, Spectators	Total
Yes	24%	87%	31% (N = 45)
No	76%	13%	69% (N = 101)
Total	100% (N = 131)	100% (N = 15)	100% (N = 146)

crime of assault already prevalent in the community, then legal activity will be sporadic at best. When the folk conception is supported by some public, the possibility for continuous sanctioning is enhanced.

The social visibility of aggressive play was intensified by folk conceptions following the introduction of the professional game in Toronto. During this period, Toronto police intervened in professional games five times, and each intervention produced public discussion and solidified folk conceptions.

Evaluation

Despite press reports that the board of governors and the president of the NHA were opposed to "foul play" and were committed to eliminating it, official action was inconsistent. As the December 25, 1912 *Toronto Globe* article indicates, some reporters considered official sanctions too lenient. Moreover, these sanctions were often rescinded. Official inconsistency was contrasted with increasing player acceptance of certain norms of aggressive play. Injury was spoken of by some as "one of the risks of the game." The most dramatic indicator of a developing incongruity between community and hockey definitions of aggressive play was the successful attempt by a hockey player to plead on behalf of his assailant before the magistrate (Coleman, 1966). In another case, the victim reportedly "refused to lay an information against his assailant" (*Toronto Globe*, December 28, 1912, p. 23). Overall, as the professional hockey world evolved, players developed an occupational culture that negated conceptions of aggressive play as routine deviance and actively circumvented legal responses.

Threat

With the incongruity between hockey and community definitions established, the threat to individuals and to league maintenance became salient. The key feature of this control pattern—its symbolic nature—lies in the lack of effective enforcement. First, a large number of aggressive incidents evoked no legal response; those that did often resulted in dropped charges, reduced charges, or nominal fines. For example, two players involved in an incident flipped a coin to determine which would pay the $1 fine. Second, in spite of editorial writers' contentions that the sport was on trial, individuals rather than the league were held legally responsible for aggressive acts. "Blood and murder games," reprinted in the *Toronto Globe* from a Montreal paper, indicted all sports for "rowdy tactics," explored causes, and proposed solutions:

> There are men playing in these different sports who are experts in nagging and using insulting epithets to opposing players, and little by little the flames of anger and passion are fanned into fury until rowdyism and brutality begin. . . .
>
> The general impression is that if any player cannot control his temper when playing in any line of sport he is not fit to be allowed to remain in action, and banishment for good is the best medicine and most suitable punishment for such an individual. . . .
>
> The poor attendance at our sports speaks in trumpet tones for a much needed change, and the quicker those concerned eradicate the great errors they have introduced, or allowed to hold sway, the better for our sports in general and our athletic organizations in particular (*Toronto Globe*, February 22, 1913, p. 26).

By attributing responsibility to individuals, suggesting solutions in terms of management repeal of deviant behavioral standards, and implying consequences for sport attendance, such editorials minimized the direct threat to the hockey organization.

Outcome

Aggressive play was treated as a mistake (albeit a grievous one) rather than as deviant behavior. Mobilization of the law occurred throughout this period; however, legal sanctions were minimal and could be more aptly labeled symbolic. Because the nascent culture of professional hockey produced increasingly homogeneous norms about the role and meaning of aggressive play, conflict was reduced. That the definition of aggression in this period enhanced solidarity may be indicated by a player's willingness to plead in his assailant's behalf. Finally, although hockey and community publics defined aggressive play differently, the lack of real sanctions diminished the potential threat to organizational autonomy.

Invisible Control and the Consolidation of the League (1922 to 1949)

Although the NHL's competition folded during the period from 1922 to 1949, professional ice hockey was well established by the 1920s. Along with the end of interleague competition came increased control by the NHL. While conflicts over the control of aggressive play continued, improvement in the rules and refereeing resulted in fewer aggressive incidents. Rough play was still prevalent but legal responses leveled off and remained almost nonexistent for the next 45 years. The determining characteristic of this external control pattern is the absence of visibility and legal reactions.

Awareness

The physical visibility of hockey decreased. While the number of games played increased, the number of leagues and teams decreased. This meant more games played by the same teams, in the same communities, to the same clientele. That clientele had fewer abnormally aggressive incidents to define as the rate decreased. Only occasional calls for arrest and a lack of trials characterized the ensuing years. The type of aggression changed in that deliberate head injuries to disabled opponents became less frequent. There were still many alleged deliberate stick swinging incidents but with less extreme results. Most of the individual players consistently involved in extreme incidents left active play early in this period. Also, players describe these years of NHL consolidation as a time of fraternization between players of opposing teams (Gitler, 1974). It is likely that the retirement of the remaining individual-expressive marauders, greater control by league authorities, and increased respect of players for their opponents resulted in less aggressive play. Hence, severe injuries that had in the past resulted in arrest were no longer present. The social visibility of aggressive play decreased with a stable clientele (who became accustomed to some aggression) and a reduction in the types of incidents likely to evoke legal responses. In short, neither the audiences nor the acts were conducive to a folk conception of aggressive play as a crime.

Outcome

With little external interference, the autonomy of the league was enhanced. Aggressive play became a "mistake" to be fined by league officials. Most important, the definition of proper conduct was now monopolized by league authority. However, this did not lead to solidarity. According to Coleman (1966) the board of governors argued incessantly over the propriety of aggressive play, and certain teams opposed aggressive tactics while others cultivated them. Regardless of intrahockey disagreements, the external control situation had no effect on solidarity or conflict.

Paternal Control and the Stable Years (1949 to 1968)

The onset of the "invisible period" (1922 to 1949) was marked by the strong authority of management, illustrated by the suspension of an entire team that attempted to go on strike (Coleman, 1966), the "paternal period" (1949 to 1968) exemplified a major shift in the mood of management, typified by patronizing actions toward players, and a change in the power structure of the league. The NHL was dominated by a family that entered the sports business in the 1930s and owned or had a substantial interest in three of six teams by the 1950s. The guiding figure in the family believed that, in business, relationships should be based on trust and the strength of his word (Fischler, 1974). When he appeared before a United States House Subcommittee on sport, the NHL president, Clarence Campbell, said that club owners do have a "sympathetic attitude" toward prestige players and their requests. Later in the hearings, player representative Ted Lindsay agreed that owners took "an overpaternalistic view toward their players" and other testimony indicated that the owners had opposed the formation of a players' association (United States Congress, 1957). Finally, fraternization among opponents was discouraged and the active elimination of more amicable relationships followed (Gitler, 1974).

Awareness

The visibility of aggressive play increased during this period. The breakdown of fraternization among players contributed to an increase in abnormally aggressive incidents. Public attention returned to hockey in 1949 when banner headlines announced the arrest of three players who assaulted a spectator during a game. Despite widespread publicity of the case, charges were eventually dropped, and public attention receded until the Montreal hockey riot of 1955. This riot occurred after NHL president Campbell suspended French Canadian hockey player Maurice Richard. Right after the suspension, Montreal fans began a protest that culminated in a destructive rampage through downtown Montreal. With worldwide attention focused on this event, some Canadians searched for causes, consequences, and solutions. Explanations were many and diverse, including a "loss of control" by enraged sports fans, the "hoodlum element" taking advantage of a chaotic situation, and a display of anti-English sentiment by French Canadians. Most important, some saw the outbreak as the inevitable outgrowth of violence in ice hockey. An editorial in the *Ottawa Journal*, reprinted widely throughout Canada, declared:

> Violence of a mob in this particular instance was an almost inevitable consequence of continued permitted violence in hockey itself. . . . We have come to a point where an act which outside the hockey rink . . . would be treated as a bodily assault and dealt with accordingly is in such forums regarded as normal, left to the punishment—if there is punishment at all—of a referee.
>
> Assault is assault; in the criminal code put down as a crime. Why should a man assaulting another with a hockey stick in a hockey rink be treated differently? Why should his punishment be outside the law, left to a referee or other officials? The locale of a crime make it any less criminal?
>
> Hockey referees are necessary to deal with infractions of rules. But assault with a hockey stick is more than the infraction of playing rules: it is assault, an attempt to do bodily harm—under the law a crime. . . .
>
> Perhaps if bodily assaults in hockey rinks were dealt with by magistrates instead of referees more of us would understand the real meaning of crime—of violence. And if the rule were applied as well to prize rings and wrestling rings—where violence runs rampant—so much the better. There might be less danger of mobs (March 25, 1955, p. 6).

Although law enforcers did not follow these suggestions, the definition of aggressive play as crime was communicated widely.

Evaluation

Hockey efforts to control aggressive play were sporadic. Occasional crackdowns were followed by periods of neglect. Hockey officials and supporters often opposed the suggestion that the sport was overly violent and refused to make changes in rules of play. In the aforementioned spectator assault case, hockey officials attributed the problem to unruly spectators and worked to release and exonerate the players. Similarly, critics of the riot blamed "the criminal element" in society rather than hockey fans. In all cases, public criticism was short-lived and hockey officials remained committed to the prevailing mode of aggressive play.

Threat

After years of scant legal attention, the threat of the application of criminal law to the area of sports raised significant questions for hockey. The current leadership had arrived after the earlier period of arrests and, in addition to their lack of experience with the law in sport, were confronted with the prospect of players being jailed for assault. Although the sporadic nature of arrests minimized threat to the organization, the league still had to contend with intense public concern and the indignity of jail.

Responsibility

This period is marked by a transition in the attribution of responsibility. Although the individual remained the primary focus of responsibility and punishment, links to the hockey organization entered public discussion. As mentioned in the Ottawa editorial, hockey officials were not seen as causing the violence but as permitting it. Despite this argument, the writer maintained that an appropriate response would focus on the individual through the uses of criminal law. Individual responsibility also came into question with the emergence of the "policeman role" in ice hockey. In this mode of aggressive play, one player on each team has the informal duty to protect his teammates. This individual-instrumental style complicated the task of determining responsibility; aggressive play became the duty of particular individuals, but was enacted for team rather than individual purposes. While links between aggressive play and the hockey organization were forming, the individual player continued to be the primary locus of responsibility.

Response

Hockey officials recognized a potential threat, but that threat was minimized by focusing on the individual. They reacted accordingly. Hockey officials averted criticism by not protesting too much, yet every effort was made to protect players from the legal system. The owner of one team made a special effort to get arrested players released from jail, and league officials carefully avoided any activity that might prejudice the case. It was clear that hockey players, like errant sons, were given the protection of a paternal management.

Outcome

With a threat added to conditions of high visibility and an incongruent evaluation, the prospect for a reduction of autonomy became real. Against a backdrop of initial public criticism of the hockey organization (but individual attribution of responsibility), the criminal sanctioning of players could proceed routinely, subject to the characteristics of individual cases. Hence, this control pattern involved a return to routine deviance.

Farcical Control and the Expansion Years (1969 to 1974)

In the 1960s, rapid change occurred in society and in ice hockey. A new management philosophy replaced the "cottage industry" character of previous decades and the six-team league expanded rapidly (Fischler, 1974). The spread of ice hockey on all levels of play was accompanied by a rapid influx of new and untested managers and players and an increase in abnormally aggressive incidents. In 1969, amid growing public criticism of hockey violence, two players were arrested for assault and a new control pattern emerged. The central characteristic of farcical control is a disjuncture between the purpose and object of control. During this period, such disjuncture occurred in two ways. First, two individuals were the objects of control, although the sport organization was to be reformed. Second, the sanctioning of player violence at the professional level had two purposes; it was intended to effect crowd control at professional contests and to improve the situation for amateur hockey. These are common tactics of criminal justice agencies—using key individuals (Stone, 1975; Krislov, 1971) or available legal doctrine (Marx, 1974) to sanction an organization or to sanction uncontrolled activity.

Awareness

The physical expansion of ice hockey was dramatic on all levels of play, because of television coverage and new franchises. An increase in aggressive play and a few noteworthy stick fights helped focus public attention on sports violence. The crucial change occurred in the social visibility of aggressive play. During this period aggressive play began to look like something completely different. Instead of activity in the rink being fit into prevailing folk conceptions of crime, a *new* folk conception of deviance (hockey violence) and a new deviant (the violent sportsman) emerged. Aggression was not new and, in some ways, became less extreme. But aggression in sport now resonated with deep-seated fears growing out of the experience of rapid and violent social change. In the ebb and flow of folk conceptions, hockey violence became, in Cohen's (1972) terms, a "folk devil," a public stereotype symbolizing social change and providing a highly visible exemplar of what to avoid. The backdrop for the folk devil came in public responses to the chaotic sixties. A general concern with and fear of violence (Mulvihill, 1969; Blumenthal, et al., 1972) coupled with widespread fear of rising crime and the emergence of "the crime problem" as a top priority (Erskine, 1974a) produced a general sensitization about violence and aggression. Although historians pointed out. "There is nothing new in our violence, only in our sudden awareness of it" (Hofstadter and Wallace, 1971: 3), public concern was fed by a sense of newness and a prediction of deterioration. One large-scale study (Blumenthal, et al. 1972) showed that this intense concern was paralleled by disagreement over which acts were violent. Hence, the stage was set for some social audience to find "violence" in ice hockey, and league expansion provided an opportunity.

The importance of physical visibility is underscored by an apparent conflict in the meaning of violence between people of different income levels in Canada. A 1970 public opinion poll in Canada indicated lack of consensus over the acceptability of types of violence. Fighting at a hockey game was the most acceptable form of entertainment-oriented violence among those included in the pool, with 60% claiming a distaste for it and 39% claiming they like to see it. Further analyses showed that the percentage enjoying hockey fights was higher among males (46%) and among low-income groups (48%). Since low-income males are the main population from which hockey draws its fans, researchers concluded that "nearly half the people who watch the game positively *want* violence." ("We're more violent than we think," 1970: 25). Their analyses of general reactions to violence indicated that people in higher income brackets are more disturbed by the sight of violence and are more likely to declare it as a basic human need. Poorer individuals are less upset by the sight of violence and less likely to define it as "part of human nature." The researchers interpreted the disparity this way:

> People in the lower income groups are pragmatic about conflict. They are less inclined to say violence is a basic human need but they are also less timid about witnessing it. Violence is something they live with (1970: 28).

These findings suggest that one impetus behind the hockey violence reform movement was the presentation of the sport to social audiences unaccustomed to aggressive behavior.

These audiences were irritated further by the style of aggressive play dominating the late 1960s and the 1970s. During the early sixties several players effectively changed the mode of aggressive play by replacing the reactive-protective "policeman" with an active-aggressive instigator of fights. This change, combined with managers' attempts to undermine fraternization among players, led to another breakdown in the informal means of violence control (Gitler, 1974). However, this individual-instrumental mode was quickly replaced by group-based modes of aggressive play. When one team (in 1968) discovered that intimidation by the team acting in concert was an effective means of winning hockey games (Chevalier, 1974), the group-instrumental mode became salient. At the same time, players' disrespect for referees and league discipline increased. These changes produced a situation conducive to increased aggressive play of all kinds, from individual stick attacks to all-out brawls.

The public's definition of the causes and consequences of this new mode of aggressive play increased their indignation. Because of the increasing popularity of ice hockey among Canadian and American youth and public concern about widespread violence in that age group, commentators began to define professional aggressive play as a bad influence on young people. This threat, together with the league's fears that aggressive play would ruin the quality of sport activity, was aggravated by insinuations that aggressive hockey was not used only to win games but, in the words of hockey assault defendant Ted Green, "to sell tickets, to fill their rinks" (*Ottawa Journal*, October 11, 1969, p. 17). It became clear that these accusations were directed at the owners of hockey teams and their representative, Clarence Campbell.

These disparate trends and conditions crystallized in the arrest of Ted Green and Wayne Maki for a stick fight in Ottawa in 1969. Prior to the Green-Maki incident, Ottawa citizens were concerned about violence and were attempting to do something about it. This concern became directed toward the area of sport by press reports on sport violence outside the city and reached the Ottawa sports scene when crowd control problems occurred at home games. The community responded with stricter enforcement, tightened security, and new municipal laws, until the Green-Maki incident refocused attention on the role of the player. After that event, in an atmosphere of heightened concern over violence in Montreal, Ottawa officials decided to press charges.

Evaluation

League officials responded negatively to court intervention but acknowledged "the primacy of the civil code." A crackdown on violence, especially stick swinging followed, but the league remained staunchly committed to the view that fighting is a legitimate part of the game. According to NHL president Campbell, it was necessary:

> Our philosophy toward fighting is that if tempers reach the point where players are not content to go on and play without some sort of assault, far better that they should drop their sticks and fight. It works as a safety valve.
>
> But, if we were to remove the safety valve, the players would no doubt develop a more subtle form of viciousness ("Maclean's interviews: Clarence Campbell, 1969: 73).

The safety valve argument was rejected by those who saw fighting as the spark of further aggression. Those people also suspected that control efforts by hockey officials were merely symbolic, aimed at covering the active promotion of violence to sell tickets, win games, and enhance personal careers.

Threat

Regardless of agreement that stick violence required more effective sanctions, league representatives were threatened by legal intervention. Some declared that legal activity would ruin sport, while the more circumspect saw it as a lack of faith in league disciplinary procedures. One Ontario judge acknowledged that applying traditional assault definitions to ice hockey would pose a direct threat:

> It is very difficult in my opinion for a player who is playing hockey with all the force, vigour and strength at his command, who is engaged in the rough and tumble of the game . . . suddenly to stop and say, "I must not do that . . . maybe I am committing an assault" (*Regina* v. *Ted Green*, 1971: 595).

Although neither Green nor Maki was convicted, Campbell emphasized that the decision was "not necessarily a vindication of the NHL and its method of operation." On the contrary, the judge in the Maki case declared that no sports league "should render players in that league immune from criminal prosecution . . ." (*Regina* v. *Maki*, 1970). Local newspaper editorials responded, "If a league in given instances doesn't police itself it is up to the laws of the country to keep order," (*Ottawa Journal*, March 6, 1970, p. 6). The threat of prosecution remained strong, as evidenced by several subsequent cases of arrest and trial at the junior hockey level.

Responsibility

Attributions of blame for hockey violence were increasingly directed at the league or the game itself. This accorded with the popular belief that players, teams, and owners used aggressive play for their advantage—they could instigate or promote it, or fail to take "proper" control actions. The widespread belief that violence was organizationally induced was not evidenced in prosecutorial strategies. Rather than focusing directly on violence in professional ice hockey (as something worthy of legal attention in its own right), prosecutorial staff emphasized the politically safer arguments of protecting youth and controlling unruly crowds. For example, the public prosecutor responsible for the Green and Maki cases justified the prosecutions thus:

> "My submission is that if, as a result of the events, two things appear: first, that there is a degree of force used which is not in the normal context of the rules of the game, and the event itself alarms and causes either a disturbance, or a situation which may give rise to public involvement in the events, then the state becomes involved for the protection of the individuals in the arena and of the participants in the event, no matter what may be their status as far as their willingness or otherwise to prosecute each other for the alleged assaults between each other.[11] (*Regina* v. *Wayne Maki*, 1970: 21).

And thus:

> I submit that the effect of this kind of event on those watching—if it did not create a disturbance or breach of the peace, is a matter in which the authorities should be involved and which the police should investigate (*Regina* v. *Wayne Maki*, 1970: 24).

And in response to the court's question whether prosecution was relevant to the issue:

> Should it be argued at some stage that there should not have been involvement in a situation of this kind I would not be put in a position of saying that what goes on in a public arena . . . that it is not of importance to the public (*Regina* v. *Wayne Maki*, 1970: 26).

The prosecutor's emphasis on crowd control was rejected by the defense and the court, but a similar idea was used in police investigation of another hockey disturbance at the junior level. This disjuncture between the objects and purposes of control exemplified farcical control. The object of control, the hockey league, was not prosecuted; rather, two individuals were tried for organizational malfeasance. The purpose of control was constantly obscured by prose-cutorial posturing but seemed to emphasize controlling junior hockey players and hockey crowds through the device of prosecuting professional players.

Response

League response to the threat was indignant but focused on the unprecedented nature of legal intervention rather than the substantive issue of aggressive play. The problem of aggressive play was defined as a problem in the discipline system, not a problem of the style of play promoted by players, managers, and owners. Assault trials were the subject of much commentary, but the league and teams made no effort to oppose the definition of the incidents as illegitimate. Campbell summed it up:

> The policy of the NHL has always been to recognize the primacy of the civil authority and the only basis for abstaining from taking criminal action is the adequacy of the discipline maintained by the league . . . (*Ottawa Journal*, March 6, 1970, p. 17).

Outcome

Although the league failed to respond to an all-out confrontation, the public attribution of responsibility to the game itself and its organizational representatives heralded the trend toward political deviance in this period. Increased public indignation and sensitization to criminal trial as an appropriate solution for hockey violence, along with the rudiments of a folk devil of hockey violence, guaranteed that nonconviction would only provide a brief respite in the absence of effective league control. A general relief over nonconviction temporarily obscured a rising conflict among professional hockey interests about violence. Suggestions for an "appropriate" response differed: the NHL Players' Association requested life suspension, others asked for stiffer fines, and some argued that the current rules could be enforced more effectively through the cessation of team indemnification of players and increased referee vigilance. Responses by league leaders were inconsistent and, with the exception of establishing a penalty to stop brawls, few changes were made. The autonomy of the league was clearly threatened, and occasional court cases reminded hockey enthusiasts that the issue was not dead.

Sacrificial Control and the End of Expansion (1974 to 1975)

During the period from 1974 to 1975, the National Hockey League competed with an upstart league for players and spectators, resulting in large increases in expenses through "bidding wars" for top players. This dramatic increase in expenses (Fischler, 1974) heightened management interest in selling hockey in the dozen expansion cities. President Campbell appeared before the McMurtry investigation into violence in amateur hockey and testified (McMurtry, 1974a) that the purpose of the NHL was to conduct ice hockey and institute rules conducive to box office support of that branch of show business. In selling a new team, one expansion investor commented:

> Southern people don't understand hockey yet, but they understand fights. We've done pretty well in three years. We've won a lot more than people predicted we would. But I'm convinced we could put another thousand people in the OMNI for every game if we had a fighting team—which we don't (Ronberg, 1975: 88).

Fighting teams were doing well in both box office and season standings. Events at the professional and amateur levels brought the submerged issue of hockey violence into the public eye more forcefully than before. The folk devil solidified and expanded while control efforts revealed a shift in definitions and a final attempt by the organization to defray any attribution of responsibility that went beyond the individual player. The league strategy of sacrificial control is characterized by a return to individual responsibility and protection in a situation of high threat.

Awareness

As the expansion of hockey continued and the frequency of aggressive incidents increased, public attention remained high. The precipitating event that catapulted hockey violence into public awareness was the incident in which Dave Forbes hit Henry Boucha in the eye with a hockey stick in Minneapolis in 1975. As the first hockey assault prosecution in the United States, it became newsworthy; events from the incident through the trial of Forbes for aggravated assault attracted a national press corps. With the newsworthiness of the case established, journalists and their readers saw the incident as connected to wider problems. The outlines of the emerging folk devil of hockey violence became clearer. Hockey violence was characterized as "the mirror of a sick society" and, in a more threatening formulation, was viewed as a possible *cause* of societal aggression. In an extreme but not unique viewpoint, a letter to the editor declared:

> The basis of today's sport seems to be to develop aggression. Children and youth caught in a critical stage in their development . . . are led into this "great world of sports," where they learn the rudiments of aggression. Add to that TV and you will have a citizenry who will not consider aggressive behavior deviant or anti-social, but rather as an appropriate way of solving real-life problems. And that is how we can be piped, perhaps, even into another war . . . (*Minneapolis Tribune*, January 26, 1975, section A, p. 11).

Investigator McMurtry voiced a similar theme:

> When all the available research to date supports the proposition that the acceptance of hockey violence encourages outside the context of hockey, then one's incredulity turns to concern.
>
> When the evidence strongly indicates that there is a conscious effort to sell the violence in hockey to enrich a small group of show-business entrepreneurs at the expense of a great sport (not to mention the corruption of an entire generation's concept of sport) then one's concern grows to outrage (McMurtry, 1974b: 24).

Motivated by the threat of hockey violence to the sport, to youth, and to society, commentators intensified efforts to publicize the problem. They marshaled support and resources to ameliorate the problem and approved the use of criminal indictments as a solution.

Evaluation

Players gaining notoriety and teams winning championships through intimidation had a vested interest in retaining a high level of aggressive play. President Campbell admitted that aggressive play was a problem:

> Something must be done to control the violence in our game. I hear 10 discipline cases each week. And over the course of a season, I suspect I hear at least 10 cases where civil authorities might think a crime was committed (Mulvoy, 1975: 16).

But he denied that civil intervention was appropriate and argued that reliance on a court would produce a situation in which "no discipline in sport would be acceptable in terms of public opinion." He emphasized that according to his records, this was only the second case of civil law intervention. He asserted that

> singular intervention is singularly inappropriate for establishment of law and order . . . . The court machinery is so ponderous. The civil authorities are just not equipped to deal with the situation (*Chicago Sun-Times*, May 5, 1976, p. 129).

But Campbell defended player intimidation (as a "fact of life") and fighting (as a "catharsis formula"). The league remained committed to the retention of certain violent activities despite growing public criticism.

Threat

The notoriety of the Forbes case and increased attention to hockey violence in the mass media, in various public forums, and in Canadian legislative bodies, were threatening to ice hockey. The possibility of more indictments by prosecutors seeking publicity through politically advantageous hockey violence crackdowns was discussed. Amid discussion that a conviction in Minnesota might produce a boycott of league play in that legal jurisdiction, Campbell intoned, "If this civil intervention is pursued to trial, we will have to give great thought to the future of our game" (Mulvoy, 1975: 16).

Responsibility

Although public discussion in the Forbes case centered on the role of the league and team management in inducing violence, prosecutors emphasized the *individual* aspects of the case. In his summary to the jury, the county attorney, Gary Flakne, said:

> The purpose of this trial is not to ask you to change or modify or ridicule the rules of the game of hockey. That's why I asked you a question about that during your selection as a juror. This action between the State of Minnesota and the defendant is not an effort to embark on a reformation of the game of hockey, nor is it meant to criticize or complain about the game of hockey . . . (*Minnesota* v. *David Forbes*, 1975: 9-10).

The defense took the opposite approach; Forbes's attorney, Ronald Meshbesher, said in his summary:

> I hold no brief for the way hockey is played today. It is a violent, bloody game where you have to have a doctor on call all the time to stitch up, have an ambulance available, players getting maimed, some even dying.

> I can't justify it. But, my goodness, don't make this man the patsy. If the sport is to be cleaned up, let the legislatures clean it up and tell the hockey league "Clean your own house" (*Minnesota* v. *David Forbes*, 1975: 52-53).

Hours of deliberation ended in a deadlock and the dismissal of the jury. Jurors disagreed about who should be held responsible. One conviction juror concurred with the prosecution when he said, "Any man is responsible for his own actions regardless . . ." (personal communication). An equally comitted nonconviction juror took a different view: "Just like if I had committed some crime because of my job then my employer should suffer or should answer it—not me" (personal communication). In a news conference following his dismissal of the Forbes case, the county attorney stated that this was a "unique event" but added that if other prosecutors were to "move into this area" of sports violence litigation, "hockey [was] going to have a look at its own house and put it in order" (press conference, Minneapolis, August 1975).

Response

This silence by the hockey league and other hockey representatives was in keeping with a definition according to individual responsibility. Since the team would not publicly announce whether or not legal support was undertaken by them, the defendant appeared to be on his own. Moreover, the NHL president testified for the prosecution, and several hockey players, including the victim of Forbes's alleged assault, publicly denounced him and approved the prosecution. President Campbell initially questioned the prosecution but repeated his deference to "the primacy of civil authority." County Attorney Flakne characterized the league response during questioning at his press conference following the dismissal:

> I'm not sure what the NHL's feelings are on it. They have been most silent on their opinions on this particular case. They haven't been either . . . officially adverse or officially for it (press conference, Minneapolis, August 1975).

Defendant Forbes was on his own. Or so it appeared.

Outcome

Legal strategies belied the public issue of violence in hockey. By sidestepping a confrontation through the timely sacrifice of one player, the hockey establishment seemingly bought time and defused public indignation and prosecutorial zeal. A league spokesman was quoted as characterizing the Forbes case as "an unusual aberration that does not escalate any fears we may have of a recurrence" (Kennedy, 1975: 17). Though the case ended in a hung jury and the organizational issues were often obscured, the outcome was indeed one of political deviance. The sacrificial strategy centers on what some commentators called "scapegoating," and in the words of one of the trial press corps:

> Meshbesher's defense caused more than a few of the newsmen at the trial to privately characterize Forbes as the Lieutenant Calley of hockey, a foot soldier forced to suffer the consequences of a battle plan ordered by the NHL brass (Kennedy, 1975: 19).

The league did gain some vindication, as revealed by an inquiry on fighting in professional sport included in a Minnesota poll conducted by Midcontinent Surveys. More respondents preferred league discipline (61%) to court intervention (26%) ("Probe," 1975). But in the hockey world the violence issue generated increased conflict, and players, team management, and league officials took divergent views on its propriety and on the role of civil courts in its control. Yet, without conviction, the Forbes case did not deter the advent of another violent season. League autonomy in defining and controlling aggressive play seemed unassailable.

Political Control and the McMurtry Crusade (1975 to 1977)

This proved to be false. While media attention focused on the Forbes case, activity in Canada moved toward a more open confrontation between legal and hockey interests. Shortly after the Forbes non-verdict, Roy McMurtry (whose brother headed the Ontario investigation into violence in amateur hockey) was elected attorney general of Ontario. He announced his intention to prosecute outbreaks of sports violence in his jurisdiction and told police officers to attend hockey games with that purpose in mind. When charges were brought in the first incident that came to police attention, the battle lines were clearly drawn. This signaled the advent of political control. This final external control pattern involves open conflict between the hockey organization and representatives of the criminal justice system over the means and ends of control of aggressive play.

Awareness

Physical visibility remained high with hockey activity going on in numerous cities. Abnormally aggressive incidents occurred with high frequency. But frequency became less important, because concerned parties were prepared to publicize and sanction *any* incident. The continued newsworthiness of hockey violence cases and surrounding commentary sensitized the public and widened the antiviolence movement until other sports also came under scrutiny, especially baseball and basketball. One political scientist, quoted in *Time* by Stefan Kanfer as an "authority on sports violence," declared:

> "People actually get hurt in televised sports programs, and the hurt cannot even be justified by a higher cause. By some standards it is the most shocking form of violence, done merely for sport or fun" (Kanfer, 1976: 64).

Kanfer himself drew a more threatening scenario:

> In the end, it is not the players who are cheapened and injured, nor even the event itself. It is the children and adults who watch and then repeat what they see on the playground and in the stands—and perhaps in their lives (Kanfer, 1976: 65).

The folk devil of hockey violence, and now sports violence, was becoming more firmly entrenched.

However, public views on the appropriate response to the problem were less clear. Regardless of public opinion, legal officials intensified their interest in sports violence. Articles appeared in legal reviews (Binder, 1975) and legal magazines (Hallowell and Meshbesher, 1977), and prosecutors became sensitized to the possibility of indicting violent athletes for ciminal offenses. A *Toronto Star* poll of head prosecutors in 12 cities where professional hockey is played revealed that an overwhelming majority—11 of 12—favored prosecution of sports violence (*Chicago Sun-Times,* May 3, 1976, p. 88). The number of assault cases increased for both professional and semi-professional play and public focus on sports violence in general and hockey violence in particular was maintained.

Evaluation

Hockey officials made a direct confrontation over legal intervention and continued a refined stance on the propriety of violence in sport. Control of extreme violence was attempted through changes in rule structure, penalties, and rule enforcement, but hockey officials maintained that fist fighting was a necessary if not "healthy" part of the game. Opponents of hockey violence accepted the proposed distinctions between tough and dirty play and between fist fights and stick fights but still disagreed with hockey representatives over the definition of acceptable aggressive play. Arguments in the media became increasingly polemical as the threat of prosecution increased.

Threat

During the period from 1975 to 1977, threat was high. A proactive enforcement procedure was established in Ontario, assault prosecutions occurred in several communities (often for less extreme events than previously sanctioned), public investigations were going on in several jurisdictions, and numerous prosecutors publicly pledged to accept sports violence indictments. Other levels of hockey play instituted rule changes partly aimed at demonstrating the untenable position of the NHL toward the acceptability and control of violence.

Responsibility

Attribution of responsibility was now fixed on the hockey organization. In the June 1976 assault prosecution of Dan Maloney for hitting Bryan Glennie during an NHL game defense and prosecution attorneys emphasized the milieu of ice hockey and the definition and legitimacy of violence in the game. The prosecution argued that a conviction would show that the community would not tolerate violence. The defense, on the other hand, characterized the violence as "part of the game" (*Toronto Globe,* July 1, 1976, p. 1). Although only one individual was on trial, the jury recognized the consequences of the verdict for the hockey organization. The defendant was found not guilty. However, in explaining the verdict, the jurors asserted that they did not condone violence in hockey but, on the contrary, hoped that "similar occurrences [would] not happen in the future" (*Toronto Globe,* July 2, 1976, p. 6). Although the criminal justice system can only control the hockey organization through the prosecution of individuals, another legal development threatened to reach the organization more directly. The victim of Forbes's attack filed a multimillion-dollar suit naming his assailant's team and the NHL as defendants. With the possibility of large monetary settlements added to the possibility of jailed players, the already financially troubled league had to accept responsibility or face numerous lawsuits from disenchanted, injured players who sought remuneration for shortened careers.

Responses

Aside from initial attempts to reduce violence through rule changes, the official response was more of an all-out confrontation. One defendant's team announced that, because the player was actively engaged in legitimate employment as a team member, the team considered the charges against their player as charges against the team. The league did not officially move to support the team or the player but representatives questioned the charges, saying that the cases were motivated by the political ambitions of legal officials. The trial effort epitomized the protective response of the hockey world when coaches, players, officials, fans—and even the victim of the attack—testified in support of the defendant.

Outcome

Despite the closing of ranks during the Maloney trial, the hockey world remained embroiled in conflict over the definition and legitimation of violence. No case had resulted in conviction, but the prospect of continued prosecutions and threats to players' careers and to the image of ice hockey led to increased agitation for control of violence within hockey. Finally, the NHL Players' Association voted for strong league action against violence, resulting in fewer fights, penalties, violent incidents, and criminal prosecutions during the following season. Criminal court intervention produced (1) a reduction in organizational autonomy, (2) a redefinition of proper conduct in ice hockey, (3) changes in internal control policies and practices, and (4) changes in external modes of control. With several cases still in the courts and antiviolence interests active, it appeared that the hockey organization would have to take outside interests into account when marketing its product. With several struggling franchises and large drops in attendance, the overall impact of these changes remained unknown, but, whether violence sells tickets or not, the hockey league no longer had the flexibility to use violence as a sales tool. Along with decreased autonomy and internal conflict, the control pattern produced political deviance: the organization's ability to marshal resources necessary for survival in a rapidly changing environment was directly threatened. Having openly confronted criminal justice representatives on the propriety of violence, hockey representatives won the battle by avoiding player convictions but lost the war by surrendering organizational mandate.

CONCLUSION

I have analyzed the social control of hockey violence as a political phenomenon. By studying the relationship between the organization of ice hockey and its external environment, I demonstrated the existence and significance of different patterns of control. The seven external control patterns are the outcomes of conditions and changes in society, the community, and the hockey organization. The emphasis on a legitimate organization and the historical approach provide an extension of traditional accounts of the collective definition of deviance. I have highlighted the importance of deviance designation as a political resource and the crucial role of resistance by the "deviants." In so doing, I have provided a counterpoint to studies that depict deviants as passive, unorganized victims of moral crusades. It is hoped that, through further study of violent occupations such as police officer, prison guard, and the military, a comparative model of external control patterns and movements to define deviance can be formulated.

NOTES

1. Hence, to the extent that this study centers on deviance, it is through the study of collective rule making (Schur, 1971) or collective definitions (Davis and Stivers, 1975). Davis (1975) criticizes labeling analysts of rule making for neglecting formal law and group conflict but concedes that the labeling view focuses on social control rather than deviant etiology. However, approaches enthusiastically embracing the trend toward conflict analyses of law-making processes run the risk of neglecting extralegal aspects of social control that support, resist, or redefine formal law. By including both legal and extralegal facets of the social control of hockey violence, we can give a more complete portrayal of the collective rule-making process.

2. Gouldner (1954) pioneered the study of patterns of control with his analysis of a gypsum plant. He found three types of bureaucratic control patterns—representative, punishment-centered, and mock—and demonstrated their link with other aspects of internal and external organizational life. Mock rules originated outside the plant and were neither legitimated nor enforced by management. Smigel (1964) followed Gouldner's lead in his study of lawyers but found a control pattern that emphasized the external source. This "professional" pattern was legitimated and enforced, although enforcement tended to be informal. Both studies indicate that organizations have several control patterns influenced by the behavior involved and other features of the organization. Contrasting the two raises the possibility that organizations have different types of control patterns, including those of external control. As Smigel's study indicates, self-regulation and autonomy are important features of the professions (Hall and Engel, 1974). But the prevailing acceptance of this

form of control as an inherent trait of a profession diverts attention from other influences on control patterns. In his critique of the professional literature, Johnson states that the type of social control to which an occupation is subject is not an inherent characteristic of certain types of occupations and that

> institutionalized forms of control of occupations are only to be fully understood historically through an analysis of the power of specific groups to control occupational activities . . . we must make a clear distinction between the characteristics of an occupational activity . . . and historically variant forms of the institutional control of such activities which are a product of definite social conditions (1972: 37).

REFERENCES

Aldrich, Howard. 1971. "Organizational boundaries and inter-organizational conflict." *Human Relations* 24: 279-93.

Aubert, Vilhelm. 1952. "White-collar crime and social structure." *American Journal of Sociology* 58: 263-71.

Becker, Howard S. 1963. *Outsiders: Studies in the Sociology of Deviance.* New York: Free Press.

Bensman, Joseph, and Israel Gerver. 1963. "Crime and punishment in the factory: The function of deviance in maintaining the social system." *American Sociological Review* 28: 588-98.

Binder, Richard. 1975. "The consent defense: Sports, violence and the criminal law." *American Criminal Law Review* 13: 235-48.

Blumenthal, Monica, et al. 1972. *Justifying Violence: Attitudes of American Men.* Ann Arbor, Mich.: Institute for Social Research.

Brentano, Lujo. 1969. *History and Development of Guilds and the Origin of Trade Unions.* New York: Burt Franklin. (Originally published in 1870.)

Chambliss, William. 1976. "Functional and conflict theories of crime: The heritage of Emile Durkheim and Karl Marx." In William Chambliss and Milton Mankoff (eds.) *Whose Law? What Order? A Conflict Approach to Criminology.* New York, John Wiley.

———. 1976. "The state and the criminal law." In William Chambliss and Milton Mankoff (eds.). *Whose Law? What Order? A Conflict Approach to Criminology.* New York: John Wiley.

———, and Robert B. Seidman. 1971. *Law, Order and Power.* Reading, Mass.: Addison-Wesley.

Chevalier, Jack. 1974. *The Broad Street Bullies: The Incredible Story of the Philadelphia Flyers.* New York: Macmillan.

Clinard, Marshall, and Richard Quinney. 1973. *Criminal Behavior Systems: A Typology.* 2nd ed. New York: Holt, Rinehart and Winston.

Cohen, Albert. 1966. *Deviance and Control.* Englewood Cliffs, N.J.: Prentice-Hall.

Cohen, Stanley. 1972. *Folk Devils and Moral Panics.* London: McGibbon-Kee.

———. 1974. "Criminology and the sociology of deviance in Britain." In Paul Rock and Mary McIntosh (eds.). *Deviance and Social Control.* London: Tavistock.

Coleman, Charles. 1966. *The Trail of the Stanley Cup.* Vol. 1. Montreal: National Hockey League.

Coser, Lewis. 1962. "Some functions of deviant behavior and normative flexibility." *American Journal of Sociology* 68: 172-81.

Cressey, Donald. 1969. *Theft of the Nation.* New York: Harper and Row.

Davis, F. James, and Richard Stivers. 1975. *The Collective Definition of Deviance.* New York: Free Press.

Davis, Nanette J. 1975. *Sociological Constructions of Deviance.* Dubuque, Iowa: William C. Brown.

De Jouvenal, Bertrand. 1957. "Sovereignty." In David Bell et al. (eds.). 1970. *Issues in Politics and Government.* Boston: Houghton Mifflin.

Dickinson, William. 1963. "Deaths and injuries in sports." *Editorial Research Reports* 6: 427-44.

Duster, Troy. 1970. *The Legislation of Morality.* New York: Free Press.

Edelman, Murray. 1967. *The Symbolic Uses of Politics.* Urbana, Ill.: University of Illinois Press.

Elias, Norbert, and Eric Dunning. 1971. "Dynamics of sport groups with special reference to football." In Eric Dunning (ed.). *The Sociology of Sport.* London: Frank Cass.

Emery, F. E., and E. L. Trist. 1965. "Causal texture of organizational environment." *Human Relations* 18: 21-32.

Erikson, Kai T. 1966. *Wayward Puritans: A Study in the Sociology of Deviance.* New York: John Wiley.

Erskine, Hazel. 1974a. "The polls: Fear of crime." *Public Opinion Quarterly* 37: 131-45.

———. 1974b. "The polls: Control of crime and violence." *Public Opinion Quarterly* 37: 490-502.

Faulkner, Robert. 1974. Making violence by doing work: Selves, situations and the world of professional hockey." *Sociology of Work and Occupations* 1: 288-312.

Fischler, Stan. 1971. *The Flying Frenchmen.* New York: Hawthorne Books.

———. 1974. *Slashing.* New York: Thomas Y. Crowell.

Gitler, Ira. 1974. *Blood on the Ice.* Chicago: Henry Regnery.

Gouldner, Alvin. 1954. *Patterns of Industrial Bureaucracy.* New York: Free Press.

Graham, James. 1972. "Amphetamine politics on Capitol Hill." *Society* 9: 14-23.

Gusfield, Joseph R. 1963. *Symbolic Crusade: Status Politics and the American Temperance Movement.* Urbana, Ill.: University of Illinois Press.

———. 1967. "Moral passage: The symbolic process in public designations of deviance." *Social Problems* 15: 175-88.

Hall, Richard, and Gloria Engel. 1974. "Autonomy and expertise: Threats and barriers to occupational autonomy." In Phyllis Stewart and Muriel Cantor (eds.). *Varieties of Work Experience.* New York: John Wiley.

Hallowell, Lyle, and Ronald Meshbesher. 1977. "Sport violence and the criminal law." *Trial* 13: 13-22.

Hay Donald. 1975. "Property, authority and the criminal law." In Donald Hay et al. *Albion's Fatal Tree: Crime and Society in Eighteenth Century England.* New York: Pantheon Books.

Hofstadter, Richard, and Michael Wallace. 1971. *American Violence.* New York: Vintage Books.

Horowitz, Irving Louis, and Martin Liebowitz. 1968. "Social deviance and political marginality: Toward a redefinition of the relation between sociology and politics." *Social Problems* 15: 280-96.

Hughes, Everett. 1971a. "Mistakes at work." In Everett Hughes (ed.). *Sociological Eye.* Chicago: Aldine-Atherton.

———. 1971a. "The study of occupations." In Everett Hughes (ed.). *Sociological Eye.* Chicago: Aldine-Atherton.

Inciardi, James. 1972. "Visibility, societal reaction and criminal behavior." *Criminology* 10: 217-32.

Johnson, Terrence. 1972. *Professions and Power*. London: Macmillan.

Kanfer, Stefan. 1976. "Doing violence to sport." *Time*. May 31: 64-65.

Kelman, Herbert, and Lee Lawrence. 1972. "Assignment of responsibility in the case of Lt. Calley: Preliminary report on a national survey. *Journal of Social Issues* 28: 177-212.

Kennedy, Marc. 1970. "Beyond incrimination: Some neglected facets of the theory of punishment." *Catalyst* 5: 1-37.

Kennedy, Ray. 1975. "Wanted: An end to mayhem." *Sports Illustrated*. November 17: 17-21.

Kirchheimer, Otto. 1961. *Political Justice: the Use of Legal Procedure for Political Ends*. Princeton, N. J.: Princeton University Press.

Koeppet, Leonard. 1973. "Sports and the law: An overview." *New York Law Forum* 18: 815-39.

Krislov, Samuel. 1971. "The Hoffa case: The criminal trial as a process of interest group leadership selection." In Theodore Becker (ed.). *Political Trials*. Indianapolis: Bobbs-Merrill.

"Maclean's interviews: Clarence Campbell." 1969. *Maclean's* 82: 15, 72-73.

McFarlane, Brian. 1973. *The Story of the National Hockey League*. New York: Charles Scribner.

McMurtry, William. 1974a. Investigation and inquiry into violence in amateur hockey. Public hearings transcript. Special commission of the Honorable R. Brunell, Ontario minister of community and social services.

———. 1974b. Investigation and inquiry into violence in amateur hockey. Report to the Honorable R. Brunell, Ontario minister of community and social services. Toronto: Ontario Government Bookstore.

Marx, Gary. 1974. "Thoughts on a neglected category of social movement participant: The *agent provocateur* and the informant." *American Journal of Sociology* 80: 402-42.

Minnesota v. David Forbes. 1975. Official trial transcript.

Moore, John. 1967. "Football's ugly decades: 1893-1913." *Smithsonian Journal of History* 2: 49-68.

Mulvihill, Donald, and Melvin Tumin. 1969. *Crimes of Violence*. Vol. 11: A Staff Report Submitted to the National Commission on the Causes and Prevention of Violence. Washington, D. C.: U. S. Government Printing Office.

Mulvoy, Mark. 1975. "Hockey is courting disaster." *Sports Illustrated*. January 27: 16-17.

"Probe: A quarterly survey of Minnesota adults." 1975. August. Minneapolis: Midcontinent Surveys.

Regina v. Maki. 1970. *Criminal Reports New Series* 10: 268-73.

Regina v. Ted Green. 1971. *Ontario Reports* 1: 595.

Regina v. Wayne Maki. 1970. Official trial transcript.

Robin, Gerald. 1967. "Corporate and judicial disposition of employee thieves." In Ernest Smigel and L. Ross (eds.). *Crimes against Bureaucracy*. New York: Van Nostrand Reinhold.

Rock, Paul. 1973. *Deviant Behavior*. London: Hutchinson University Library.

Ronberg, Gary. 1975. *The Violent Game*. Englewood Cliffs, N. J.: Prentice-Hall.

Schur, Edwin. 1971. *Labeling Deviant Behavior*. New York: Harper and Row.

Smelser, Neil F. 1963. *Theory of Collective Behavior*. New York: Free Press.

Smigel, Ernest. 1964. *The Wall Street Lawyer*. New York: Free Press.

Smith, Michael. 1975. "The legitimation of violence: Hockey players' perceptions of their reference groups sanctions for assault." *Canadian Review of Sociology and Anthropology* 12: 72-80.

Stone, Christopher. 1975. *Where the Law Ends: The Social Control of Corporate Behavior*. New York: Harper Colophon Books.

Stone, Gregory P. 1971. "Wrestling: The great American Passion Play." In Eric Dunning (ed.). *The Sociology of Sport.* London: Frank Cass.

Terryberry, Shirley. 1968. "The evolution of organizational environments." *Administrative Science Review* 12: 590-613.

Turk, Austin. 1976. "Law as a weapon in social conflict." *Social Problems* 23: 276-91.

Turner, Ralph. 1969. "The public perception of protest." *American Sociological Review* 34: 815-31.

United States Congress. 1957. House Committee on the Judiciary: Hearings before the Antitrust Subcommittee. Washington, D. C.: U. S. Government Printing Office.

"We're more violent than we think." 1970. *Maclean's* 81: 25-28.

Wilson, Kent, et al. 1977. "Facial injuries in hockey players." *Minnesota Medicine.* January: 13-19.

Chapter 5

Official Violence during the Watts, Newark, and Detroit Race Riots of the 1960s

Albert Bergesen

INTRODUCTION

The race riots of the 1960s are obvious examples of collective violence, and we have expended much effort trying to determine their cause. We have examined the social characteristics of riot participants (see the literature reviewed in Sears and McConahay [1973] and Fogelson [1971]) and looked at the structural characteristics of cities that might be conducive to riots (Lieberson and Silverman, 1965; Spilerman, 1970, 1971, and 1976; Downes, 1968, 1970; Morgan and Clark, 1973). In all these studies, and in our more general theorizing as to causes of racial violence, we matter of factly focus upon black violence as the reality of racial violence: to speak of riot participants is to speak of black civilians. This is an assumption we rarely question. Violence during a race riot, though, is not always initiated by civilians. Law enforcement officials also act violently. In fact, if one looked at the number of people killed during the 1960s riots, one would see

Note: An earlier version of this paper was presented at the Research Symposium on Social Indicators of Institutional Racism-Sexism, University of California, Los Angeles, April 29 and 30, 1977. I would like to thank Otis Dudley Duncan and Beverly Duncan for assistance, advice, and encouragement throughout this research. Ron Hopley assisted in the coding for Watts, and Ronald Schoenberg provided helpful comments on an earlier draft of this paper. I would also like to thank Sandy Goers for her graphic work.

that the overwhelming number are black civilians who have been killed by law enforcement officials. The excessive use of force by police officers and other law officers has been discussed in terms of the lack of training in riot control methods, the long hours of duty for inexperienced officers, and the racial hostility between white police and black ghetto residents (Kerner, 1968; Skolnick, 1969; Stark, 1972). In general the violence of officials is viewed as an overreaction to the riot situation and a temporary departure from professional standards and behavior. This is undoubtedly true. But, in viewing official violence solely in this framework we limit our application of various theories of collective violence to noninstitutional actors, such as black civilians. The assumption that processes of collective violence apply largely to noninstitutional actors has a long tradition rooted in studies of the preindustrial crowd (Hobsbawm, 1959; Rudé, 1959; Tilly, 1969) and in the sociological study of mobs, crowds, fads, and panics, (Smelser, 1963). But what of institutional actors, such as the police and the National Guard? Are their actions only deviations from professional roles? Is it not also possible that they too are susceptible to the very same sociological processes that generate collective violence in civilians? The answer, I want to argue, is yes.

Sociological theories of collective violence are as applicable to institutional actors such as the police as they are to unorganized actors such as the classic mob or crowd or, in our case, black civilians. The question is not why blacks rioted, although that question is important, but why law enforcement officials also were violent? Before we can go on and discuss causes of either civilian or official violence, we need to determine just who killed whom during these riots. There has been a lot of discussion about police violence, and it was identified by the Kerner Report (Kerner, 1968) as one of the underlying causes of the 1960s riots. The Kerner Commission also suspected that law enforcement behavior during the riots was not what it could have been: "In their anxiety to control disorders, some law enforcement agencies may resort to indiscriminate, repressive use of force against wholly innocent elements of the Negro community" (Kerner, 1968: 335).

Much of the issue of police violence has remained at the level of charges and countercharges, and what would be most helpful is some systematic data on just what the police did and did not do. In this regard it is the purpose of this paper to systematically examine the specific circumstance of death for each person (civilian or law enforcement official) killed during the Watts, Newark, and Detroit race riots of the 1960s.

METHODS

Data on the specific circumstances of death were taken from sources that used police reports, eyewitness accounts, and information from news media to reconstruct each event. For the Newark and Detroit riots, the circumstances of death have been laboriously reconstructed in two books. For Newark, we relied on Hayden's *Rebellion in Newark* (1967) and, for Detroit, on Sauter and Hines's *Nightmare in Detroit* (1968). There was no equivalent single compilation of incidents for Watts, so three sources were consulted: Parker's *Violence in the U. S.*, Volume I: 1956-1967 (1974), Cohen and Murphy's *Burn Baby Burn* (1966), and Crump's *Black Riot in Los Angeles* (1966).

The rapidity of unfolding events along with the emotional character of racial violence provides obvious room for error, misinterpretation, and bias in the reconstruction of the events of these riots (see Danzger [1975] and Snyder and Kelley [1977] for a discussion of coding news accounts). One means of checking reliability is to compare different accounts of the same event. For Watts there were three sources that were cross-checked, and for Newark and Detroit the accounts were compared with those provided by the National Advisory Commission on Civil Disorders (the Kerner Report). That report specifically discussed 8 deaths in Newark and 23 in Detroit. In all of these cases, the Kerner Report matches Hayden and Sauter and Hines.

Bias can also be reduced by excluding questions of motive or attitudinal disposition of both civilians and officials who initiated fatal violence. In this fashion we avoid making unnecessary judgments and evaluations as to the motives for the killings. Only the more public aspects of each death will be examined. From these accounts we can distinguish (1) whether the deaths were initiated by civilians or officials; (2) what the general circumstance of death was (e.g., whether the victim was shot while looting or shot in a car, or whether the victim was accidentally killed, as by being trapped in a burning building); and (3) the date on which the death occurred. The final data set will be those deaths for which we can determine both the general circumstance of death and the date on which it occurred.

For some of the deaths the information was incomplete, and for others there were conflicting reports. In Watts, the following deaths could not be coded. On August 13 a youth died in the hospital from gunshot wounds, but there was insufficient information to determine the general circumstance under which he was shot. On August 14 there were 3 deaths and again insufficient information in the report to determine the exact circumstance of death. A National Guardsman shot a man, but the circumstance wasn't mentioned. A youth was found dead from gunshot wounds, but his killers could not be determined. Finally, police shot a youth fleeing a store being looted, but the day of death could not be determined. This left 28 deaths during the Watts riot that could be analyzed by circumstance of death and date of riot.

In Newark there were reports of 4 deaths that could not be coded. One man was shot, but there were no eyewitnesses; another was shot looting, but the date of death could not be determined. A woman was reported to have died from a heart attack, but that didn't seem directly attributable to the riot. Finally, there were conflicting reports on the death of one man. This left 21 deaths that could be analyzed.

In Detroit there was one incident that was quite different from all others. Rather than create a new category for only one incident, I treated it as a deviant case and left it out of the later analysis. In this incident the police broke into a man's apartment and the man, after wounding the first officer through the door, was shot by the other officers. This left 42 deaths that could be analyzed in Detroit and a total of 91 deaths from all three riots that can be examined in terms of the date and circumstance of death.

CIRCUMSTANCE OF DEATH

The first and most general finding was that, although some 91 different deaths in three separate riots were involved, there was a great deal of similarity in the circumstances of death. Some of the killings were by civilians, both white and black, and some were the result of accidents. Most, though, were initiated by officials. There were four general situations that appeared in the accounts studied: (1) persons were shot as looters; (2) persons were shot in cars and standing in crowds; (3) persons were shot in their homes; and (4) persons were shot in what could only be described as personal attacks by officials. These categories were not created prior to looking at the accounts of the violence; they arose from the data. The effort was to describe as accurately as possible the different ways in which people died during these race riots. I will now turn to the specific deaths that make up these general categories.

Civilians or Officials Killed by Civilians

In Watts there was only one incident in which a civilian or an official was killed by a civilian: a store employee shot a looter entering the store. In Newark there were two cases in this category: a policeman and a fireman were claimed by authorities to have been shot by snipers. Eyewitnesses did not see the actual sniper fire, and Hayden (1967: 84-88) suggests that they may have been hit by stray bullets from other law enforcement officers shooting in the area. In this analysis, though, they were coded as deaths caused by civilians. In Detroit there were six such cases: a white store owner was beaten by a black youth; a white woman was shot in her car as it passed through a milling crowd of black civilians (although no one saw her shot, I am accepting the assumption that she was shot by someone in the crowd); a white looter was shot by a white store owner; a black youth was shot by a black private guard; a black looter was shot by a white store owner; and a black man was shot by an unprovoked white civilian.

Of the nine deaths initiated by civilians, three were looters shot by store personnel. Only four situations involved black civilians in anything approaching "riot" behavior—the store owner beaten by a black youth, the woman shot in her car as it passed through a milling crowd, and the policeman and fireman who were possibly shot by snipers. Of the total number of incidents coded, only 10% were initiated by civilians, and, more striking, only 4.4% were initiated by black civilians in what would commonly be considered as riot behavior.

Accidents

There were five incidents classified as accidents in Watts: a fireman was crushed under a fallen wall as he battled a fire; a woman died in her apartment, which had caught fire; two policemen, on different occasions, were shot by two other policemen when their shotguns accidentally discharged as they were struggling with black civilians; and a 14-year-old girl was crushed when she leaned out of a moving loot-filled car and struck a parked truck.

There were two accidents in Newark: a fire engine struck a parked car killing the occupant, and a black civilian, shooting at a white civilian, hit a black woman sitting on her porch.

In Detroit there were seven such accidental deaths: two looters died in the collapse of a burning building; a fireman and a black civilian, on different occasions, bumped into high-voltage wires; a fireman and a guardsman were shot in National Guard cross fire; and a policeman accidentally shot another policeman while he was struggling with a looter.

Persons Shot as Looters by Officials

There were 14 incidents in Watts: police shot a man crouched behind a truck in front of a store being looted; police shot a man standing in a looted liquor store; police shot a man fleeing a looted department store; police shot a looter fleeing a store (in this case police reported they were under fire from elsewhere at the time they shot the fleeing looter); police shot a looter fleeing a looted auto supply store; police shot a man as a looter in a looted shoe store; police shot a man as a looter in a men's store; police shot a man as a looter in a liquor store; police shot two men fleeing a looted appliance store; police shot a man as a looter in a hardware store; police shot a man fleeing a looted store; police shot a man fleeing a looted furniture store. Of the 14 persons shot for looting in Watts, 1 was shot in front of the looted store, 5 were shot in the stores, and 8 were shot fleeing the premises.

There were three incidents in Newark: police shot a youth looting a store; police shot a looter running from a car into which he had been loading loot; and police shot a looter carrying beer from a looted store. Of the 3 persons shot for looting in Newark, none were shot in front of the store, 1 was shot in the store, and 2 were shot while fleeing.

There were 18 incidents in Detroit: the National Guard shot a man with a gun in his hand standing in front of a store that had been looted (he was suspected of looting but was actually guarding the store); police, on eight different occasions, shot looters fleeing a looted store; police shot a looter running to the back of a store; on two different occasions, police shot a looter in a looted store; police shot one looter running from a store and another coming out of a store; police shot two men in a looted store; police shot a looter running from a junkyard; and a paratrooper shot a suspected looter running from a house where looted goods were stored. Of the 18 persons shot for looting in Detroit, 1 was shot in front of the store, 5 were shot in the store, and 12 were shot fleeing.

Finally, of the 34 persons shot for looting in all three riots, 2.9% were shot in front of a looted store, 32.4% were shot in a looted store, and 64.7% were shot while fleeing the premises.

Persons in Crowds Shot by Officials

There was one incident in Watts: police fired down a street and hit a man standing by a car. There were six deaths in this category in

Newark: police fired down a street, hitting a man looking at the wreckage of a bar; police fired down a street, hitting a woman who had come out of her home to look for her children; police fired down a street hitting a 74-year-old man walking toward his car; police fired from rooftops, hitting a man standing with his relatives; police and the Guard fired down an alley hitting a man getting into his car; and police fired down a street hitting a man standing on a corner. There were no incidents in this category in Detroit.

In none of these cases were the individuals either provoking officials or engaging in riotous behavior such as sniping, throwing objects, or setting fires. They were all bystanders, not participants.

Persons in Cars Shot by Officials

There were five incidents in Watts of persons in cars being shot by officials: the Guard shot a man in his car when he refused to stop; police and the Guard shot a man in a car as it swerved past a trash can barricade; the Guard shot a man as he gunned his car toward a barricade; a woman coming home from a party was shot by the Guard as she approached a roadblock; and a white milkman, on his way to work early in the morning, was chased and shot by Guardsmen with a machine gun mounted on a jeep.

There was one incident in Newark: the National Guard fired upon a car approaching a roadblock, killing a 10-year-old boy inside. There were two incidents in Detroit: a man was killed when his car was fired upon as it proceeded slowly through an intersection after halting at a stoplight, and a car approached a parked National Guard jeep and the Guard opened fire, riddling the car with bullets and killing an occupant.

Persons Shot in Homes and Hotels by Officials

There were two incidents in Watts: a Guardsman shot a man in the doorway of a hotel, and police shot a man in the doorway of his home.

There were three cases in Newark: a woman was shot in her second floor apartment when troopers fired on the building; a woman looking out the window of her tenth-floor apartment was killed when police strafed her building with bullets; and a woman was killed in her home when Guardsmen fired at her apartment building.

There were two cases in Detroit: a four-year-old girl was hit in her living room when a 50-caliber machine gun fired from a tank strafed her apartment building (someone standing in a window had lit a match and the Guard thought it was sniper fire), and a woman visiting the city looked out her window and was killed as a Guard unit fired a volley of shots at her motel.

In Newark and Detroit police and the National Guard, supposedly responding to sniper fire, strafed apartment houses and one motel with gunfire. In none of these instances were snipers hit or captured when the buildings were later searched. According to the Kerner Report the presence of snipers seems to have been largely exaggerated. In Newark, for example, the director of police told the Kerner Commission, "As a matter of fact down in the Springfield Avenue area it was so bad that, in my opinion, Guardsmen were firing upon police and police were firing back at them . . . . I really don't believe there was as much sniping as we thought" (Kerner, 1968: 66). In Detroit, of the 27 individuals charged with sniping, 24 had charges dropped, another was given a suspended sentence, and at the time of the Kerner Report the trials of the other two were pending. Perhaps the most significant evidence was the fact that few officers were actually killed by snipers. There were none in Watts or Detroit, and only two were reportedly shot by snipers in Newark. This amounts to 2 sniper deaths out of a total of 91 deaths for all three riots.

Persons Killed in Personal Attacks by Officials

The remaining incidents seemed significantly different from the others. The killings were not the result of indiscriminate firing at cars, crowds, buildings, or looters. They could only be characterized as personal attacks by law enforcement officials. There were no such cases in Watts. There were four incidents in Newark: a man stepped out of a restaurant and was shot by plain clothesmen driving past, a youth was shot at point-blank range by police when they confronted him in a tavern (photos showed 39 bullets in his chest alone); a 12-year-old boy, taking out the garbage, was killed by a Guardsman after the boy's companion said derogatory things to one of the Guardsmen; police chased a man by car, and, after he got out of his car and ran toward an alley, they fired shots, striking him in the back.

There were seven deaths in Detroit: a man walking toward his 4:30 a.m. bus was confronted by a Guardsman and shot for no apparent reason; police and Guardsmen stormed the Algiers Motel and killed three men at a range of 15 feet or less (two white girls found inside the motel were also severely beaten by authorities); one eyewitness said he saw a Guardsman raise his gun, aim, and fire, killing a man who had been walking toward him (the man was unarmed, not looting, and not breaking any laws); Guardsmen, searching a building for snipers, confronted a man in the hallway of his apartment, bayoneted him and then shot him; police stopped a man on the street, marched him into an alley, and shot him (the medical examiner's report said he was shotgunned from about 10 feet).

DATA ANALYSIS

Table 8 presents the frequency of these different circumstances of death for all three riots. In general about three-fourths of the total violence was initiated by officials (78.6% in Watts, 80% in Newark, and 69% in Detroit). The remaining deaths are fairly evenly split between accidental deaths and deaths caused by civilians for Newark (two accidental and two civilian) and Detroit (seven accidental and six civilian), but not for Watts (five accidental and one civilian).

Among deaths initiated by officials, shooting of looters accounted for nearly half of all deaths in Watts (50%) and Detroit (42.9%) but for only 14.3% in Newark. Conversely, 33.3% of all deaths in Newark were from officials shooting at people in cars and crowds, but only 21.4% in Watts and 4.8% in Detroit died in that manner. For all three riots there was a similar number of persons shot in buildings—two in

Table 8. Percentage Distribution of the Total Number of Persons Killed During the Watts, Newark, and Detroit Race Riots by Circumstance of Death

Circumstance of Death	Watts Percentage	N	Newark Percentage	N	Detroit Percentage	N	All Three Riots Percentage	N
Killed by officials								
In personal attacks	0.0	0	19.0	4	16.7	7	12.1	11
In homes and hotels	7.1	2	14.3	3	4.8	2	7.7	7
In cars and crowds	21.4	6	33.3	7	4.8	2	16.5	15
As looters	50.0	14	14.3	3	42.9	18	38.5	35
Killed in accidents	17.9	5	9.5	2	16.7	7	15.4	14
Killed by civilians	3.6	1	9.5	2	14.3	6	9.9	9
Total	100.0	28	100.0	21	100.0	42	100.0	91

Table 9. Number of Persons Killed by Day of Riot for the Watts,
Newark, and Detroit Race Riots

Day	Watts*	Newark†	Detroit‡
First	6	1	4
Second	17	11	17
Third	3	6	9
Fourth	2	2	10
Fifth	0	1	1
Sixth	0	0	1

*The Watts riot began on the night of August 11, 1965, and August 13 was the first day someone was killed.

†The Newark riot began on the night of July 12, 1967, and July 13 was the first day someone was killed.

‡The Detroit riot began on July 23, 1967, and that was the first day someone was killed.

Watts (7.1%), three in Newark (14.3%), and two in Detroit (4.8%). There were no personal attacks in Watts. Four people in Newark (19%) and seven people in Detroit (16.7%) were killed by officials in personal attacks.

Along with recording the general circumstance of death, the date of each death was coded, making it possible to examine the changing character of death as the riot unfolded. Table 9 presents the total number of persons killed by day of riot for all three riots. The killing seems to reach a peak on the second day of violence and then tapers off. We can also examine the changing circumstances of death as the riot progresses for each city.

Detroit

During the first two days of killing in Detroit 6 persons were killed by civilians, 5 died in accidents and 10 were killed by officials. Combining the civilian and accidental deaths, they are about equal to the violence of officials for the first two days. But, for the remainder of the riot, there were 19 more officially instigated deaths, no more civilian-initiated deaths, and only 2 more accidental deaths. The official violence continued in the virtual absence of either civilian killings or accidents. There was also an escalation in official violence. If we take July 23, the first day someone was killed, as day one, then the average days on which persons were killed ranged from 2.7 for persons shot as looters, to 3.5 for persons shot in cars and in homes, to 4.0 for persons shot in personal attacks (figure 3).

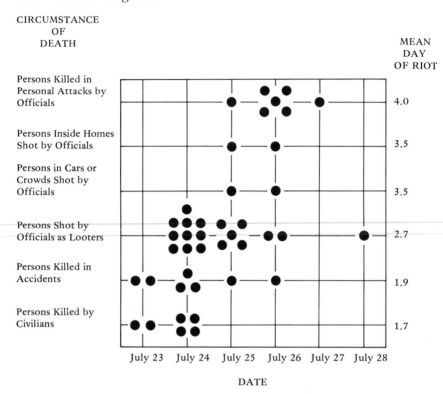

CIRCUMSTANCE
OF
DEATH

MEAN
DAY
OF RIOT

Persons Killed in
Personal Attacks by
Officials 4.0

Persons Inside Homes
Shot by Officials 3.5

Persons in Cars or
Crowds Shot by
Officials 3.5

Persons Shot by
Officials as Looters 2.7

Persons Killed in
Accidents 1.9

Persons Killed by
Civilians 1.7

July 23   July 24   July 25   July 26   July 27   July 28

DATE

Figure 3. Fatalities (N = 42) of the Detroit race riot of 1967 classified by circumstance of death and date.

The statistical significance of this overall linear progression of violence was examined using a method Simon (1974) proposed based on the likelihood-ratio chi-square statistic, χ^2, for singly ordered contingency tables, that tests for independence and the goodness-of-fit of a linear model. The null hypothesis of independence was rejected ($\chi^2 = 36.8$ with 20 d.f., $p < .02$) and a good fit of the linear model was found ($\chi^2 = 15.6$ with 16 d.f., $p > .3$), so that the linear effect was highly significant ($\chi^2 = 36.8 - 15.2 = 21.6$ with 4 d.f., $p < .01$). (These goodness-of-fit statistics should be interpreted cautiously for this and the Watts and Newark analyses, since several of the expected frequences are very small.)

We can examine the escalation of violence itself in more detail by looking at the odds on each kind of official violence versus the residual violence by civilians and the accidental deaths for each day of the riot. Expected frequencies of official and residual violence were computed under Simon's model. The expected odds on the occurrence of each type of official violence are plotted (figure 4). Figure 4 shows that for all categories of official violence the odds on their occurrence increase as the riot continues.

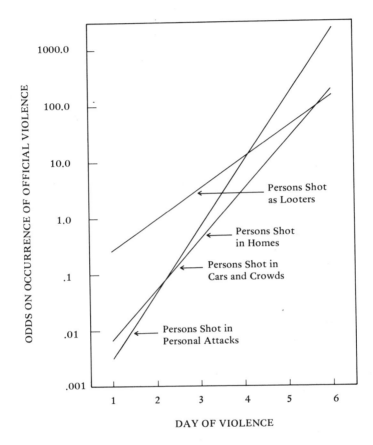

Figure 4. Odds computed from the expected frequencies of a log-linear model fitted to the data from the Detroit riot in figure 3 on the occurrence of each type of official violence against the combined civilian and accidental violence.

Watts

The pattern of violence in Watts was generally similar to that of Detroit, as seen in figure 5. On the first day of killing there was 1 civil-

ian-initiated death, 3 accidental deaths and only 2 officially instigated deaths. For the remainder of the riot there were 20 officially
instigated deaths, 2 accidental deaths, and no civilian-initiated deaths.
Much of the killing by officials occurred early Saturday morning and
could be considered part of the violence of Friday night, which was
described by the McCone Commission as the "worst" night of violence. Figure 5 also presents the average day for each circumstance
of death, and there was again a change in the character of official
violence as the riot progressed. Counting August 13, the first day
someone was killed as day one, figure 5 shows that the average days
on which persons were killed went from 2.0 for persons shot as

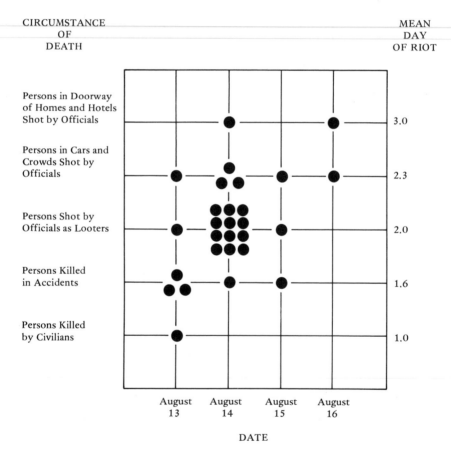

Figure 5. Fatalities (N = 28) of the Watts race riot of 1965 classified by circumstance of death and date.

looters, to 2.3 for persons shot in cars and crowds, to 3.0 for persons shot in doorways.

The Simon method to test for independence and goodness-of-fit of a linear model was applied to the data in figure 5. The null hypothesis of independence was rejected ($\chi^2 = 10.0$ with 3 d.f., p $<$ .02) and a more marginal fit of the linear model was found ($\chi^2 = 5.4$ with 2.0 d.f., .05 $<$ p $<$ .1), with the linear effect being significant ($\chi^2 = 10.0 - 5.4 = 4.6$ with 1 d.f., p $<$ .05).

The odds on each kind of official violence versus the residual violence by civilians and the accidental deaths was also examined. The expected frequencies of official and residual violence were computed under Simon's model, and the expected odds on the occurrence of each type of official violence are plotted in figure 6. This figure shows that the odds on the occurrence of the three categories of official violence (shooting persons as looters, shooting persons in cars and crowds, and shooting persons in doorways) increased as the riot progressed.

Newark

Although somewhat less pronounced, the data in figure 7 for Newark show a pattern similar to that of the other riots. Again, approximately the same number of official killings occurred both before and after the second day (nine before and eight after), but only one civilian-initiated death occurred after the second day. The official violence continued in the absence of civilian and accidental deaths. As with the other riots, the character of the official violence changed as the riot progressed. Counting July 13, the first day someone was killed as day one, figure 7 shows that the average day of violence for shooting was 2.0; for shooting persons in cars and crowds, 2.1; for shooting persons inside their homes, 3.0; and for killing persons in personal attacks, 3.8.

Applying the Simon method to test for independence and the goodness-of-fit of a linear model to the data of figure 7, we marginally fail to reject the null hypothesis of independence ($\chi^2 = 25.7$ with 16 d.f., .05 $<$ p $<$ .1) and found a good fit of the linear model ($\chi^2 = 12.6$ with 12 d.f., p $>$ .05), with the linear effect being significant ($\chi^2 = 25.7 - 12.6 = 13.1$ with 4 d.f., p $<$ .01).

The odds on each type of official violence versus the combined violence by civilians and accidental deaths was also computed. The expected odds on the occurrence of each type of official violence

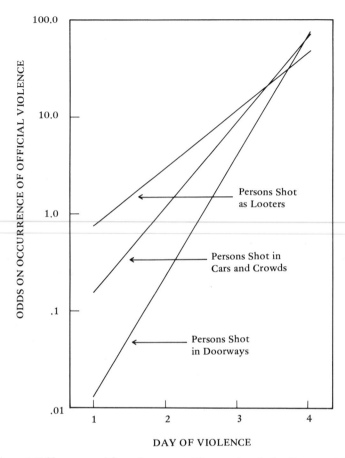

Figure 6. Odds computed from the expected frequencies of a log-linear model fitted to the data from the Watts riot in figure 5 on the occurrence of each type of official violence against the combined civilian and accidental violence.

are plotted in figure 8. The odds on the killing of persons in their homes and in personal attacks increased as the riot progressed and decreased for shooting persons in cars and crowds and as looters (figure 8).

THE STRUCTURE OF VIOLENCE

Two general trends appear in this data. First, violence initiated by civilians occurs during the early stages of a riot, and violence by po-

CIRCUMSTANCE
OF
DEATH

MEAN
DAY
OF RIOT

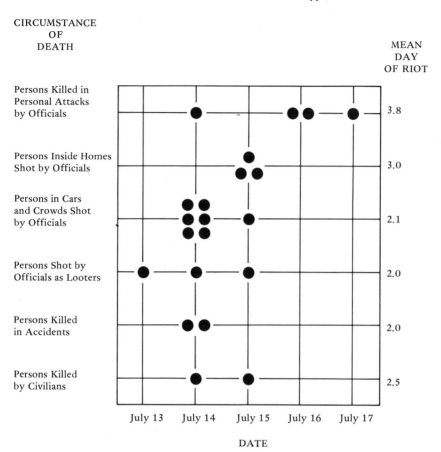

Persons Killed in
Personal Attacks
by Officials — 3.8

Persons Inside Homes
Shot by Officials — 3.0

Persons in Cars
and Crowds Shot
by Officials — 2.1

Persons Shot by
Officials as Looters — 2.0

Persons Killed
in Accidents — 2.0

Persons Killed
by Civilians — 2.5

July 13   July 14   July 15   July 16   July 17

DATE

Figure 7. Fatalities (N = 21) of the Newark race riot of 1967 classified by circumstance of death and date.

lice and the National Guard comes later. Second, officials become
increasingly indiscriminate, random, and personal in their killing as
the riot progresses. There is an order in the violence of these riots:
civilian-initiated and accidental deaths occur first, followed by officially instigated deaths, which become more random and indiscriminate. The violence is not randomly distributed over the course of
the riot.

The Breakdown of Police Controls: White Officials Riot

It appears that the normative and organizational constraints upon
law enforcement officials disintegrated as the riots progressed. Vio-

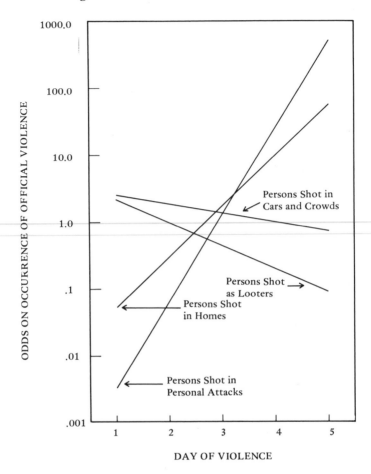

Figure 8. Odds computed from the expected frequencies of a log-linear model fitted to the data from the Newark riot in figure 7 on the occurrence of each type of official violence against the combined civilian and accidental violence.

lence by law enforcement officials seemed to progress from actions that were "legal" and could be seen as part of the law enforcement role, such as the shooting of looters, to acts that represented the complete opposite of organizational roles, such as the personal attacks upon black civilians. Consider the sequence of official violence. During the early stages of the riot, law enforcement officials shot looters, which, in some sense, could be seen as part of an officer's job. (Even here, though, some 64.7% of the persons shot for looting were running from the premises when they were killed.) As the riots progressed, shooting of looters declined and persons were increasingly shot standing on street corners and in cars as they approached or ran past National Guard roadblocks. This activity is a departure from the more "legal" activity of shooting looters. The people shot standing on street corners were not riot participants. They were bystanders. They were not shot while throwing objects, setting fires, harassing police, or sniping. Most lived in the neighborhood and had either come out to see what was going on or were going about their own business when they encountered the indiscriminate and random shooting by police. A similar situation existed with persons shot in cars. The roadblocks were not well lighted and were often no more than an overturned ash can and a few boards. Some persons were shot at when they merely approached roadblocks, and others were shot at when they attempted to run roadblocks. The cars were indiscriminately riddled with bullets; in Newark such indiscriminate shooting killed a 10-year-old boy riding in a car. As the riots progressed and as the organizational controls continued to dissolve, the next general kind of violence to appear involved law enforcement officials indiscriminately spraying apartment houses with bullets. Here women and children were killed (five deaths out of seven) and though officials claimed that they were shooting at snipers, none were either hit by officials or found when buildings were later searched. One could conceive of people on the streets or in cars as possible participants in ongoing riot activity and as possible threats to law enforcement officials, but this seems much less likely for women and children shot in their living rooms. Finally, with seemingly all professional restraint on the part of officials gone, there appear those killings characterized as personal attacks. These were not a matter of indiscriminate shooting but of very deliberate, almost vindictive, killing. At this point it appears that the transition from role-prescribed behavior (as in shooting of looters) to strictly private attacks is complete. The other cases (shootings of persons in crowds, cars, and buildings) seem to represent an area halfway between role-prescribed behavior and private behavior. Although each type of official killing can be considered in isolation, its temporal order suggests the breakdown of normative constraints as the riot progressed. In short, the appearance of rioting by white law enforcement officials.

RETHINKING THE CAUSES OF THESE RIOTS

The racial violence of the 1960s remains an enigma. Numerous empirical studies have been conducted, and these have generated quite varied explanations as to the causes of racial violence. Yet none seem totally satisfactory. The underlying model has been quite simple: black Americans, economically deprived and excluded from political participation, reacted against these conditions in the inner city with protest and violence. This account, in its most general outline, is the same across the political spectrum. For radicals it is a matter of "internal colonialism" and "ghetto revolt." For liberals it is more a matter of political communication through violence: blacks are signaling that they are fed up with depressed conditions and that if something isn't done soon the whole system is likely to break down. In these arguments the two assumptions everyone makes are that it is blacks who are protesting and that it is something about their depressed condition that is the cause of their discontent. One problem, though, is that our research efforts haven't supported these assumptions, particularly the second one. Consider, for instance, the general notion that it is something about the depressed condition of the inner city that is generating racial unrest. To test this idea researchers have looked at the association between the social condition of both individuals and cities and their propensity for racial violence. So far, studies that have compared rioters with nonrioters (see the literature reviewed in Fogelson [1971]) have found that, except for being young, rioters are by and large no different from the average ghetto resident:

> Depending on the riot, roughly two thirds to nine tenths of the arrestees were teen-agers or young adults, one half to two thirds single or otherwise unattached, one half to three quarters unskilled, one fifth to two fifths unemployed, and one third to two thirds uprooted; and one third to nine tenths had prior criminal records. *But these figures do not sharply distinguish the rioters from the potential rioters;* and to the extent that they do this reflects mainly the extremely heavy involvement of young adults who are more likely than their fathers to be single, unskilled, and unemployed. . . (Fogelson, 1971: 41) [emphasis added.]

If the social condition of individuals does not predict riot participation, what about the social condition of cities? Are there any structural characteristics of cities that make them more riot prone? A number of studies (Lieberson and Silverman, 1965; Spilerman, 1970, 1971, and 1976) have shown that there is no systematic relationship between depressed conditions—unemployment, dilapidated housing, etc.—and the propensity for, or severity of, riots. Spilerman has concluded, "Although we would not claim that local conditions never influenced disorder-proneness or disorder severity, we do assert the absence of a systematic tendency for either of these facets of the racial turmoil to be associated with the extent of Negro deprivation in a community" (Spilerman, 1976: 789).

Another problem is the one we have examined in this chapter so far: most of the killing during the three major riots of the 1960s was initiated by law enforcement officials and followed a definite pattern. *In short, there seems to have been an "official riot" accompanying the civilian riot.*

These findings of an absence of association between racial violence and depressed conditions and the presence of a possible "white riot" create doubts that we are dealing simply with blacks reacting to their depressed environment and suggests that we need to revise our conception of the racial violence of the 1960s in two ways. First, we need to shift the unit of analysis from cities to the nation as a whole. Since most major American cities experienced some sort of racial unrest during the 1960s, the comparison should not be between cities but between different periods in American history. Why should such violence have erupted from 1964 to 1968? Why not during the 1950s or the 1970s? Second, we must consider reasons for the official violence other than the notion of a temporary departure from professional behavior. White police are just as much a part of history as black civilians, and they are just as much animated by the forces of social change into outbursts of collective violence. With these two revisions in mind, I will devote the rest of this paper to examining the expansion of the state during the early 1960s and the resistance and reaction this generated in both blacks and white who were alternately mobilized and dispossessed by this expansion of state power. Comparisons will also be made with the expansion of state power during the early phases of nation building in Europe and the collective violence that was generated. Finally, I will articulate the complex interrelationship between the violence of whites and blacks, as each group responded to the tottering status order that was being subverted by the expanding national polity.

EXPANDING NATIONAL AND RESISTING LOCAL POLITICAL ORDERS

Nation Building and Collective Violence

The construction of the modern nation-state involves two general processes, state formation and nation building (Bendix, 1964; Tilly,

1975). The former precedes the latter and involves the emergence of a national bureaucracy, army, and educational system through which the power and authority of the central state is established over a defined territorial unit. Once the encompassing institutional framework of the state is established, the process shifts to the incorporation of new groups, largely through the extension of the franchise to ever-widening circles of the population (Rokkan, 1970). The process of state formation, involving the initial domination of local authorities to establish the sovereignty of the state and build a national economy and polity, has already been linked to the protest and riot of local polities resisting the claims of the central state (Tilly, 1969 and 1971). The subsequent process of nation building, involving the mobilization and incorporation of new groups, has been viewed largely in terms of the gains made by these groups and of a country's expanding definition of national citizenship (Lipset and Rokkan, 1967).

The extension of the rights and duties of citizenship to ever-widening circles of the population simultaneously involves a direct attack by the state upon intermediary authorities that stand between the discrete citizen and the sovereign state, making the history of nation building in the West largely a matter of eroding and breaking down local authorities (Marshall, 1948; Bendix, 1964; Nisbet, 1953). Social groups are often embedded within local political systems, and the extension of national citizenship involves breaking down the sovereignty of these polities to incorporate the individuals within as discrete national citizens.

In this process the incorporation of one group may simultaneously involve the loss by other groups of some traditionally held rights and privileges. As such, it may generate reactionary violence. Although the disruption of local politics need not always accompany the incorporation of new groups, this appears to have been the situation with the extension of the rights of national citizenship to black Americans during the early 1960s.

In this context I want to argue that what Charles Tilly has termed "reactionary" collective violence, of groups losing traditionally held rights and privileges to the state, does not necessarily cease with the institutionalization of the claims and authority of the victorious state. The specific forms of riot and protest—food and grain riots, anticonscription riots, or antitaxation riots—may have ceased, but the more general sociological conditions that brought them forth remain, because the process of nation building *also* involves the intervention of the state in local affairs. In short, *state intervention is not limited to the process of state formation, and, therefore, neith-er is the appearance of reactionary collective violence.*

French Grain Riots and American Race Riots

Consider for a moment the similarity of the grain riots that swept France from the seventeenth century to the middle of the nineteenth century and the American racial violence in the 1960s.

Louise Tilly (1971) has described how the emerging French state deregulated the grain trade as a means of building a national econo-my. With the growing demands of an expanding bureaucracy, court, and army, Paris intervened in local economic relationships to serve its own national needs. Grain was in some sense embedded in the structure of the traditional medieval economy, much as blacks can be considered embedded in local social and political stratification systems that had existed largely untouched by the federal govern-ment since the period immediately following the Civil War. In France, the paternalistic protection of the small buyers was removed, allow-ing speculators and large buyers to purchase grain to feed growing urban centers. "The crown supplanted local authority in one area after another. Royal officials took over the administration of tradi-tional local laws and made them serve the needs of the state" (Tilly, 1971: 28). With the state removing its previous regulation of both the commerce and pricing of grain, the result was to create supply and distribution problems for small towns and small buyers who could not compete with the increasing demands of large urban areas and the growing number of large grain speculators. They reacted to the interference of the state in their local affairs with riot—overturn-ing grain carts, breaking into the homes of bakers, and forcing the sale of grain and bread at what they considered a just price.

A similar situation existed in the construction of a national citi-zenry in the United States. Extending and enforcing the rights of national citizenship to blacks embedded in local status structures similarly involved resistance, protest, and riot by local political orders against the claims of the federal government. The building of a national polity, like the building of a national economy earlier in France, involves the disruption of local social arrangements and the loss by local groups of traditionally held rights. The rights at stake in the 1960s were the substance of black-white race relations as they manifested themselves in questions of employment, schooling, wel-fare, and the control of city hall. The group threatened was local *whites,* for whom the redefinition of the political status of blacks accomplished by the federal legislation of the early 1960s involved a direct attack upon their local political order. As local groups in France protested their loss of rights by attacking the symbols of the encroaching state through grain riots, so have those whites who in mid-twentieth-century America found their political position being undermined by the encroaching national polity engaged in protest and riot against the symbol of their loss of control, urban blacks.

White Ethnic Protest and Riot

The protest by whites is not limited to the violence of police during the major race riots. Since about the time of George Wallace's 1964 primary campaigns and the emergence of the "white blacklash," America has experienced an almost unending succession of demonstrations, protests, complaints, and collective violence by white ethnics against the intrusion of the federal government into local affairs to improve the status of blacks.

> Whether we say "blue collar" or "lower middle-class" or "home-owner" in New York City, or whether we say "Italian" or "Irish" is not unimportant, and yet we know we are talking about roughly the same people. So the mass media discourse about the "white ethnic groups" or the "white working- and lower middle-class"—the people are the same, and the issues are the same: their feelings that they have been ignored, have received little from government in recent years, and have borne the brunt of the costs involved in the economic and political rise of the Negroes (Glazer and Moynihan, 1970: xxvi).

There have been protest marches, demonstrations, and violence in resistance to court-ordered busing, as in Boston; conflicts between white teacher associations and black administrators, as in the Ocean Hill-Brownsville fight over decentralization (Ravitch, 1974); struggles over who will control the police, as seen in the resistance to police review boards (Abbott et al., 1969); increased militancy by associations of police officers (Bop, 1971); bitter mayoralty elections between white ethnic and black candidates (Levy and Kramer, 1972); a new militancy among voluntary associations that have traditionally been of the self-help variety; and support for national politicians, such as Wallace and Spiro Agnew, who opposed the extension of federal power into local politics and reaffirmed the sanctity of family, neighborhood, church, and authority in general (Lipset and Rabb, 1970).

Many of the local heroes of the new ethnicity, such as Louise Day Hicks of Boston, Frank Rizzo of Philadelphia, Antony Imperiale of Newark, or Albert Shanker of the AFT, have gained their fame by engaging in defensive political activity, supporting the position of ethnic groups in the structure of local politics. Their ethnic pride is generated largely out of a defensive reaction to an external threat. The Irish of south Boston, for example, do not express ethnic solidarity simply because they have similar occupations and residential stability but because they are reacting to an attack upon the local privilege of controlling schools.

The protest of white ethnics during the past decade can be seen as another instance of the resistance of local polities to the expansion of state power. George Rudé's (1959: 225) observations on the protest of the Parisian "little people" during the French Revolution is applicable to the ethnic protest of today. Parisians protested "not to renovate society or to remodel it after a new pattern, but to *reclaim traditional rights and to uphold standards* which they believed to be imperilled by the innovations of ministers, capitalists, speculators, agricultural 'improvers,' or city authorities [emphasis added]." The ethnic protest over schools, police, city hall, and shifting moral standards was a similar reactionary protest to *reclaim traditional rights* that were being *imperiled* by the intrusions of the government and by the growth of black political power.

Ethnicity is so merged with the substance and structure of city politics that the federal intervention became not only a crisis in local authority but also a crisis in ethnicity itself. Ethnicity has persisted in an *organizational* form, along with its usual form as a cultural heritage, in the reality of city politics. The ousting of native Yankee-Protestant control from large northeastern cities was one of the principal means for immigrant mobility and the institutionalization of ethnicity in political forms (Hofstadter, 1955). "Public employment was a major channel for the Italian, the Irish, and the Jew, each of whom by successively taking over whole sectors of the public services, gave various municipal agencies their distinctive ethnic coloration. Now blacks are the newcomers" (Cloward and Piven, 1975: 227). The political machine and patronage system provided a means for perpetuating ethnic control over cities, a control that is only now being challenged by the new "immigrants," the blacks. In America, city politics have been ethnic politics (Banfield and Wilson, 1966) in that they are both the institutionalization of group advantage (controlling city hall, schools, etc.) and a symbol of the presence and persistence of ethnicity in America.[1] Ethnic protest emerges as a means of reaffirming the collective identity of the social system that is being attacked and as a more literal means of resisting this loss of control.

It is interesting to note that the Yankees and the old middle class who earlier lost control of the cities to the immigrants engaged in a similar kind of reactionary protest. As Hofstadter (1955) has so brilliantly pointed out, much of the progressives' complaint against political machines, patronage, and the moral corruption of city life was actually a protest against the immigrant takeover of city politics. Similarly, concern in the 1960s over crime in the streets, lawlessness, permissive attitudes toward sex, declining respect for the family and for authority in general is quite similar to the progressives' suspicions about city life at the turn of the century. As earlier, much of this fear is attributed to the presence of newcomers. From Yankee to immigrant, and now from white ethnic to black, the history of city politics seems to be one of group succession and reactionary protest by those losing control.

RACIAL VIOLENCE AND THE EXPANDING STATE

This general process of encroaching national and resisting local political orders can be broken down into three stages involving the three major participants: the federal government and the action it took during the early 1960s; the blacks, the group toward whom federal attention was directed; and the local whites, the group who resisted the changes sought by the state. There is a complex interrelationship among these social actors. The action of the federal government directly threatened the substance of local politics in large cities and caused the complex action-reaction between rioting blacks and rioting white law enforcement officials.

Stage I: Federal Intervention in Local Politics

Since the initial effort by the federal government to incorporate blacks as national citizens immediately following the Civil War, the political structuring of race relations had been left almost exclusively to local authorities up until the Brown decision of 1954. During the early 1960s, a massive federal effort was directed toward changing the social, economic, and political status of blacks. The key legislation was the Great Society programs, which differed from earlier welfare acts in their concern for the political participation of the poor in local politics and the belief that the poor must acquire power in order to transform their own social and economic position. Speaking of this federal intervention in city politics, Marris and Rein observed:

> It was less an answer to poverty, than to a sense of breakdown in the open, democratic structure of society. Each of its successive formulations—in the grey areas projects, the delinquency programme, in the Economic Opportunity Act and Model Cities legislation—implied a need to reform the process of government itself. This was its consistent purpose (1967: 251).

The principal way that the power of the poor was built into this federal legislation was through "maximum feasible participation" of the poor in the administration of local poverty programs. Such participation posed a direct threat to local political arrangements, for it implied the relinquishing of control by local whites over employment practices, housing policy, schools, welfare agencies, and the police. It also threatened to mobilize new groups, leaders, and sources of political power that would challenge the city's very structure of power and authority (Greenstone and Peterson, 1973; Piven and Cloward, 1971; Cloward and Piven, 1975).

Federal intervention into city politics took different forms. One of the most explicit was the withholding of poverty money from those cities that did not allow for the participation of the poor in the administration of poverty programs. This enraged local white power holders.

> By the summer of 1965, the U.S. Conference of Mayors had become a determined lobby against any conception of community action which threatened their authority. It accused Shriver of "fostering class conflict," and denounced his attempts to fund agencies apart from the agencies approved by city hall (Marris and Rein, 1967: 251).

Another source of pressure was the Community Action Projects established by the poverty program. They organized demonstrations, rent strikes, boycotts, marches, petitions for the removal of public officials and suits against the city and its agencies. The manifestation of black-white status relations in schools, welfare agencies, housing boards and city government itself was under constant political pressure.

For example, antagonism between the poverty programs and local white authorities characterized both Detroit and Newark before their major riots in 1967. In both of these cities the black population had been steadily growing. Detroit went from being 16% black in 1950 to 29% black in 1960 and 44% black in 1970. Similarly, Newark went from being 17% black in 1950 to 34% black in 1960 and 54% black in 1970. This growth of the black population was not reflected in increases in political participation. The Kerner Report (Kerner, 1968: 91) commented about Detroit: "In elective offices the Negro population was still underrepresented. Of nine councilmen, one was a Negro. Of seven school board members, two were Negroes." As for Newark, after noting the dramatic increase in the black population, the Kerner Report (Kerner, 1968: 57) commented: "The white population, nevertheless, retained political control of the city. On both the City Council and the Board of Education seven of nine members were white. On other key boards the disparity was equal or greater." There was also tension between local poverty programs and the city. As the Kerner Report commented about Newark:

> Largely excluded from positions of traditional political power Negroes, tutored by a handful of militant social activitists who had moved into the city in the early 1960's, made use of the anti-poverty program, in which poor people were guaranteed representation, as a political springboard. This led to friction between the United Community Corporation, the agency that administered the anti-poverty program, and the city administration (Kerner, 1968: 59).

The whites, and the municipal political system in which they enjoyed positions of power and privilege, were being undermined in yet another fashion. Along with the direct pressure from the federal government to share power and increase the participation of blacks, the alteration of the political status of blacks resulting from the federal attention had an indirect effect upon the status of whites and the larger stratification system in which both blacks and whites were embedded. The black-white status order was disrupted when the institutionalized interchanges supporting the definition of this stratification system were subverted by the intervention of the federal government in city politics during the early 1960s. *The extension of the rights of national citizenship to blacks redefined one of the groups in the status equation and created an imbalance in the whole structure of race relations.* The result of this intrusion was a chain reaction of violence whereby both groups responded literally and, more importantly, symbolically, to the tottering political and status order. Blacks, and the local political order as represented by the police, were both involved, although each had different social realities they were attempting to maintain. Blacks were reacting to their status and moral position as national citizens, while whites were attempting to restore the traditional black-white status order that was crumbling from pressure of the encroaching national polity. Local politics were becoming nationalized, and that brought about a severe disruption in the black-white status order on which local power and authority were predicated. The data on the circumstances of death in the first part of this paper suggest that the first reaction was by black civilians and that this in turn triggered white violence.

Stage II: Status Uncertainty and Black Protest

Race relations involve the structured interaction of status groups. A status order is maintained on a daily basis through ceremonial interaction between the status groups (Goffman, 1956). When this racial status order is politically institutionalized, it is expressed in such institutional forms as housing and job discrimination, limited educational opportunities, and limited participation on school boards or in police forces.

Relations between status groups of an institutional character, such as police relations with black citizens, have at least two dimensions. There is the literal content of these relations, which, for example, would refer to issues of police brutality and harassment. There is also the ceremonial or ritual meanings carried by police-civilian encounters. All relations between blacks and whites carry some ceremonial significance, even if they originate for purely instrumental purposes, and as such reaffirm the positional location of these groups in the organization of local politics.

Police Brutality

The actions of the police have been isolated as the single most important precipitating incident for most of the black violence during the 1960s (Kerner, 1968; Fogelson, 1971). The significance of police-civilian relations has been studied largely as a question of police harassment and the use of excessive force. The traditional reasoning has been that blacks were protesting or rebeling against the excessive and unfair treatment they received from the police. There are, though, two problems with this reasoning. First, abuses of police power seem to have decreased over the past century (Fogelson, 1971 and 1977), and if anything there is probably less abuse of the rights of minorities than at any previous time in police history. This raises the question of why protest against police harassment occurred during the 1960s and not earlier, when the treatment was more severe and the police were less professional. Second, and perhaps more significant, the precipitating incidents for most of the riots during the 1960s appear to have been quite ordinary police-civilian encounters and not matters of excessive use of force. As Fogelson has observed:

> Most of the 1960's riots were triggered by commonplace, reasonable, and trivial police actions . . . . The Rochester (1964), Philadelphia (1964) and Los Angeles (1965) riots are cases in point. So are the Jersey City riots which erupted after the police attempted to break up a fight between two Negro women; the Omaha riots of 1966, which broke out after the police tried to stop a fireworks display on the July 4th weekend; and the Chicago riots of 1966, which started after the police turned off a few fire hydrants on a hot summer evening. Moreover, most of these actions were taken in response to complaints by Negroes. They may or may not have been wise, but they were certainly not extraordinary; the police break up fights, stop fireworks dislays, and turn off fire hydrants all the time. Nor, the press reports reveal, did the police use excessive force, show insufficient respect, or otherwise behave improperly in most of these incidents (1971: 50-51).

This general situation was also true for Watts, Detroit, and Newark. The precipitating incident in Watts was the arrest of a drunk driver. In Detroit it was the raiding of an after-hours drinking place. In Newark it was rumors about police beating a cabbie in a precinct house. The problem with the police brutality explanation is that there simply wasn't much of it immediately before these riots. The sociological question now becomes why, if police normally break up fights, stop fireworks displays, turn off fire hydrants, and raid after-hours drinking places, these ordinary events generated such a collective outburst. The answer lies, I think, in the ceremonial component of police-civilian relations.

The ritualistic interchanges between status groups (in our case white police and black civilians) constitute the daily means for the rejuvenation of police and black identities. The nature of political authority within the city and the general relations between police and citizens are daily transmitted through the accepted interchanges between the two groups. The federal attention toward blacks during the early 1960s (stage I) guaranteeing them the rights of national citizenship, involved a change in their political and moral status. This change had direct implications for police actions toward blacks, particularly the quite ordinary ones.

Disconfirming the Status Order.

Normal police activities lost their ability to validate the status order, not because they themselves had changed (the police brutality argument) but because the definition of one of the groups in the status equation had changed. The police continued to perform the traditional status rituals—breaking up fights, turning off fire hydrants, etc.—but the status order that these acts usually confirmed had been changed from the outside, and this transformed the police activity into acts that no longer validated the status relations of blacks and whites. Police actions had temporarily lost their ceremonial significance and appeared to be a source of uncertainty, threat, and danger. The situation is somewhat like Durkheim's notion of anomie, where rapid change creates a confusion and uncertainty over what is considered appropriate and legitimate. The traditional status order as encased in police-civilian relations had been upset by the intervention of the government, which be redefining the status of blacks implicitly redefined the meaning of ordinary police activity.

The federal intervention had been directly aimed at the position of blacks in the local political system and at the treatment they received by the administrative structures of that political order. It was not just the actions of the police but all sorts of traditional prerogatives of the city that became illegitimate. For example, in Newark prior to the riot there had been extensive controversy between blacks and the city over the "appropriateness" and legitimacy of city actions (Kerner, 1968: 57-59). There were controversies over the establishment of a police review board, the expansion of a medical school into black neighborhoods, and the appointment of a new secretary to the board of education. Local privilege and authority was illegitimate, not because it was "out of line," or excessive, but because blacks' relationship to it had been altered by the federal attention.

Status Protest

By conceptualizing the black violence as a ritualistic response to the now illegitimate and uncertain character of police-civilian interchanges we can better understand some of its most distinctive characteristics. For all the depictions of black rioting as a colonial revolt or revolution, black violence was not specifically directed at either white institutions or individuals. The riots didn't surge into white suburbs, nor was city hall stormed. Again, the astute Fogelson:

> What is remarkable is that thus far the rioters have been so restrained and selective. By restrained I mean that for all the rioting and assault very few blacks attempted to kill white passers-by, policemen, or National Guardsmen. And by selective I mean that for all the looting and burning, even fewer sought to destroy banks, insurance companies, courthouses, and city halls . . . . A few radicals aside, they did not renounce membership in American society; nor did they challenge its economic organization or political legitimacy (1971: 96).

Black violence was not a focused attack or protest. It was diffuse, undirected, and localized. Its properties of being prompted by police actions and yet being largely disorganized and undirected have resulted in seemingly contrary interpretations as to cause. Its precipitation by the police suggests revolt, protest, and revolution, as in the explanations of Blauner (1969) and Rubenstein (1970); yet its diffuse and unorganized character has also prompted explanations such as Banfield's (1974) characterization "Rioting Mainly for Fun and Profit." The solution to these seemingly contradictory approaches lies in the ceremonial significance of both the police actions and the subsequent black response. From this perspective, both Banfield and Blauner or Rubenstein are correct; black violence was precipitated by activity of officials and it was also unorganized and largely symbolic in character. But, since the question at hand is the definitional status of the political order, the symbolic character of black violence is, in fact, the important dimension. Blacks protested what appeared to be an illegitimate infringement upon their status as national citizens.

Stage III: Threatened Whites Riot

The focus now shifts to the white violence that followed the initial black outbursts in Watts, Newark, and Detroit. White violence had two causes. First, the cities had been on the defensive during the early part of the 1960s (stage I) because of federal demands to relinquish power and authority to blacks. The ever-encroaching national polity was attacking the roots of local power arrangements as manifested in the control of schools, police, welfare, housing, and jobs. In the most general sociological sense this is the primary source of the instability in American cities. Second, the effect of federal attention not only directly threatened whites but also altered the status of blacks. The sociological process here is much like the earlier black protest, but now the stakes are more serious and the violence accordingly more severe. For the local whites, the failure of blacks to confirm the status order by accepting the ordinary actions of police called into question the substance of political authority in general and, as such, the whole system around which it was built. If the federal government's encroachment upon the prerogatives of local government can be considered the underlying cause of the white riots, then the actions of the blacks during the first few days can be considered the immediate precipitating incident.

What is ironic is that the threat blacks posed with their failure to accept ordinary police activities was greater than if they had responded to more obvious examples of police brutality and racial discrimination. Clear examples of police brutality are not part of the *ceremonial* interchange between public authorities and their citizens, whereas breaking up fights, shutting off fire hydrants, and raiding after-hours drinking spots are. Failure to accept police excesses does not undermine the status order, since they are not part of its ceremonial props. But failure to accord validity to the most ordinary police activities is to deny their social reality and the reality of the political and status order itself.

The white response to this crumbling status order was the ritual violence of indiscriminate shooting and personal attacks. This process is very similar to the one observed by Erikson (1966) in his study of witch-hunting in Salem. There, following a crisis in social boundaries, the community responded with an outpouring of ritual persecutions to reaffirm the dissolving social order. Similarly, the formal agents of the local corporate order—the police—responded to the crises in the status order by persecuting blacks. This notion that police respond to threats to their authority has some support in studies conducted at the individual level of analysis. Westley (1953) found that police officers, when asked under what conditions violence on their part was justified, most often responded "disrespect for police." Similarly, Piliavin and Briar (1964), while observing encounters between officers and juveniles, found that a youth's presentation of self, or demeanor, was related to whether he would be arrested or merely admonished. Finally, Reiss (1968: 18), after observing instances of the excessive use of force by police officers on patrol, concluded that "almost one-half of the cases involved open defiance of police authority (39%) or resisting arrest (9%)."

Crisis in White Identities.

The exact nature of the crisis in race relations involves the basic Meadian idea of the reciprocity of selves and actions individuals take in confirming both their own identity and that of others. The general point is best put forward by Goffman.

> The individual's failure to encode through deeds and expressive cues, a *workable* definition of himself, one which closely enmeshed others can accord him through the regard they show his person, is to block and trip up and threaten them in almost every movement that they make. *The selves that had been the reciprocals of his are undermined* (1971: 366) [Emphasis added.]

Blacks, as part of the local political order, are reciprocally linked to the identities of whites. The interactions encoded in police-civilian relations provide selves that both blacks and white police can accord each other. Black violence in the 1960s threatened whites because it implied a self-concept on the part of blacks that whites, and for that matter public authorities in general, could not accord if they were to maintain their own identity and the broader structure of public authority. Race relations, as stated before, are matters of social definition, and are largely maintained by the ceremonial significance of interchanges between participating groups. The actions of each group reinforce and make possible the very identity of the other. In America, a large part of being defined as black is the relation one has to another group defined as white. As long as each group plays out its part in the system of structured identities, the status order persists. The crisis comes when the meaning of one of the statuses change (stage I), which implicitly changes the meaning of the ritual interchange (stage II), or when the interchange itself changes (stage III). In the first case the interchange remains the same, but its meaning is altered. In the second case the interchange is altered. Both situations created a disequilibrium in the local status order and generate a collective response. In the 1960s blacks protested what seemed illegitimate activity, and whites engaged in ceremonial violence to reconstruct the dissolving system of race relations. White protest, like the earlier black protest, was essentially diffuse and unorganized.

The idea of "restoring order" or putting blacks in "their place" has important symbolic significance, for it is the definition of race relations that is really under attack, not the actualities of white institutions. As mentioned earlier, blacks didn't attack public buildings, banks, or prestigious stores, nor by and large were individuals attacked. A literal attack upon white institutions and its symbols was not necessary to trigger the counterreaction. Black rioting was behavior "out of place" and a violation of the symbolic structure of race relations. *In effect, blacks, by not being themselves, kept whites from being themselves, and as such they constituted a direct threat to both the identity of whites and the larger status and political order in which those identities were embedded.*

From this perspective we can now explain why these riots involved relations between black civilians and police rather than between black civilians and white civilians, as in earlier American race riots. The police in America are largely under local control (Wilson, 1968) and are agents and literal members of those local white groups that control large cities. Race relations are merged with political relations, and the separation of the two is quite difficult. In a way the riots of the 1960s were race riots in the classic sense of encounters between status groups, yet at the same time they were actions by local polities protesting their loss of privilege and authority to the claims of the central state.

CONCLUSION

Was much of the racial violence of the 1960s in fact a protest of whites against the dissolution of the local status order resulting from the expansion of the national polity? Certainly there was black violence, but in the perspective of time it seems that the racial violence was at least as much a protest by whites as by blacks. We are back to the riots and revolts of eighteenth-century France. The small polities, like the famed "little people" of Paris, who rioted to protest the coming of the revolutionary regime and the centralization and nationalization of local life, have appeared again in the form of local white ethnics in large American cities. They protested the intrusion of the central state into their affairs much as Parisians had done 200 years earlier.

Recent work on the riots and protest of revolutionary France has forced a reevaluation of the traditionally held notions that it was the marginal classes and Parisian riffraff who participated in these popular uprisings. Painstaking research has shown that it was in fact the small shopowners and guildsmen from the stable neighborhoods who comprised the mob and participated in much of the revolutionary violence. Today, we may likewise have to revise our understanding of the 1960s and see the violence of that decade not so much as black revolt, although there was much of that, but also as white riot and protest.

NOTES

1. A classic example of both the power and symbol of ethnic politics is New York, about which Glazer and Moynihan comment:

"Ethnic considerations have always been primary in New York City politics, where the three top spots of each party are regularly divided among a Jew, an Italian, and an Irishman . . . the Borough presidency of Manhattan has been reserved to Negroes for some years; where the old Board of Education was regularly divided among three Jews, three Catholics, and three Protestants" (1970: xxviii).

REFERENCES

Abbott, D. W., L. H. Gold, and E. T. Rogowsky. 1969. *Police, Politics and Race: The New York City Referendum on Civilian Review.* New York and Cambridge, Mass.: The American Jewish Committee and the Joint Center for Urban Studies of M.I.T. and Harvard University.

Banfield, E. C. 1974. *The Un-Heavenly City Revisited.* Boston: Little, Brown.

———, and J. Q. Wilson. 1966. *City Politics.* New York: Vintage Books.

Bendix, R. 1964. *Nation-Building and Citizenship.* New York: John Wiley.

Blauner, R. A. 1969. "Internal colonialism and ghetto revolt." *Social Problems* 16: 393-408.

Bop, W. L. 1971. *The Police Rebellion.* Springfield, Ill.: Charles C. Thomas.

Cloward, R. A., and F. F. Piven. 1975. *The Politics of Turmoil: Poverty, Race, and the Urban Crisis.* New York: Vintage Books.

Cohen, J., and W. S. Murphy. 1966. *Burn Baby Burn.* New York: E. P. Dutton.

Crump, S. 1966. *Black Riot in Los Angeles.* Los Angeles: Trans-Anglo Books.

Danzger, M. H. 1975. "Validating conflict data." *American Sociological Review* 40: 570-84.

Downes, B. T. 1968. "The social characteristics of riot cities: A comparative study." *Social Science Quarterly* 49: 504-20.

———. 1970. "A critical reexamination of the social and political characteristics of riot cities." *Social Science Quarterly* 51: 349-60.

Erikson, Kai T. 1966. *Wayward Puritans: A Study in the Sociology of Deviance*. New York: John Wiley.

Fogelson, R. M. 1971. *Violence as Protest*. Garden City, N. Y.: Anchor Books.

———. 1977. *Big-City Police*. Cambridge, Mass.: Harvard University Press.

Glazer, N., and D. P. Moynihan. 1970. *Beyond the Melting Pot: The Negroes, Puerto Ricans, Jews, Italians, and Irish of New York City*. 2nd ed. Cambridge, Mass.: M.I.T. Press.

Goffman, Erving. 1956. "The nature of deference and demeanor." *American Anthropologist* 58: 473-502.

———. 1971. *Relations in Public*. New York: Harper and Row.

Greenstone, J. D., and P. E. Peterson. 1973. *Race and Authority in Urban Politics*. New York: Russell Sage Foundation.

Hayden, T. 1967. *Rebellion in Newark: Official Violence and Ghetto Response*. New York: Vintage Books.

Hobsbawm, Eric J. 1959. *Primitive Rebels*. Manchester: Manchester University Press.

Hofstadter, R. 1955. *The Age of Reform*. New York: Alfred A. Knopf.

Kerner, O. 1968. *Report of the National Advisory Commission on Civil Disorders*. New York: Bantam Books.

Levy, M. R., and M. S. Kramer. 1972. *The Ethnic Factor: How America's Minorities Decide Elections*. New York: Simon and Schuster.

Lieberson, S., and A. R. Silverman. 1965. "The precipitants and underlying conditions of race riots." *American Sociological Review* 30: 887-98.

Lipset, S. M., and E. Rabb. 1970. *The Politics of Unreason: Right-Wing Extremism in America, 1790-1970*. New York: Harper and Row.

Lipset, S. M., and S. Rokkan. 1967. "Cleavage structures, party systems, and voter alignments: An introduction." In S. M. Lipset and S. Rokkan (eds.). *Party Systems and Voter Alignments*. New York: Free Press.

Marris, P., and M. Rein. 1967. *Dilemmas of Social Reform*. Chicago: Aldine.

Marshall, T. H. 1948. *Citizenship and Social Class*. Garden City, N. Y.: Doubleday.

Morgan, W. R., and T. N. Clark. 1973. "The causes of racial disorders: A grievance-level explanation." *American Sociological Review* 38: 611-24.

Nisbet, R. A. 1953. *The Quest for Community*. New York: Oxford University Press.

Parker, T. F. 1974. *Violence in the U. S.* Vol. 1: 1956-1967. New York: Facts on File.

Piliavin, I., and S. Briar. 1964. "Police encounters with juveniles." *American Journal of Sociology* 70: 206-14.

Piven, F. F., and R. A. Cloward. 1971. *Regulating the Poor: The Functions of Public Welfare*. New York: Pantheon Books.

Ravitch, D. 1974. *The Great School Wars: New York City, 1805-1973*. New York: Basic Books.

Reiss, A. J. 1968. "Police brutality: Answers to key questions." *Trans-Action* 5: 10-19.

Rokkan, S. 1970. *Citizens, Elections and Parties*. New York: David McKay.

Rubenstein, R. E. 1970. *Rebels in Eden: Mass Political Violence in the United States*. Boston: Little, Brown.

Rudé, G. 1959. *The Crowd in the French Revolution*. Oxford: Oxford University Press.

Sauter, V. G., and G. Hines. 1968. *Nightmare in Detroit*. Chicago: Henry Regnery.

Sears, D. O., and J. B. McConahay. 1973. *The Politics of Violence: The New Urban Blacks and the Watts Riot*. Boston: Houghton Mifflin.

Simon, G. 1974. "Alternative analyses for the singly-ordered contingency table." *Journal of the American Statistical Association* 69: 971-76.

Skolnick, J. H. 1969. *The Politics of Protest*. New York: Ballantine Books.

Smelser, Neil F. 1963. *Theory of Collective Behavior*. New York: Free Press.

Snyder, David, and W. R. Kelley. 1977. "Conflict intensity, media sensitivity and the validity of newspaper data." *American Sociological Review* 42: 105-23.

Spilerman, S. 1970. "The causes of racial disturbances: A comparison of alternative explanations." *American Sociological Review* 35: 627-49.

———. 1971. "The causes of racial disturbances: Tests of an explanation." *American Sociological Review* 36: 427-42.

———. 1976. "Structural characteristics of cities and the severity of racial disorders." *American Sociological Review* 41: 771-93.

Stark, R. 1972. *Police Riots.* Belmont, Calif.: Wadsworth.

Tilly, Charles. 1969. "Collective violence in European perspective." In Hugh Graham and Ted Gurr (eds.). *Violence in America.* New York: Signet Books.

———. 1975. *The Formation of National States in Western Europe.* Princeton, N. J.: Princeton University Press.

Tilly, L. 1971. "The food riot as a form of political conflict in France." *Journal of Interdisciplinary History* 2: 23-57.

Westley, W. A. 1953. "Violence and the police." *American Journal of Sociology* 49: 34-41.

Wilson, J. Q. 1968. *Varieties of Police Behavior.* Cambridge, Mass.: Harvard University Press.

Chapter 6

Theories of the Political Creation of Deviance
Legacies of Conflict Theory, Marx, and Durkheim

James Inverarity

INTRODUCTION

Sociological analysis of law, crime, and deviance has long been segregated from the analysis of political power. As David Matza has cogently observed:

> The criminological positivists succeeded in what would seem impossible. They separated the study of crime from the workings and theory of the state (1969: 143).

In the sixties the New Left spawned several attempts to politicize and radicalize the sociology of law. The civil rights movement, the Berkeley free speech movement, the anti-Vietnam War movement, women's liberation, and gay liberation each raised questions about the relationship between crime and politics that had, for the most part, been dormant in standard American criminology. Within sociology the conflict theorists, played an important role in directing attention to these critical, but long neglected, problems in the sociology of law. Nevertheless, it is becoming increasingly clear that conflict theory has major limitations both as a coherent theoretic perspective and as a basis for empirical investigation.

This paper proposes to transcend the limitations of conflict theory by reconsidering some of the ideas of Karl Marx and Emile Durkheim on the role of political entities in defining crime. The first part of this essay examines some of the basic limitations of current conflict theories of the political nature of deviance. The second part of the essay outlines some themes from Marx and Durkheim that so far have been obscured by the preoccupations of conflict theory.

THE CURRENT CONFLICT THEORY OF LAW

One of the key statements of the current theory in the sociology of law is Chambliss's essay "The functional and conflict theories of crime: the heritage of Marx and Durkheim." It will be useful to begin with this essay, since it is among the most thorough statements of current American conflict theory.[1] Chambliss reduces the central issues in the sociology of law to two general theories of society, functional and conflict. The functional model (which includes the anomie, differential association, and other theories of crime) assumes a society stable through time, integrated around a set of common values and concerns, but periodically faced with deviance on the parts of individual members who have failed somehow to become properly socialized. The conflict model, on the other hand, views society as an arena of conflicting groups that employ the criminal law to stigmatize their opponents in the conflict over scarce resources. All discussions of law and social structure, Chambliss maintains, can best be viewed as "a gigantic struggle between proponents of the previously dominant functional paradigm and proponents of the newly emerging conflict paradigm" (Chambliss, 1976: 1).

The first part of this essay will raise four issues concerning Chambliss's presentations of the central theoretical problems in the sociology of law. The goal here is not to defend the "functional paradigm" against the "conflict paradigm" but rather is to demonstrate that Chambliss's functional/conflict polarity is a misleading division of issues, which creates a series of essentially intractable problems and paradoxes that hinder adequate analysis of law and society.[2] In brief the four issues are these:

1. Chambliss's discussion equivocates between explaining punishment and explaining crime. These two questions are independent: What causes crime, that is, why do people engage in activities that society has defined as criminal? And why are these particular activities subjected to the criminal sanction in the first place?

2. Chambliss's discussion commits fallacies of reification, confounding theoretic concepts with empirical variables. He takes, for example, Durkheim's concept of mechanical solidarity and Marx's concept of class conflict as alternative literal descriptions of American society. This paper will show that neither concepts can be literally applied and that any attempt to do so as a test of "paradigms" is totally misguided.

3. The dichotomy between conflict and functionalist orientations has preoccupied sociologists since Dahrendorf (1959) and arguably (e.g., Turk, 1977) has had a long run in social philosophy. Recently, however, Giddens (1976) and others have questioned the reduction of *sociological issues* to such a dichotomy. It is the contention of this paper that in the sociology of law the conflict/functionalist dichotomy warps our vision and constrains our imagination. Furthermore, the best reason for reading Marx and Durkheim is not to find harbingers of this false polarity but rather to free ourselves of contemporary warps and constraints.

4. Conflict theory emphasizes the increasingly repressive and coercive nature of the criminal law under advanced capitalism. It will be shown that this thesis is not only contrary to fact but inconsistent with the Marxist analysis that is alleged by Chambliss to be its basis.

Crime or Punishment

A basic source of confusion in the sociology of law is the equivocation between attempting to explain deviant behavior and attempting to explain the societal reaction to it (cf. Roshier, 1978; Akers, 1968). For example, Chambliss characterizes Durkheim's argument as follows:

> Criminal behavior, when it occurs, reinforces the sacredness of the customs within the society (Chambliss, 1976: 6).

For Durkheim, however, it is not criminal behavior that affects solidarity but the social reaction to crime. "Punishment brings together the upright consciences and concentrates them" (Durkheim, 1964: 108). This point would be nothing more than a question of style if Chambliss did not continue down the wrong track by stating that Durkheim's position

> emphasizes the acquisition of norms and values and the social psychological experiences of individuals that lead to this acquisition as the most important feature of social relations in understanding crime (Chambliss, 1976: 6).

We have now moved entirely from an explanation of punishment to an explanation of individual criminal behavior. As we will see below, the motivation of individual criminals is an issue that is irrelevant to Durkheim's and Marx's theories of criminal law.

It may be worthwhile to consider the contrast between explanations of crime and explanations of punishment more concretely. Consider the interesting case of the man who becomes sexually aroused by women's handbags and baby carriages (Raymond, 1956). This case poses two distinct issues. The first issue is how such uncommon preferences were developed. Tied to the motivational question are a series of issues of praxis: for example, how can the client be exorcised of his deviant sexuality (or alternatively, how can these particular delights be made more accessible to conventionals)? The second issue is quite different. It concerns why any given society imposes sanctions (criminal, moral, psychiatric) on the sexual fetishism of these two particular commodities, handbags and baby carriages. An adequate answer to the first question will not necessarily tell us much about the second. A discussion that equivocates between motivational issues and definitional issues, therefore, is likely to be stillborn.

Reification

Chambliss's version of Marx posits a conflict between the class that rules and those that work for the ruling class. In marshaling evidence for this argument, however, the class conflict model dematerializes and law becomes the product of

> a small minority occupying a particular class or stratum but sharing a viewpoint and a set of social experiences which brings them together as an active and effective force of social change. For example, Joseph Gusfield's astute analysis of the emergence of prohibition in the United States illustrates how these laws were brought about through political efforts of the downwardly mobile segment of America's middle class (Chambliss 1976: 10).

Chambliss's use of Gusfield's study of the temperance movement as evidence for the class conflict position is curious since Gusfield prefaces his analysis with the observation that "our social system has not experienced the sharp class organization and class conflict which have been so salient in European history" (1963: 1); the whole point of *Symbolic Crusade* is to demonstrate that a class conflict perspective is inadequate for explaining the phenomenon of status politics exemplified in the temperance movement.

In effect, Chambliss treats "class" as a descriptive category, thus commiting the fallacy of reification, confusing an analytic concept with a descriptive category.[3] Why did Chambliss commit this error? It appears to be due to his attempt at a "Marxist" analysis derived entirely from *The Communist Manifesto*. In this work Marx and Engels present an analytic model in which social change is the outcome of conflict between two antagonistic classes (capitalists and working class; nobility and bourgeoisie, etc.). Chambliss takes this model as universally applicable, which not only results in nonsensical empirical analysis but is entirely contrary to Marx's analysis of specific historical societies. When faced with the task of examining French politics, for example, Marx abandons the Manifesto's schematic of a simple dichotomy for a more complex analysis in which industrial capitalists battle finance capitalists, in which peasantry whose class organization resembles a sack of potatoes plays a major political role. The discussion of classes and class conflict in the American conflict theory of law has, in short, been inadequate both as an explanation of the criminal law and as a reading of Marx.

The reification of "class" has recurrently spawned tautological forms of explanation in the American conflict approach. For example, Quinney writes:

> What, then, is the nature of this ruling class as reflected in criminal matters? It is composed of (1) members of the upper economic class (those who own or control the means of production) and (2) those who benefit in some way from the present capitalist economic system (1973: 55).

Conflict theory explanations of criminal law are frequently based on the nebulous idea of an elite consisting of all who benefit "in some way" from the system. Such a line of argument is a tautology: What determines the enactment and enforcement of the criminal law? The interests of the ruling class! And who are the ruling class? Why, those who determine the laws, be they corporate elites, international bankers, or downwardly mobile middle classes.[4] At best such tautologies serve as orienting statements, injunctions of where a researcher ought to begin looking to discover the determinants of the criminal law. Too often, however, both the proponents and critics of the conflict approach have taken these statements as the finished product of the analysis. For example, the problems of reification and tautology recur throughout Chambliss's analysis of law in Seattle, Washington, and Ibadin, Nigeria.[5] Two convenience samples are used to argue that law enforcement (variously interpreted) serves the (undefined) interests of (unidentified) ruling classes in both Nigeria and the United States. The central finding in Seattle turns out to be that "over 70 percent of all arrests during the time of the study were for public drunkenness. The police were actually arresting drunks on one side of a building while on the other side a vast array of other offenses was being committed" (Chambliss, 1976: 23). This observation is supposed to demonstrate that law enforcement in Seattle reflects "the ruling class's effort to see that those acts most often committed by the lower classes are defined as crime, whereas typically 'immoral' acts [e.g., political corruption] will not be" (1976: 23). The observation, however, is at best a slender reed on which to base the argument that law enforcement is a product of ruling class interests. First, it fails to consider alternative explanations. It is just as plausible to account for the high incidence of arrests for public drunkenness in terms of visibility (cf. Stinchcombe, 1963), since legally admissible evidence in the case of public drunkenness is much easier to obtain than legally admissible evidence for political corruption (unless, of course, one of the culprits is tape recording the transaction).[6] To demonstrate bias in law enforcement, it is essential to examine individuals of different classes committing the same offense, or at least to control for alternative factors, such as visibility of the behavior. Second, Chambliss fails to define who constitutes the ruling class in Seattle. Presumably it would include the board of directors of Boeing Aircraft, but does it also include petite bourgeoisie who complain about drunks standing in front of their hardware stores? Or just plain folk who complain to the police about being accosted on the street by a drunk? Without specifying the composition of the elite and its interests, it would be impossible to provide a noncircular explanation of why 70% of the arrests in Chambliss's study were for drunkenness or why drunkenness has recently been decriminalized (see Pittman [1974]).[7]

As Hopkins observes:

> The outcome of the [conflict/functionalist "debate"] depends more on definition and the way terms are used that it does on empirical research. For example, if we allow that interests[8] of the powerful may on occasion coincide with the interests of the less powerful groups or alternatively that the community itself is a powerful interest group, then even laws which reflect widespread consensus can be interpreted as expressions of the interests of the powerful. But such a formal resolution of the issue is trivial and unenlightening (1975: 614).

Conflict/Functional Polarity

The heuristic value of the conventional conflict/functional polarity is questionable. Percy Cohen (1968: 166-73) suggested a decade ago that the conflict/functional polarity rests upon semantic quibbles; similarly, Anthony Giddens recently wrote that the conflict/functional "debate"

> not only rests upon misleading interpretations of past [theorists], but is also a wholly inadequate way of conceiving our present tasks (Giddens, 1976: 717).

The conflict/functional polarity confounds several distinct issues, some of which are analytic and others of which are empirical. For example, one component of the conflict/functional polarity is the *empirical* issue of the extent of political or moral consensus in any given society. Thus, Chambliss argues (1976: 9) that empirical studies of the sociology of law fail to show that "criminal law is a body of rules which reflect strongly held moral dictates of society." These studies, therefore, support the conflict position, as against the functionalist position. Unfortunately, the studies referred to are historical studies of the origin of particular criminal laws (e.g., Chambliss's study of vagrancy laws), which are not representative of the criminal law[9] but are often inconsistent with the conflict thesis. Chambliss invokes Gusfield's study of the Prohibition movement to exemplify the conflict hypothesis that law is shaped by powerful minority interest groups rather than societal consensus. The Prohibition lobby was unquestionably successful in maneuvering Congress into passing the Eighteenth Amendment despite the opposition of most Americans to national Prohibition. Leaving aside the fact that Prohibition was counter to the interests of a multimillion-dollar beverage industry, this case seems to support the conflict hypothesis. Unfortunately, history ends for Chambliss in 1919. He conveniently ignores the repeal of Prohibition in 1933, a change in the law resulting from substantial consensus on the part of the public that Prohibition was unworkable, unnecessary, and undesirable. If conflict theory is confirmed by the passage of the Eighteenth Amendment, then consensus theory is confirmed by the passage of the Twenty-first Amendment. Such historical myopia raises serious questions about the whole conflict/consensus opposition. How are we to determine on the basis of empirical observation whether conflict or consensus is the underlying force of society? Do we add up the number of cases to see whether conflict or consensus positions have a preponderance of cases supporting them? How do we go about choosing an unbiased sample of such cases?

More relevant to the empirical question of consensus are studies of public perceptions of the seriousness of offenses (e.g., Rossi et al., 1974) demonstrating that, while consensus is not perfect, there is a remarkable amount of agreement among various segments of the population about what constitutes serious crime. The weight of the empirical evidence here is for the "consensus" position, but this empirical question does not even address the Marxist theoretical issue that is Chambliss's implicit concern. Given the fact of consensus, the theoretical problem becomes how to account for it. By making the "Marxist interpretation" rest upon the empirical degree of consensus, Chambliss overlooks the central problem of accounting for hegemony.

The second distinct issue underlying the conflict/functionalist polarity is the relative predominance of conflict as opposed to integration. Again a theoretic issue is confused with an empirical question. This confusion typically takes the following form: if student revolts, riots in urban ghettos, and crime in the streets occur, then a sociological theory of stability or integration is inadequate. Conversely, if these convulsions recede, as they have in the seventies, then a sociological theory of conflict bites the dust. We choose between theories, in other words, on the basis of current events.[10] As Percy Cohen pointed out, this is nonsense. A sociological theory of stability is simultaneously a theory of instability.

> The truth of the matter is that if functionalists have not produced adequate theories of social change this is largely because they have not produced adequate theories of social persistence. Insofar as they have gone some way to explaining why social systems persist, they have also, I submit, contributed to the theory of social change . . . if functionalism could really state the conditions under which social systems persist then it could also explain change simply by showing that some of those conditions are sometimes absent (Cohen, 1968: 57-58).

The third independent issue underlying the conflict/functionalist dichotomy is the appropriateness of functional explanation. Functional explanations seek to account for the persistence of a social structure in terms of its consequences for its social environment. A functional explananation of punishment, for example, asks what consequences punishment has on a society that lead to the recurrence of this particular form of punishment over time.

While functional explanations have generic difficulties,[11] conflict theorists frequently raise irrelevant criticisms. For example, a common misconception (e.g., Becker, 1963) is that a functional explanation entails an assumption that if X is functional it is good for the society. This misconception is commonly associated with a second stereotype, namely, that a functional explanation invariably postulates consensus in the society. These two misconceptions can be dispelled by a careful reading (see Matza [1969: 41-66]) of Merton's functional explanation of the urban political machine. Merton explains the persistence of the political machine despite recurrent reform efforts to clean up city hall. Merton shows how diverse, even *antagonistic* interests (business, labor, the poor) are each served in their own distinct way by symbiotic ties to the political machine. As Matza points out, there is no implication here that the urban political machine is an optimal solution to the conflicting needs of these constituents; indeed, a high price is often paid for the machine's inefficiencies.[12]

Furthermore, functional explanations abound in Marx's analyses that seek to show how the capitalist system has been able to survive its contradictions. In current Marxist analysis, this set of issues is referred to as the problem of *reproduction*.

Empirical Problems of Conflict Theory: Increasing Repression

In addition to the methodological and theoretic problems with conflict theory discussed above, there are empirical problems, situations in which the central arguments of the perspective fail to come to grips with the realities of criminal law. The most important of these, for purposes of our later discussion of Marx and Durkheim, is the postulate of increasing repression. This postulate states that, as capitalism matures and class conflict becomes more intense, the severity of coercion increases. Thus, Chambliss writes that "criminologists and legal scholars have noted an increasing reliance in capitalist societies on penal law to solve disputes of all kinds, including matters of personal morality" (1976: 16). In the first part of this paper I wish to raise some questions about the empirical validity of this diagnosis; in the next secion I will show that this thesis is contrary to Marx's own analysis of bourgeois law.

We ought first to examine the evidence used by Chambliss and other conflict theorists for asserting that the law under capitalism tends toward increasing coercion, that is to say, increasing criminalization of a wider range of activities and increasing use of imprisonment as a mode of controlling surplus population (cf. Quinney, 1977: 134-35). The only support Chambliss provides for his assertion that penal law is increasingly invoked is one citation to Edwin Schur's

(1965) *Crimes without Victims.* Has there, in fact, been a secular increase in American society in the enactment and enforcement of the criminal law? Probably not. The use of Schur's book as evidence of such a trend in 1976 is particularly unfortunate, since victimless crimes have undergone extensive decriminalization since Schur published his study. A comprehensive review of this trend would be out of place in this paper, but a brief review of the specifics may be useful. Arrests for most forms of victimless crime have sharply declined (table 10). Public drunkenness has been decriminalized in most jurisdictions following the *Robinson* v. *California* case in 1962, in which the Supreme Court argued that the state could no more justly imprison someone for an addiction than it could imprison someone for a common cold. Abortion was decriminalized nationally in *Doe* v. *Bolton* in 1973. Here the Supreme Court ruled that abortion in the first trimester was a decision legitimately made only by the woman and her physician; after the first trimester, the individual states were free to establish restrictions. Homosexuality has been decriminalized in several jurisdictions by state laws permitting sexual acts between consenting adults. Even in those cases in which the courts and legislatures have failed to take the initiative, law enforcement agencies have tended to become less rigorous in prosecuting victimless crimes. In the case of private use of marihuana, Oregon passed the first decriminalization statute in 1973, followed by 10 other states over the next five years. Outside these states, there has been a decrease in the prosecution of marihuana use, despite its high incidence. All of this does not suggest that a civil liberties paradise suddenly appeared after 1965; victimless crimes remain the focus of restrictive efforts, states are restricting public funding for abortions, local ordinances deny homosexuals civil rights, and so on. The minimal conclusion that one can draw from

Table 10. Arrest Trends in the United States, 1967-1976

	Percentage in 1967	Percentage in 1976
Victimless crimes	37.5	23.4
Gambling	1.4	0.9
Drunkenness	31.1	14.0
Vagrancy	2.1	0.5
Narcotic drug laws	1.3	6.6
Sexual vice	1.0	0.7
Prostitution	0.6	1.0
Other crimes	62.5	76.6
	100.0 (3,712,909)	100.0 (4,448,521)

Source: Adapted from Kelly (1976: 175).

the recent history of victimless crimes is that, if Chambliss wants to demonstrate secular trend toward increasing repression and coercion, a simple citation to one study written in the previous decade is not very compelling evidence.

Furthermore, if we move beyond a parochial concern with recent trends in American criminal law, the thesis of a relationship between capitalist development and legal coercion finds itself on even thinner ice. Capital punishment is the most extreme form of state coercion. Chambliss's conflict theory predicts that as capitalism matures executions will increase and that socialist societies will have relatively lower rates of capital punishment (Chambliss, 1976: 8-9). Neither of these predictions is consistent with the evidence. Capital punishment has largely been abandoned in Western industrialized societies, in practice if not in law. The thesis that advanced capitalism becomes more coercive cannot be reconciled with two basic facts about capital punishment in the United States: executions by 1967 virtually ceased, and executions in this century have taken place disproportionately in the South, the region least penetrated by advanced capitalist modes of production. Not only is the hypothesis linking capitalism and coercion wrong, the hypothesis about coercion and socialism is equally unrealistic. The Soviet Union, for example, was in the sixties executing 250 individuals annually for economic crimes alone (Berman, 1963: 86). Cuba imposes capital punishment not only for counterrevolutionary crimes but for rape, homicide, and child molesting (Cantor, 1973: 3-4).[13]

There is, then, little systematic evidence to support the conflict theory thesis of increasing coercion in the criminal law of capitalism. Conflict theorists have often been careless in their use of evidence, taking sensational instances of government repression such as the Chicago Seven trial as representative of an evolving trend on the part of advanced capitalist states toward more blatant repression (a stance Balbus [1973] labels the "fascist core" stereotype). Reliance on such single instances on which to base generalizations about the system has led conflict theorists to develop characterizations of capitalist legal systems that are not only contrary to fact but, as we will see below, contrary to Marxian analysis of the law.

Conflict theory thus distorts central theoretic and empirical problems concerning the relationship between law and social structure. In its attempt to oppose functionalism it confounds distinct issues into a simple polarity of functional versus conflict approaches. In so doing, it becomes blind to some of the most important issues for contemporary Marxist analysis of law, politics, and the state, such as how legal institutions serve to maintain hegemony and reproduce capitalist social relations. This is not to deny that conflict theorists have made major contributions. They have been primarily responsible for the renewed interest in the sociology of law and in the historical development of statutes, judicial decisions, and enforcement practices. These contributions, however, have been made despite, rather than because of, conflict theory. Heuristically, conflict theory has proven to be detrimental, "for nothing takes so long to resolve as a problem which does not exist or has been badly posed" (Althusser and Balibar, 1970: 184).

We have seen in Chambliss's essay an attempt, predominant in the current literature in the sociology of law, to develop explicit theories around the themes of conflict and functionalism. The remainder of this essay is devoted to spelling out the nature and implications of an alternative, structural analysis of law and society. This mode of analysis, to be found in Marx and Durkheim, has been overlooked by American conflict theorists in their haste to bury their functional antagonists.

TOWARD A REASSESSMENT OF MARX AND DURKHEIM

This discussion proceeds on three assumptions; first, that the character and behavior of the legal system are phenomena ascertainable through systematic empirical investigation; second, that the work of Marx and Durkheim are points of departure rather than finished solutions in understanding the relationship between law and social structure; third, that the law of diminishing returns operates for exegesis as for the production of any other commodity. The problem is not—or ought not to be—separating the orthodox from revisionist interpretations of classical scholars or developing a catechism for the faithful. It is rather to use the ideas of those scholars to develop theories that can be verified empirically.[14]

Whatever else one may find in the work of Marx and Durkheim, there are significant conceptions of the relationship between law and social structure, conceptions that can illuminate many of the problems that sociology of law now confronts.

Marx on Law and Social Structure

The first thing to be said about Marx's work on law is that it is isolated and fragmented. Chambliss claims, "Clearly Marx recognized [law as an important source of data and theoretical refinement] when he devoted much effort to analysis of law." Chambliss (1976: 27) cites references of some sixty pages to support this claim. These writings range from comments on current events to observations on law in historical analysis. The plain fact of the matter is that there is no sustained discussion of the law in Marx. Marx did appreciate the significance of legal institutions but never devoted time to a systematic analysis of law. In the Paris Manuscripts of 1848 Marx lays out the long-range goal of his studies:

> I shall, therefore, publish my critique of law, morals, politics, etc. in a number of independent brochures; and finally I shall endeavor, in a separate work, to present the interconnected whole, to show the relationships between the parts, and to provide a critique of the speculative treatment of this material (Tucker, 1978: 67).

Marx never got beyond the first section on economics. Only the first of four volumes of the initial section of his project was published in his lifetime. For this reason, any attempt to treat the scattered pages of Marx's observations on law as a finished product, a source of a Marxist litany, is misguided. As Marxist historian Eugene Genovese has pointed out:

> It is not their fault that later generations of epigoni have canonized them and insisted on the value of every word, have mistaken political commitment for historical analysis, and have done violence to Marxism by defending positions taken by Marx and Engels on matters to which they devoted very little study (1972: 321).

It is a testimony to Marx's work, however, that despite the fragmentary discussion of law, many ideas are to be found which can be useful for analyzing current problems in the sociology of law. Combined with his general approach toward social phenomena, these writings constitute a resource virtually untapped by contemporary sociologists.

This discussion will be limited to two themes in Marx's writings on law and social structure, themes that appear to have the greatest significance for an understanding of the social definition of deviance. The first theme is that there is a correspondence between modes of production and legal forms. This theme has particular importance for the understanding of ascriptive discrimination in the law, which has been of particular concern for conflict theory. The major conclusion of this discussion will be that Marx's writing on modes of production and legal forms leads to predictions antithetical to the hypotheses of the conflict theorists. Beyond the textual exegesis, a careful reading of Marx on this issue lays bare the basic deficiencies of current empirical research on bias in legal decision making. The second theme in Marx that has important implications for an understanding of deviance definition derives not from his explicit consideration of legal institutions but from his discussion of the social bases of political (i.e., class) consciousness. Marx's discussion of these bases will be examined, and the implications of his discussion for the phenomenon of political deviance will be suggested.

The relation between legal forms and modes of production was stated clearly in two of Marx's best-known passages:

> In the social production which men carry on, they enter into definite relations that are indispensible and independent of their will; these relations of production correspond to a definite stage of development of their material powers of production. The sum total of these relations of production constitutes the economic structure of society—the real foundation, on which rise legal and political superstructures and to which correspond definite forms of social consciousness. The mode of production in material life determines the general character of the social, political and spiritual processes of life. It is not the consciousness of men that determines their existence, but, on the contrary, their social existence determines their consciousness (Marx, 1970: 20-21).

> Each special mode of production and the social relations corresponding to it, in short, the economic structure of society, is the real basis on which the juridical and political superstructure is raised, and to which definite social forms of thought correspond; the mode of production determines the character of the social, political, and intellectual life generally; all this is very true for our own times, in which material interests preponderate, but not for the middle ages, in which Catholicism, nor for Athens and Rome, where politics, reigned supreme . . . . This much, however, is clear, that the middle ages could not live on Catholicism, nor the ancient world on politics. On the contrary, it is the mode in which they gained a livelihood that explains why here politics, and there Catholicism, played the chief part. For the rest, it requires but a slight acquaintance with the history of the Roman republic, for example, to be aware that its secret history is the history of its landed property. On the other hand, Don Quixote long ago paid the penalty for wrongly imagining that knight errantry was compatible with all economical forms of society (Marx, nd: 94n).

The theme that the legal form coincides with the dominant mode of production is, perhaps, most fully advanced in Marx's essay on the

Jewish question. This essay concretely explores the significance of the emancipation of the Jews in Western Europe, which begins in the eighteenth century as part of the Age of Reason. Marx points out that this emancipation is part of a general trend in the capitalist societies to create a division between civil and political realms, that political and legal equality is a structural necessity for an economy based on contractual relations and the exchange of commodities through market transactions. At the same time, formal equality has the consequence of preserving the existing inequality in the distribution of productive property and providing the conditions for the continued expansion of capital.[15]

In describing the essential characteristics of the modern bourgeois state, Marx noted that

> the state abolishes, after its fashion, the distinctions established by birth, social rank, education, occupation, when it decrees that [these factors] are nonpolitical distinctions; when it proclaims, without regard to these distinctions, that every member of society is an equal partner in popular sovereignty, and treats all the elements which compose the real life of the state from the standpoint of the state. But the state, nonetheless, allows private property, education, occupation, to act after their own fashion . . . and to manifest their particular nature. Far from abolishing these effective differences, the state only exists so far as they are presupposed (Tucker, 1978: 33).

This character of the liberal state is revealed by comparing its mode of operation with that of the state in feudal society. Feudal society

> had a directly political character; that is, the elements of civil life such as property, the family, and types of occupation had been raised, in the form of lordship, caste and guilds, to elements of political life. They determined, in this form, the elevation of the individual to the state as a whole; that is, the individual's political situation, or in other words, his separation and exclusion from the other elements of society. For this organization of national life did not constitute property and labor as social elements; it rather succeeded in separating them from the body of the state and made them distinct societies within society. Nevertheless, at least in the feudal sense, the vital functions and conditions of civil society remained political. They excluded the individual from the body of the state, and transformed the particular relation which existed between his corporation and the state into a general relationship between the individual and social life, just as they transformed his specific civil activity and situation into a general situation and activity. (Tucker, 1978: 44-45).

The legal forms of the society, then, are linked to the mode of production. The law under capitalism comes increasingly to celebrate human rights and due process. To the extent that the capitalist mode of production predominates, to the extent that the dominant form of productive activity is capital intensive, dependent upon market transactions and employing wage labor, the legal system will be more egalitarian, discriminating less among individuals on ascriptive criteria. Marx sees this development as an important step in the evolution of human emancipation but is careful to point out the ways in which this equality in the legal system serves to perpetuate existing inequalities in the civil society.

In addition to dealing with the relations between legal institutions and mode of production, Marx developed ideas about the conditions under which individuals would come to recognize their objective interests and organize collectively to engage in political activity that furthered those interests. While this discussion focuses exclusively on occupational statuses, the same conditions appear to be significant for understanding how certain categories of deviants come to share a collective redefinition of their position and organize politically to improve their position. Briefly, the conditions are as follows:

1. Opponents must be perceived as posing a direct conflict of interest with the members of the category. Thus, industrial workers express greatest hostility toward the management rather than the owners of the means of production, who directly benefit from the workers' subordinate position. By extension, deviants will be unable to define their actions as political to the extent that a direct conflict of interest cannot be shown between themselves as a group and their therapists, custodians, detectors, etc.

2. The status must be shared by a large number. Consciousness of kind is a basic ingredient of class consciousness. Pluralistic ignorance inhibits political definition. Thus, strikes and other labor protests increase with the concentration of workers into large productive units where they associate on a daily basis with individuals who share their objective circumstances. By extension, deviants (e.g., homosexuals) are more open to political organization if it becomes known that a large number of individuals share in the activity or life-style.

3. There must be opportunities for networks of communication to develop. Oppressed peasants are less likely to develop class consciousness than factory workers because they are physically isolated and lack means of effective communication. By extension, the political mobilization of deviance is likely to depend on ecological and technological factors that facilitate the growth of communication networks.

An analysis of the transformation of deviants into political actors could thus follow Marx's discussion of the transformation of a class-in-itself to a class-for-itself. An empirical Marxian examination of the transformation of deviants is likely to be more fruitful than the chimeras produced by conflict theorists. The following section briefly discusses how these two themes from Marx (the relation between mode of production and legal forms and the social bases of class consciousness) might be translated into researchable issues.

Some Research Implications of the Marxian Approach

Marx's discussion of the Jewish question contains a possible solution to some impasses that now exist in the literature concerning discrimination in the law. Proponents of labeling and conflict theories have contended that the racial and class disparities in arrest, conviction, and sentencing in the American legal system could be best explained by systematic biases in legal decision making. Thus, for example, Chambliss and Seidman (1971: 475) argue that "when sanctions are imposed, the most severe sanctions will be imposed on persons in the lowest social class. A considerable number of empirical studies have called into question the validity of the labeling/conflict perspective on discrimination. The weight of the evidence suggests that class and race differentials in crime rates are reflections more of differential involvement than of differential treatment by the legal system.[16] Although the current debate over how the variance in convictions, arrests, or police homicides is to be partitioned between legal bias and differential involvement may be an important issue, from the standpoint of Marx's discussion, as outlined above, this issue is secondary. Conflict theory's contention that capitalist law is intrinsically and increasingly coercive and racist bears little relationship either to Marx's ideas or to empirical reality (cf. Balbus, 1973: 1-4). The capitalist mode of production, Marx argues, banishes from the law consideration of birth, social rank, and other ascriptive characteristics of the defendent. Any given capitalist society does not fulfill the ideal type of bourgeois law. Thus, though the bourgeois authors of the United States Constitution did, for tactical reasons, provide legal protections for slavery, the central tendency in the capitalist law is to abolish discrimination. What distinguishes Marx from the standard American pluralist who makes similar observations is Marx's contention that we must go a step further and analyze how the norms of equality serve to perpetuate the existing inequalities of the society. Balbus (1973) has carried out such an analysis in his study of the reaction of liberal capitalist legal systems to urban riots in the sixties. These systems maintained adherence to due process procedures and equality before the law, Balbus argues, as a means of legitimizing coercion and preventing the riots from being defined as political rather than criminal.

> This strategy offers important advantages to the elite in its struggle to minimize revolutionary potential and maximize long-run legitimacy. To begin with, the successful adaptation of the ordinary criminal justice system to the threat of collective violence is likely to have a profound impact on the consciousness of the participants in the violence . . . the ideological coherence of participants in collective violence is not necessarily fixed, but rather is shaped by the nature of the elite response. Repression by formal rationality, insofar as it attempts to affix the label of "crime" on the behavior of the participants, is likely to help convince participants that their violent acts represent nothing more than massive outbreaks of common "criminality." To recall the insight of Lukacs, the legal system in the liberal state tends to "confront individual events as something permanently established and exactly defined"; the effort to apply the routine administration of justice to the problem of collective violence represents nothing less than an effort to fit the violent events under the rubric of previously established, general categories of proscribed behavior, i.e., to deprive the violence of its special, hence political, character by defining it as ordinary "crime." Repression by formal rationality thus serves to depoliticize collective violence and to mitigate against the growth of the consciousness and solidarity of the participants.
>
> The "criminalization" process entailed in repression by formal rationality also serves to delegitimate whatever demands emerge from the collective violence. Demands which arise from "criminals" are unlikely to receive a hearing and thus less likely to be voiced in the first place. Once the process of criminalization is under way, public debate is not likely to center over the substantive grievances of the participants but rather over the severity of punishment which they merit: criminals do not have just grievances; criminals deserve to be punished. Repression by formal rationality thus makes it unlikely that the claims and grievances of the participants in collective violence will be addressed to, or accepted by, significantly large numbers of the population at large (1973: 12).

In addition to legitimizing, legal equality can be seen as preserving the social conditions necessary for the continued operation of a market in which individual laborers are free to contract out their labor power according to the variable needs of producers.

Pursuing Marx's line of argument further suggests that *variations* in discrimination among jurisdictions may in large part reflect variations in the mode of production dominant in that jurisdiction (cf. Stinchcombe, 1976). This hypothesis is of particular importance because the conflict versus anticonflict empiricist debate over discrimination in the law seldom pays any attention to the time and locale of the studies cited as evidence for the respective positions. Quite often the locations are disguised, as in "Rainfall West" or "a typical middle-size city in the South." The failure to attend to the location of the observations is yet another indication of the atheoretic character of this research literature.

The fact that most executions in this century have been carried out in the South (see table 11) provides some *prima facie* evidence of the Marxist hypothesis that modes of punishment correspond to modes of production. Forms of extralegal punishment also appear to vary according to predominant mode of production; lynchings in the South, for example, were most common in small towns and decreased with increasing urbanization (Inverarity, 1976). These observations suggest that Marx's writings on law and social structure can help us to transcend the current conflict theory discussion of discrimination in the criminal law, a discussion that has been largely atheoretic and ahistorical. Examination of historical and regional *variations* in discrimination and the relationship of such variations to social structure is likely to be more fruitful than treating discrimination as a constant, timeless feature of capitalist legal systems.

Durkheim on Punishment, Solidarity, and the State

Around the turn of the century Durkheim began to elaborate a theory of law and social structure that has long been recognized as a classical piece of sociological analysis. Durkheim (1950 and 1964) argues that

Table 11. Executions in the United States by Decade

Decade	Legal Executions	Percentage in the South	Lynchings	Total Executions
1890s	1,214	. . . .	1,540	2,754
1900s	1,176	. . . .	885	2,061
1910s	1,031	. . . .	621	1,652
1920s	1,162	. . . .	315	1,477
1930s	1,667	56	130	1,787
1940s	1,284	65	5	1,289
1950s	717	59	2	719
1960s	191	53	. . . .	191

Source: Adapted from Bowers (1974: 25, 40).

crime is a product of punishment rather than an instigator of punishment. The social act of punishment has the primary consequence not of deterring potential troublemakers but rather of reaffirming commitment and solidarity among the virtuous. Furthermore, the dialectic of crime and punishment are normal, natural consequences of the division of labor in society.

Our point of departure for elaborating Durkheim's argument is his parable of the community of saints.[17]

> Imagine a society of saints, a perfect cloister of exemplary individuals. Crimes, [commonly] so called, will there be unknown; but faults which appear venial to the layman will create there the same scandal that the ordinary offense does in ordinary consciousnesses.[18]
>
> If, then, this society has the power to judge and punish, it will define these acts as criminal and will treat them as such (Durkheim, 1950: 68-69).

Underlying this parable are the following propositions:

1. "Crime brings together the upright consciences and concentrates them" (Durkheim, 1964: 19); that is, the *punishment* of crime increases solidarity in the community.

2. Every society (even a community of saints) requires some level of solidarity.

3. Therefore, the punishment of deviance will be found to some degree in all societies [from 1 and 2].

4. The behavior and character of the individual deviant are irrelevant. "Deviance is not a property *inherent* in any particular kind of behavior; it is a property *conferred upon* that behavior . . . (Erikson, 1966: 6). In the purest case, that of "primitive societies,"[19] people "punish for the sake of punishing . . . It is thus that they punish animals which have committed a wrong act, or even inanimate beings which have been its passive instrument" (Durkheim, 1964: 85-86).

5. The behavior that is defined as criminal may bear no objective relationship to the negative consequences of that behavior for society.

> The amount of harm that [a crime] does is [not] regularly related to the intensity of the repressions which it calls forth. In the penal law of the most civilized people, murder is universally regarded as the greatest of crimes. However, a stock-market crash, even a failure can disorganize the social body more severely than an isolated homicide . . . if we compare the significance of the danger, real as it is, and that of the punishment, the disproportion is striking (Durkheim, 1964: 72).

(This last proposition, interestingly enough, is one of the central new discoveries of conflict theory.)

It takes no great exercise of imagination to discover cases exemplifying Durkheim's thesis that the creation of deviance by organizations is intimately related to the organization's solidarity. For example, Vogel and Bell (1968) provide case studies of families in which emotionally disturbed children are essentially created and maintained by their parents as scapegoats for resolving strains in the marriage. Dentler and Erikson (1959) review case studies of this general phenomenon in small groups. Becker notes that among jazz musicians there is a tendency to

> derive a good deal of amusement from sitting and watching squares. Everyone has stories to tell about the laughable antics of squares . . . . Every item of dress, speech and behavior which differs from that of the musician is taken as new evidence of the inherent insensitivity and ignorance of the square [,thus fortifying] their conviction that musicians and squares are two kinds of people . . . . The jazz fan is respected no more than the other squares. His liking is without understanding and he acts just like the other squares; he will request songs and try to influence the musicians playing, just as other squares do (1963: 91).

Examples of this sort could be readily multiplied.

Systematic investigation of Durkheim's thesis begins with Kai Erikson's attempt to "see if [Durkheim's] insights can be translated into useful research hypotheses" in his monograph *Wayward Puritans* (1966). Erikson's research hypotheses specifically address not Durkheim's argument that solidarity increases following punishment[20] but rather his corollary thesis that

> when a society is going through circumstances which sadden, perplex or irritate it, it exercises a pressure over its members, to make them bear witness, by significant acts, to their sorrow, perplexity or anger. It imposes upon them the duty of weeping, groaning or inflicting wounds upon themselves or others, for these collective manifestations, and the moral communion which they show and strengthen, restore to the group the energy which circumstances threaten to take away from it, and thus they enable it to become settled. This is the experience which men interpret when they imagine that outside them there are evil beings whose hostility, whether constitutional or temporary, can be appeased only by human suffering. These beings are nothing other than collective states objectified; they are society itself seen under one of its aspects (Durkheim, 1947: 459).

Deviance becomes a major problem, Erikson argues, when the moral boundaries of the community become, for one reason or another, questioned.

The occasion which triggers this boundary crisis may take several forms—a realignment of power within the group, for example, or the appearance of new adversaries outside it—but in any case the crisis itself will be reflected in altered patterns of deviation and perceived by the [members] of the group as something akin to what we now call a crime wave (1966: 68-69).

He then proceeds to show how three boundary crises resulted in the three major crime waves of seventeenth-century Massachusetts,[21] emphasizing the phenomenon of displacement. Punishment of deviance is a method by which communities act out conflicts that they cannot deal with on a more "realistic" basis.[22] For example, in the trial of Anne Hutchinson,

> the two principals were trying to speak a language which had not yet been invented, to argue an issue which had not yet been defined. In many ways, the magistrate's decision to banish Mrs. Hutchinson was a substitute for words they could not find (Erikson, 1966: 93, 107).

This then, is the state of the argument bequeathed by Erikson. Strains or conflicts arise in a community from a variety of sources. Unable to deal with these conflicts realistically, the members of the community displace the conflict onto some form of deviance, which provides a tangible incarnation of the conflict. The community then moves to repress this form of deviance through the dramatic form of ritual repressive justice. Massachusetts in the seventeenth century provides persuasive evidence for such a process.

Although Erikson successfully translates Durkheim's argument into researchable problems, he fails to consider the problem of scope. In particular, Erikson offers no explicit criteria for his choice of Puritan Massachusetts as a research site. Consequently, we are left uncertain about the external validity of his conclusions. Do boundary crises produce crime waves only in seventeenth-century Massachusetts, in theocracies in general or in all social systems?[23] Erikson's analysis ends in 1692 with the last crime wave episode. After the seventeenth century, Massachusetts is rapidly transformed into a more differentiated society and is secularized, urbanized, and ethnically diversified (see, for example, Thernstrom [1964: 33-56]). Can crime waves in nineteenth-century Massachusetts be understood in the same terms Erikson applies to seventeenth-century Massachusetts?

This problem may be clarified by considering other cases in which variations in repressive justice seem to be unrelated to variations in solidarity. Three such cases will be reviewed: capital punishment, the Soviet purges, and the McCarthy episode. I will then return to Durkheim's original formulation of the problem and examine the solutions he provided eighty years ago.

Capital punishment in modern society differs fundamentally from capital punishment in the kind of society that Durkheim envisioned. Trial and execution involve only a small segment of the population, and the general public is only remotely involved through mass media. The failure of modern capital punishment to have any public impact is the basis for Camus's polemic against judicial murder. If capital punishment is to affect the general public, Camus argues:

> Executions [should] be given the same promotional campaign ordinarily reserved for government loans or a new brand of apertif. Yet it is well known on the contrary that in France executions no longer take place in public-they are perpetrated in prison yards *before an audience limited to specialists* (Camus, 1957). [Emphasis added.]

Camus's statement captures the essential distinction between modern capital punishment and repressive justice. Where punishment is limited to an audience of specialists and excludes the general public it will not have the same impact as diffuse punishment in a homogeneous society.[24]

A similar case can be made for the Soviet purge trials of the 1930s in which there was

> a radical asymmetry of power, and, by implication, an extremely narrow monopoly on decisions about what constitutes deviance, its proofs, and how society will proceed against it. Characteristic of the Soviet Union was a radical monopoly of such powers—their concentration in the hands of Stalin and a handful close to him. His own personality, rather than the collective interests and apprehensions of the Soviet upper elite (many of whom were purge victims), shaped the purge to a large degree. In such situations, over the short run at least community sentiment counts little, and leadership decisions more (Connor, 1972: 410).

The McCarthy "witch hunt" of the early 1950s involved a variety of state and federal bodies investigating Communist influence on various sectors of American life. This episode is commonly interpreted as an instance of mass displaced aggression or as an attempt at national reintegration following the political, social, and economic crises of the early Cold War years. In examining the impact of the McCarthy hearings and related government activities on public opinion, however, Stouffer found that

> the number of people who said they were worried either about the threat of

Communism in the United States or about civil liberties, even by the most generous interpretation of occasionally ambiguous responses is less than one per cent (1955: 59).

As Hyman (1964) points out in examining the McCarthy episode, it is essential to distinguish between the reaction of the *general* public and the reaction of *specialized* population groups. Treating a society with differentiated subgroups as if it were mechanically a solidarity leads to a form of synecdochic fallacy: attributing erroneously to the whole properties common only to a segment (Wenkert, 1961).

Other cases could be cited, but the above three should be sufficient to demonstrate the necessity of qualifying Durkheim's theory, of distinguishing in general terms those kinds of social systems to which it is applicable from those to which it is not. Durkheim's work began the task of providing the necessary qualifications. First, he distinguishes between two forms of social solidarity, mechanical and organic, a distinction Erikson ignores. Mechanical solidarity is based on similarity of individual characteristics and is characterized by consensus on values, harmony (if not identity) of interest, and unity of purpose. Differences exist among members in their attributes, but such differences are regarded as secondary or peripheral, not as bases for organization and action. In contrast, organic solidarity is based on diversity of individual interest and is characterized by interdependence and exchange. While mechanical solidarity is associated with *repressive justice*, which reaffirms a common value through diffuse forms of ritual punishment, organic solidarity is associated with *restitutive justice*, which is characterized by restorative sanctions (i.e., sanctions such as damages and fines, which seek to restore the disrupted relationship) and organized administration. Durkheim suggests that in mechanical solidarities deviance automatically arouses sentiments in the group as a whole.

> The functioning of repressive justice tends to remain more or less diffuse. In very different social systems it does not function through the means of special magistracy, but the whole society participates in rather large measure. In primitive societies where . . . law is wholly penal, it is the assembly of the people which renders justice . . . . It is true that, in other cases, the power is wielded by a privileged class or by particular magistrates . . . . Organized repression is not opposed to diffuse repression, but is distinguished from it only by a difference of degree; the reaction has more unity . . . the nature of punishment has not been changed in its essentials. All that we can say is that the need of vengeance is better directed than heretofore . . . . More clarified, it depends less on chance. One no longer sees it turn against the innocent to satisfy itself (1950: 76-77, 90).

Even when carried out by a small specialized staff, adjudication in mechanical solidarities remains diffuse.

There are, however, circumstances in which organized repression is unrelated to mechanical solidarity.

> Some actions . . . are more strongly repressed than they are strongly reproved by general opinion. There is nothing in us which protests against fishing and hunting out of season, or against overloaded conveyances on the public highway . . . . [The state] can become an autonomous factor in social life . . . treating as criminal, actions which shock it without, however, shocking the collective sentiments in the same degree (1950: 82-83).

This fundamental qualification of his theory in effect means that the conviction rate for a given offense may be independent of collective sentiments, that is, that boundary crises will not produce crime waves. If Durkheim's proposition is not to be applied in an ad hoc manner, the general conditions under which it holds must be specified in advance.

Durkheim offers two leads. In "Two Laws of Penal Evolution" (1973b) he argues that the form of justice depends not only on the type of solidarity but on the degree of centralized political authority. In particular, repressive justice is associated not only with mechanical solidarity but with power centralization. Repressive justice may vary with the centralization of political power quite independently of mechanical solidarity. This qualification would cover the Soviet purge trials, for example. The second major lead can be found in his distinction between mechanical and organic solidarity and especially the differences between the state in mechanical solidarity versus organic solidarity. In organic solidarities,

> [the state] no longer has the same character as in [mechanical solidarities], for, if the others depend upon it, it in its turn, depends upon them. No doubt, it still enjoys a special situation and, if one chooses so to speak of it, a privileged position, but that is due to the nature of the role that it fills and not to some cause foreign to its functions, nor to some force communicated to it from without. Thus, there is no longer anything about it that is not temporal and human (1950: 181-82).

This suggests the following general condition of the relationship between repressive justice and mechanical solidarity. In predominately organically solidary societies, the state operates independently of collective conscience and there is no relationship between variation in the conviction rates and variation in mechanical solidarity.

This general condition does not imply that mechanical solidarity is completely absent in differentiated social systems.[25] Rather, mechanical solidarity may be less significant in integrating the total society for heterogeneous differentiated systems than it is for homogeneous segmental systems. For example, criminal trials, psychiatric case conferences, and similar proceedings may have far less impact on the solidarity of contemporary American society than their counterparts had on Puritan Massachusetts. The relevant publics in contemporary society are specialized. Following this line of argument, the crime statistics of differentiated society are irrelevant to Durkheim's theory.

Durkheim's position on the precise role of mechanical solidarity in complex social systems is characterized by "ambiguity and ambivalence" (Bellah, 1973: xxv). Two alternative positions can be found in Durkheim's work. The first, which Ralph Turner (1967) labels the "replacement thesis," is that as social systems become differentiated mechanical solidarity is displaced by organic solidarity. The second position, which Talcott Parsons (1960) identified as a "differentiation thesis," states that as social systems become more differentiated the character of mechanical solidarity changes but it does not disappear.[26] In the latter interpretation, which will be pursued here, the "cult of the individual" becomes a predominant value throughout the society, replacing the community as the basic moral unit of the society.[27]

Accompanying this new form of mechanical solidarity is a secularization of criminal law. The relationship between the cult of the individual and secularization of law is not spelled out in Durkheim's work but is readily apparent. The cult of the individual is clearly reflected in the attention paid to due process and proportionate sanction. In an undifferentiated society, repressive justice could be satisfied with victims innocent of any offense. When the focus of moral values changes from the collectivity to the individual, however, severe constraints are placed on the exercise of repressive justice. These constraints can be summarized as follows:

1. The movement from segmental to differentiated structures (i.e., increased differentiation) will be accompanied by a decrease in the amount of repressive justice.

2. As organic solidarity increases relative to mechanical solidarity, the criminal law will be transformed from a punitive orientation to a restitutive orientation (cf. Rusche and Kirchheimer, 1968: 166-76). This will be manifested by increasing emphasis on efficiency in processing cases in a rational fashion (e.g., growth of plea bargaining) and increasing emphasis on restoring relationships rather than ostracizing individuals, which in turn will be manifested by increased tendency to redefine criminal acts as torts (e.g., victim compensation laws), in-

creased use of rehabilitation rhetoric combined with increased use of probation, and increased tendency to seek psychiatric and other medical definitions of criminal acts.

Some Research Implications of Durkheim's Analysis

This section will briefly outline some implications of Durkheim's analysis for the sociology of law, in particular some central trends in American criminal law. The discussion will be, at best, suggestive. Empirical study of law and social structure at the macro level lacks at this point the refinement of method and the cultivation of systematic evidence that exists in the micro level, social-psychological studies of crime.[28]

Some indicators are available. Consider, for example, the number of inmates in federal and state penal institutions. Table 12 shows that from 1939 to 1970 there was in the United States a marked secular decline in number of inmates from 137 per 100,000 to 97 per 100,000. Table 13 suggests that a similar change took place in Germany. Net of changes in the age composition and changes in the occurrence of felonies, does this apparent decline in the prison population represent a change in the way the legal system deals with criminal cases, a trend from penal sanction to restitutive sanction?

In one of the most careful discussions of the central tendencies in American criminal law, Nicholas Kittrie summarizes the major changes as "a divestment of the criminal law" (1971). Surveying the transformations of the populations subject to criminal and noncriminal sanctions as well as trends in case law both at the federal and the state level, Kittrie concludes that

> in recent years . . . America has seen a departure from criminal sanctions and a concomitant utilization of a different system or model of social controls, described as "civil," "therapeutic," or *"parens patriae"* . . . (1971: 3).

The decline of penal sanctions that Kittrie describes is roughly congruent with Durkheim's theory on the relationship between the form of law and the nature of social structure. Contemporary American society is increasingly differentiated, and such differentiation may have profound consequences for the nature and level of mechanical solidarity. As Lieberson has noted:

> Populations within advanced industrial societies are atomized into a highly diverse set of groups, with interests that are neither fully harmonious with one another nor fully competitive (1971: 577).

Table 12. Adult Prisoners in Institutions per 100,000 Civilian Population
in the United States by Year, 1939-1979

Year	All Institutions	Federal Institutions	State Institutions
1939	137.1	15.0	122.0
1940	132.0	14.6	117.3
1941	126.0	14.1	112.0
1942	116.4	12.9	103.5
1943	108.0	12.7	95.3
1944	104.2	14.3	89.9
1945	100.5	14.0	86.5
1946	99.7	12.5	87.2
1947	105.2	11.9	93.3
1948	106.6	11.2	87.2
1949	110.0	11.3	98.6
1950	110.3	11.4	98.9
1951	108.9	11.4	97.4
1952	108.8	11.6	97.1
1953	110.2	12.3	97.9
1954	113.8	12.4	101.3
1955	113.4	12.3	101.1
1956	113.5	12.1	101.4
1957	114.9	12.0	102.9
1958	118.8	12.5	106.3
1959	120.8	13.0	107.8
1960	118.6	12.9	105.7
1961	120.8	13.0	107.8
1962	118.3	12.9	105.3
1963	115.7	12.3	103.4
1964	112.6	11.4	101.2
1965	109.5	10.9	98.6
1966	102.7	9.9	92.8
1967	99.1	10.0	89.2
1968	94.3	9.9	84.3
1969	97.6	9.7	87.8
1070	96.7	9.8	86.8

Source: U.S. Federal Bureau of Prisons "Prisoners in state and federal institutions for
adult felons, 1968-1970." National Prisoner Statistics. No. 47 (April 1972).
Tables 1 and 2.

Mary Douglas captures this notion quite well in contrasting the significance of ritual in complex differentiated societies with ritual in relatively undifferentiated tribal societies:

> We moderns operate in many different fields of symbolic action. For the
> Bushman, Dinka and many primitive cultures, the field of symbolic action is
> one. The unity which they create by their separating and tidying is not just
> a little home, but a total universe in which all experience is ordered. Both
> we and the Bushmen justify our pollution avoidances by fear of danger. They

Table 13. Type of Criminal Sanction Imposed by German Courts
on Adult Offenders by Year, 1882-1972

Year	Percentage Imprisoned Immediately	Percentage On Probation	Percentage Fined	Percentage Given Death Penalty	Absolute Figures
1882	74.40	. . . .	25.57	0.03	. . . .
1890	65.49	. . . .	32.69	0.02	. . . .
1900	56.50	. . . .	41.09	0.01	445,009
1913	45.07	. . . .	52.43	0.01	. . . .
1921	58.25	. . . .	39.33	0.02	. . . .
1925	35.98	. . . .	64.00	0.01	. . . .
1930	44.19	. . . .	55.77	0.01	. . . .
1935	40.32	. . . .	59.66	0.02	426,343
1939	44.34	. . . .	55.61	0.05	. . . .
1950	37.29	. . . .	62.71	. . . .	298,874
1955	19.08	10.31	70.60	. . . .	. . . .
1960	19.13	11.69	69.18	. . . .	496,326
1965	23.07	11.52	65.41	. . . .	. . . .
1970	7.57	8.48	83.95	. . . .	565,379
1972	7.01	9.31	85.55	. . . .	591,719

Source: Kaiser (1976: 198).

believe that if a man sits on the female side his male virility will be weakened.
We fear pathogenicity transmited through microorganisms. Often our justification of our own avoidances through hygiene is sheer fantasy. The difference between us is not that our behavior is grounded on science and theirs
on symbolism. Our behavior also carries symbolic meaning. The real difference is that we do not bring forward from one context to the next the same
set of ever more powerful symbols: our experience is fragmented. Our rituals
create a lot of little subworlds, unrelated. Their rituals create one single,
symbolically consistent universe (1966: 85).

Following the argument developed above, we might expect corresponding consequences for the criminal law. For example, differentiation results in esoteric forms of harmful activity that cannot evoke
strong reactions of collective sentiments.

[White-collar crimes] are not obvious, as is assault and battery, and can be
appreciated readily only by persons who are expert in the occupations in
which they occur (Sutherland, 1945: 138).

Rossi et al. (1974) discovered that white-collar crimes are generally
regarded as relatively low in seriousness regardless of the respondent's
race or occupation.[29] Edwin Sutherland observed that

white-collar crime is similar to juvenile delinquency in respect to the differential implementation of the law. In both cases, the procedures of the crim-

inal law are modified so that the stigmas of crime will not attach to the offenders. . . .

In part the emergence of quasi-criminal categories reflects a general trend away from reliance on penal methods. This trend advanced more rapidly in the area of white-collar crime than of other crime because—due to the recency of the statutes—it is least bound by precedents. . . . This trend is seen in the almost complete abandonment of the most extreme penalties of death and physical torture; in the supplanting of conventional penal methods by nonpenal methods, such as probation and the case work methods which accompany probation (Sutherland, 1945: 138-39).

Thirty years later we might add trends toward decriminalization of such "victimless crimes" as abortion (Humphries, 1977) and drug consumption (Bayer, 1978), trends toward ensuring due process procedures (*Miranda, Mapp* v. *Ohio*), a growing concern with victim compensation (i.e., viewing crime as problematic for the individual complainant rather than simply as a collective offense). All of this suggests a secularization of criminal law, a replacement of repressive sanction with restitutive sanction. The precise nature of these trends and their relationship to changes in the social structure require further, more systematic investigation.

CONCLUSION

When she was booked at the San Mateo County jail, Patricia Hearst defiantly listed her occupation as "urban guerilla." In the course of the legal proceedings against her involving bank robbery, assault, and kidnapping, Patty Hearst came to accept an alternative psychiatric definition of her behavior as illness induced by traumatic episodes of solitary confinement and extreme anxiety. Ultimately, her behavior was defined as criminal in nature and intent. The moral career of Patricia Hearst played out over a series of months on the front pages is in itself a study in social definition. What makes this particular episode unusual is the ease and rapidity with which a single actor moved from political to medical to criminal definition of the same behavior. The movement we witness in the case of a millionaire's wayward daughter repeatedly occurs on a less dramatic but much larger scale. In the United States, for example, there has been over the past several decades a movement toward psychiatric definitions of problematic behavior, the growth of what many observers see as a therapeutic state (Szasz, 1963; Kittrie, 1971). While these trends have been discussed in terms of their implications for civil liberties, little attention has been paid to their implications for theories of law and social structure. In large part this has been due to the preoccupation of sociology of law with tangential issues. In this paper I have attempted to direct attention to the question of social definition: under what conditions will an act be seen as a political act, a symptom of illness, or a crime? What has been the central tendency of such definitions in advanced capitalist society? How can we account for these tendencies? We are a long way from being able to offer adequate answers to these questions at the present time. This paper has had the modest objective of suggesting some lines of analysis in the work of Marx and Durkheim that may be fruitful to pursue.

I began by examining the dominant contender for a theory of criminal law in sociology, American conflict theory as represented in an essay by Chambliss. This approach, it was argued, is fatally flawed by its reliance on anecdotal evidence, its oversimplified dichotomy of theoretic issues into conflict and functionalist camps, and its consequent failure to analyze empirically systematic variation in criminal law and social structure.

A more adequate foundation, it was argued, could be laid by returning to the works of Marx and Durkheim. Both theorists struggled with the still unfinished task of defining the essential features of the criminal law under capitalism and comprehending the relationship between these features of the law and the characteristics of the social structure (complex division of labor, allocation of productive resources through various types of markets, centralization of political power). Both Marx and Durkheim place heavy emphasis on the role of the individual in the capitalist order and see this as a sharp break from previous types of social order. Marx phrases his basic contrast in terms of a dichotomy between feudal and bourgeois relations of production, while Durkheim's dichotomy is between mechanical and organic solidarity. There are fundamental differences in orientation inherent in these two formulations. Thus, for example, Marx saw economic transformation as the source of future social change, whereas Durkheim believed that any economic change would in itself be of no significance without corresponding, independent transformation of the moral order. Despite these differences, their analyses converge on important points.

The intent of this comparison has not been to suggest that the formulations of Marx and Durkheim are fully adequate to our present concerns. Rather, they above all exemplify a structural approach to the criminal law, an approach that seeks to understand the nature of the insititutional arrangements of a society and the constraints that these institutions create on the criminal law.

NOTES

1. For a review and critique of this school on ideological grounds, see Taylor, Walton, and Young (1973: 237-67).

2. This discussion is motivated in large part by a previous empirical study of lynching in the American South (Inverarity, 1976). An examination of lynching and its political context made the inadequacies of the standard conflict/functionalist polarity apparent and led to a search for an alternative theoretic perspective.

3. As Balbus succinctly points out, for Marx the concept of "class"

is not primarily a category for describing how a particular capitalist society look[s] at any given point in time, but above all an analytic tool for elucidating the sources of structural change within the capitalist system, a theory of the direction in which capitalist societies are [developing] . This is why the Marxist model of capitalist society is normally a two-class model: the two classes represent the two sides of a fundamental contradiction which is assumed to be the source of conflicts sufficiently important to produce significant structural change (1971b: 38).

4. According to Allen:

There is a large tautological element in [the conflict theorists'] propositions. The criminal law is formulated and applied by public agencies; in the long run and for the most part, therefore, it may be expected to reflect, or at least not seriously to offend, the views and interests of those capable of influencing public policy. Indeed, on occasion the criminal law may be used directly as a device to attain the political objectives of those possessed of political power. These observations, however, do not carry one far toward understanding the basic power relations of any particular society (1974: 17).

The pervasiveness of tautology in conflict theory explanations has been noted by numerous critics, such as Gibbs (1975: 37) and Offe (1972: 77).

5. This comparison is incompatible with Chambliss's own characterization of conflict paradigm. "The most fundamental error of functional analysis is that it is ahistorical" in the sense that functionalists "see society as a reality which is unconnected with a particular historical period and look for those social needs which all societies have." This methodological principle does not prevent Chambliss from moving freely back and forth between a capital-intensive industrialized society and a commodity export society to demonstrate the universal character of political corruption.

6. Since the ruling class and their interests are never identified, the alternative explanations for the police behavior that Chambliss observed are far more compelling than his "conflict" explanation. As Rubinstein points out:

For the policeman, the determining factor of any crime's importance is its setting. He defines the location of all crimes by the deceptively simple distinction between "inside" and "outside." These terms have nothing to do with his notion of privacy or with the legal definitions of private and public places, but derive from his conception of his work.

A crime committed outside may actually take place inside a building, while a crime committed inside may take place on a public street. Outside means any location a patrolman can be reasonably expected to see while on patrol. If a burglar breaks into a building through a rear door or cuts a hole in a roof, his act is considered an inside crime, because the patrolman had no chance to notice anything amiss, even if he was patrolling alertly. If a person is assaulted in his backyard or mugged in an alley, it is an inside crime, despite its occurrence in a place legally defined as public (1973: 339-40).

Chambliss also fails to consider the possibility that vice and corruption are variables, rather than constant features, of (capitalist?) cities like Ibadin and Seattle. Not only is there such variation in American cities, but these variations probably have very little to do with varia-variations in interests of the ruling class. Wilson (1968) suggests that the variations are related to the type of police department and contrasts "Eastern City" with a fraternal departmental organization, with "Western City," with a professional-bureaucratic departmental organization. He points out that

> for several years at least, Western City has had a department free from the suspicion of political influence and a court system noted for its "no-fix" policy. In Eastern City, reports of influence and fixes are not infrequent (of course a scholar without the power of subpoena cannot confirm such charges) (Wilson, 1968: 13).

7. The criticism here is methodological; by failing to specify the composition of the ruling class and its interests independently of the legal outcome, Chambliss's explanation of law enforcement in Seattle becomes circular. This does not rule out the possibility of demonstrating that the arrest practices of the Seattle police are determined by some powerful interest group or groups. The difficulty is not with this argument per se but with Chambliss's misuse of evidence to substantiate the argument. However, recent Marxist writings on the state lead to an even more fundamental objection to Chambliss's line of analysis. Chambliss, along with most of the American conflict writers, adopts what Gold et al. (1975) categorize as an "instrumental Marxist" approach to the law. Law enforcement and law enactment are viewed as determined by competing, identifiable interest groups. The alternative "structural Marxist" position, advanced by Poulantzas (1973) and others, views the identification of specific interest groups as impossible in many instances. For the structuralists, Marx's observation in *The Communist Manifesto* that "the executive of the modern state is but a committee for managing the common affairs of the whole bourgeoisie" (Tucker, 1972: 337) does *not* mean that law is to be explained in terms of the interests of some specific "interest group" or "power elite." Rather, for the structuralists, "the common affairs of the whole" requires the sacrifice of particular bourgeois interests for maintaining the system. This in turn requires a degree of autonomy on the part of the legal institutions to maintain legitimacy and to adjudicate between competing interests of the bourgeoisie themselves. If the structuralists like Poulantzas are right, the instrumentalist strategy pursued by Chambliss and the conflict theorists is doomed to failure, for it will be impossible, given an autonomous legal system, to determine legal decisions from the interests of individual parties. Whoever wins the struggle will be defined after the fact as "the powerful"; a list of "the powerful" so defined will provide an inconclusive and contradictory picture of the structure of domination in capitalist society. A thorough examination of the difficulties created by the instrumental Marxist strategy of conflict theory would be beyond the scope of this paper, but an examination of the membership of Chambliss's "ruling class" (e.g., downwardly mobile middle classes, bureaucrats, owners of the means of production) suggests that this approach to criminal law is unlikely to be fruitful.

8. By "interests," Hopkins means the objective interests, not interests as subjectively conceived. Thus, the issue here cannot be facilely resolved by invoking Engel's notion of *false*

consciousness. For example, it may be in the interests of wage laborers and the bourgeoisie to have laws against homicide or to have laws regulating employment of wage labor. Marx (nd: 304ff) discusses a specific case of the latter. In the nineteenth century, the landed aristocracy in England was locked in conflict with the industrial bourgeoisie. Parliamentary regulation of industry was for a period of time the common interest of both the aristocratic elite and the urban proletariat. To put the point briefly, politics continues to make strange bedfellows in a Marxist analysis.

9. As Wellford (1975: 334) points out, "Murder, forcible rape, aggravated assault, robbery, burglary, larceny, and auto theft, the focus of 'true criminal law' do not fit the conflict paradigm. At best the conflict theorists may be constructing an explanation of some victimless crimes." Carson (1974: 71) has similarly observed that "the recent tendency to concentrate upon relatively marginal and frequently controversial areas of criminality has possibly fostered neglect of the consensus which may still prevail in more central regions of the criminal law."

10. According to Becker and Horowitz (1972: 61), "An adequate analysis of how things stay the same is thus at the same time an analysis of how to change them."

11. The actual methodological problems with functional forms of explanation have been spelled out by Hempel (1965). As Hempel points out, lack of awareness of these methodological problems often leads to an explanation that is either tautological or empirically vacuous.

12. Gouldner has made an analogous observation about Merton's paper on social structure and anomie. He criticizes Taylor, Walton, and Young for pigeonholing Merton's analysis, pointing out that

> Merton developed his generalized analysis of the various forms of deviant behavior by locating them within a systematic formalization of Durkheim's theory of anomie, from which he gained analytic distance by tacitly grounding himself in a Marxian ontology of social *contradiction.* It is perhaps this Hegelian dimension of Marxism that has had the most enduring effect on Merton's analytic rules, and which disposed him to view *anomie* as the unanticipated outcome of social institutions that thwarted men in their effort to acquire the very goods and values that these same institutions had encouraged them to pursue. In its openness to the internal contractions of capitalist *culture* few Lukacians have been more incisive (Taylor et al., 1973: x-xi).

13. It could be argued that the Soviet Union and Cuba are not representative of socialist societies because of their peculiar historical position—being surrounded by hostile forces, having had a long tradition of autocratic rule, etc. One can easily turn this argument around to contend that the United States is equally unrepresentative of monopoly capitalism because of the frontier tradition of violence, ethnic diversity, etc. Serious questions can be raised about the appropriateness of drawing generalizations about types of society (socialist, monopoly capitalism) from an examination of the characteristics or trends of a particular historical society, but such questions are based on empirical rather than polemical grounds. For example, Giddens (1973: 20) points out that much of the discussion about changes in the composition of the labor force in advanced capitalist societies is based solely on United States trends and that these changes are not comparable to changes occurring in Western Europe.

14. Thus, the exchange between Hirst (1972) and Taylor et al. (1975) is, from this standpoint, fatuous. Hirst argues that there can be no genuine Marxist theory of crime because Marx's major concern was with class conflict:

> Any attempt to apply Marxism to this pre-given field of sociology is therefore a more or less "revisionist" activity . . . the notion that Marx's writings are open to any "interpretation" we care to impose upon them is patently false and can be demonstrated by detailed reference to an analysis of the texts themselves (1972: 204-5).

Hirst fails to acknowledge the historical progression this scholastic approach to the sacred writings has produced in Marxism. A half century of sectarian debate over the mature Marx of *Capital* as opposed to the young Marx of the 1844 manuscripts has brought us no closer to a solution. Hirst's claim to have resolved all such issues through his careful textual analysis ought to be taken with a firm grip on the saltshaker. Taylor and Walton reply to the charge of revisionism with a pathetic plea for "socialist diversity." Ideological sectarianism and quietistic tolerance may be noble activities, but they are not sociology. A sociology of law must be concerned with evaluating theoretic ideas by their logic, their coherence, their empirical implications—not by their pedigrees or their ideological resonances. The position taken in this essay, thus, is positivist, but only in the sense that it assumes that empirical investigation is capable of resolving theoretic conflicts. This view is not universally accepted. Platt (1973) for example argues that theories are to be judged by their implications for praxis rather than subjected to systematic investigation. For example, the power elite thesis is wrong not because it is inconsistent with observable facts or because it leads to false predictions about policy decisions of the federal government but because it takes the wind out of the sails of revolutionary activity by encouraging a sense of cynicism and defeatism over the possibility of effective readical challenge. It is beyond the scope of this paper to do more than acknowledge the difference between the positivist orientation of this paper and the critical orientation toward the sociology of law developed by Platt, Quinney, and others.

15. There are formal parallels between Marx's analysis of bourgeois law and his analysis of bourgeois forms of exploitation. Under feudalism the law directly and specifically favored certain classes (e.g., the benefit of clergy exempted nobility from the penalties of the criminal courts in England). Similarly, exploitation was a matter of direct coercion in the form of feudal dues, tithes, etc. Under capitalism, however, exploitation is disguised in the free market transaction between wage labor and capital and can only be detected through subtle economic analysis of the sort Marx attempted in the first volume of *Capital*. Similarly, the legal system under capitalism operates on the basis of an analogue of the free market transaction of the capitalist economy but has hidden consequences that preserve the existing unequal distributions of wealth and power. For a recent attempt to draw parallels between Marx's analysis of economic transactions and his analysis of law, see Balbus (1977). For a recent elaboration of themes in the essay on the Jewish question, see Marcuse (1965).

16. This literature has grown rapidly in the past couple of years and a review would require a separate paper in itself. In general, these studies, with some exceptions, point to a lack of discrimination at all levels from arrest to conviction. The evidence of discrimination cited by labeling and conflict theorists has been shown to be an artifact of inadequate study designs that fail to control for legally relevant variables such as seriousness of offense and prior offenses. For a review of these findings see, for example, Hindelang (1978), and Hagan (1974).

17. Chambliss (1976) ignores the parable of the community of saints and its implications. His criticism of Durkheim seems to be directed more towards Durkheim's concept of anomie as a cause of deviance, particularly as reformulated by Merton. According to Chambliss, Durkheim viewed crime "as an aberration shared by some minority which had failed to be properly socialized or adequately integrated into society or, more generally, which suffered from 'social disorganization' " (1976: 26). The social disorganization account of deviance can be found in *Division of Labor* (1964: 353-54), but Durkheim (1950: 72n) subsequently repudiated this statement. Chambliss's *bête noire* is found not in Durkheim but in Devlin (1965).

As with his treatment of Marx, Chambliss's discussion of Durkheim confuses empirical description with theoretic analysis. Chambliss draws entirely on book two of *The Division of Labor in Society* (Durkheim, 1964), which is not a description of industrial society but a presentation of an ideal type of solidarity. In fact, Durkheim takes as his central problem the absence of harmony, the predominance of conflict in industrial society. Contrary to the conservation image that Chambliss conjures up, Durkheim advocates the abolition of inherited wealth as a means of reducing class conflict in industrial society (Durkheim, 1957: 217). Marx and Durkheim differ on several fundamental issues, issues that are obscured by Chambliss's conflict/functionalist dichotomy.

18. This is not entirely a hypothetical situation. For example, Goffman (1961) has discussed the process of the moralization of minutiae, attaching massive significance to small acts and traits frequently found in total institutions.

19. Evans (1906) enumerates several hundred cases of criminal prosecution of animals in Western Europe. The diffuseness of punishment is thus not confined to "primitives." Moreover, such cases can be viewed as revealing a central characteristic of ritual punishment that is often masked in more complex societies.

20. Such analysis is not beyond the realm of possibility, however. See, for example, the imaginative study of the growth of American national consciousness in the eighteenth century by Merritt (1966).

21. Thus, in the late 1630s the increasing power of the clergy became incompatible with the Puritan doctrine of the priesthood of all believers. During the resulting boundary crisis, the colony prosecuted a group of Antinomian heretics led by Anne Hutchinson, who took the extreme position that the laity could challenge the authority of the clergy. Some twenty years later a second boundary crisis occurred as the New Englanders found themselves increasingly in conflict with the progressive tendencies of their Old World brethren, particularly on the issue of religious tolerance. During this second crisis, the colony prosecuted Quakers, people who refused to defer to authority, who disrupted church services, who paraded naked through the streets, and who otherwise challenged the Puritan establishment. Finally, toward the end of the century, the colony suffered a period of domestic turmoil: political disputes, Indian war, administrative upheaval. Massachusetts now became plagued with invisible demons, who in 1692 materialized in the witchcraft prosecutions in Salem Village. Through the seventeenth century, then, the outstanding occurrences of deviance were directly connected to boundary crises.

22. This orientation is only vaguely implicit in Durkheim's discussion of crime. It becomes most developed in his later examination of the ways in which religious belief distill the inexpressible experiences of moral constraint and invigoration produced by participation in social organization. Erikson's displacement notion itself is not explicitly examined in his work. Such an examination can, however, be found in Smelser (1963) since there is a close correspondence between Erikson's concept of boundary crisis and Smelser's concept of structural strain as "impairments of relations among and consequently inadequate functioning of components of action" (1963: 47). Smelser expresses the notion of displacement in the following terms:

The general principle for reconstituting social action is this: when strain exists attention shifts to higher levels of the components to seek resources to overcome this strain. . . . The principle of moving up the levels of generality, then, is that when any given level (e.g., technology) reaches a limit and becomes inadequate to deal with the condition of strain (e.g., missile gap), it is necessary to move to the next higher level (e.g., basic research or a new national philosophy) in order to broaden the facilities for attacking the strain (1963: 67, 69).

23. Erikson suggests the latter when he writes that

in theory, at least, the argument being made here should fit all kinds of human collectivity—families as well as whole cultures, small groups as well as nations—and the term community is only being used in this context because it seems particularly convenient (1966: 9).

He suggests the argument applies insofar as

> criminal trials, excommunication hearings, court-martials, or even psychiatric case conferences . . . act as boundary-maintaining devices in the sense that they demonstrate to *whatever audience is concerned* where the line is drawn between behavior that belongs in the special universe of the group and behavior that does not (1966: 11). [emphasis added.]

This suggestion, however, only raises the issue in different terms: how is the relevant audience to be determined? Does the whole community react to deviance or simply the magistrates? Was the Puritan colony organized around a common conception of a mission as Erikson portrays it, or is this portrayal simply the ideal conception of the magistrates, from whom Erikson derives his information about the social organization of the colony?

24. The Gary Gilmore case in Utah in 1977 raised publicly the issue of the publicity of capital punishment. What had for Camus been a surrealist proposal—the televised coverage of public executions—was discussed as a serious possibility. For the most part, however, only rarely does the general public in contemporary capitalist society become involved in the affairs of its criminal justice system. The cases in which this has occurred—Gilmore, Watergate, the Rosenbergs—are outstanding because they are exceptions.

25. According to Durkheim:

> In [mechanical solidarity] what we call society is a more or less organized totality of beliefs and sentiments common to all the members of the group: this is the collective type. On the other hand, the [organically solidary society] is a system of different, special functions which definite relations unite. These two societies really make up only one and the same reality, but nonetheless they must be distinguished (1964: 129).

> Social life comes from a double source; the likeness to conscience and the division of labor (1964: 226).

26. The persistence of mechanical solidarity in complex societies is, perhaps, best illustrated by Durkheim's conception of the "non-contractual elements of the contract" (1964: 211). Although modern society consists of individuals and corporate actors pursuing discrete and frequently conflicting interests, they are constrained by more than simple expedient calculations of immediate gains and losses. They maintain some level of commitment to common values and shared understandings over, for example, the kinds of transactions that are possible. Slavery, for example, is a morally bankrupt institution, even though it might conceivably be an economically rational solution to certain problems of labor supply in contemporary agribusinesses.

27. This position did create some theoretic difficulties for Durkheim. In *Suicide* (1951: 336, 363-64), for example, he struggles with the issue of whether the cult of the individual increases suicide because the celebration of the individual encourages egoism or decreases suicide since common beliefs (whatever their object) provide a moral focus for the integration of the society. In a later paper Durkheim resolves this problem by distinguishing between utilitarian individualism and moral individualism, the latter based on the fulfillment of individual potentials rather than the aggrandizement of immediate interests.

28. Although Durkheim proposed a study design emplying a ratio of the number of repressive statues to the number of restitutive statutes, he did not report this study in any detail and the methodological difficulties surrounding such an approach have not even been addressed in the literature (for an early discussion of these problems see Bentham [1942]). This explains why the discussion must be highly speculative.

29. This theme is a variation on Durkheim's famous observation that "the gods are growing old or already dead, and others are not yet born" (1947: 475). Lawrence Friedman has recently made the same observation about legal institutions in complex industrial societies:

"Rules of a modern legal system are not, in the main, 'shared norms.' This is so in two distinct ways. First of all, there are culture clashes in every modern society . . . . In addition, literally thousands of rules in a modern state have purely technical content" (1975: 147).

REFERENCES

Akers, Ronald L. 1968. Problems in the sociology of deviance: Social definition and behavior." *Social Forces* 46: 455-65.

Allen, Francis A. 1974. *The Crimes of Politics: Political Dimensions of Criminal Justice.* Cambridge, Mass.: Harvard University Press.

Althusser, L., and L. Balibar. 1970. *Reading Capital.* London: New Left Books.

Aubert, Vilhelm. 1952. "White-collar crime and social structure." *American Journal of Sociology* 58: 263-71.

Balbus, Issac D. 1971a. "The concept of interest in pluralist and Marxian analysis." *Politics and Society* 1: 151-77.

———. 1971b. "Ruling elite theory vs. Marxist class analysis." *Monthly Review* 23: 36-46.

———. 1973. *The Dialectics of Legal Repression: Black Rebels before the American Criminal Courts.* New York: Russell Sage Foundation.

———. 1977. "Commodity form and legal form: An essay on the 'relative autonomy' of the law." *Law and Society Review* 11: 571-88.

Bayer, Ronald. 1978. "Heroin decriminalization and the ideology of tolerance." *Law and Society Review* 12: 301-18.

Becker, Howard S. 1963. *Outsiders: Studies in the Sociology of Deviance.* New York: Free Press.

———, and Irving Louis Horowitz. 1972. "Radical politics and sociological research: Observations on methodology and ideology." *American Journal of Sociology* 68: 48-66.

Bellah, Robert N. 1959. "Durkheim and history." *American Journal of Sociology* 24: 153-76.

———. 1973. "Introduction." In Robert N. Bellah (ed.). *Emile Durkheim on Morality and Society.* Chicago: University of Chicago Press.

Bentham, Jeremy. 1942. *The Limits of Jurisprudence Defined.* New York: Columbia University Press. (Originally published in 1782.)

Berman, Harold J. 1963. *Justice in the U.S.S.R.: An Interpretation of Soviet Law.* Cambridge: Harvard University Press.

Black, Donald J., and Albert J. Reiss. 1970. "Police control of juveniles." *American Sociological Review* 35: 63-77.

Bowers, William J. 1974. *Executions in America.* Lexington, Mass.: D. C. Heath.

Cain, Maureen. 1974. "The main themes of Marx' and Engels' sociology of law." *British Journal of Law and Society* 1: 136-48.

Camus, Albert. 1957. "Reflections on the guillotine." *Evergreen Review* 1: 5-55.

Cantor, Robert. 1977. "New laws for a new society." New York: Center for Cuban Studies 5 and 6.

Carson, W. G. 1974. "The sociology of crime and the emergence of criminal laws." In Paul Rock and Mary McIntosh (eds.). *Deviance and Social Control.* London: Tavistock.

Chambliss, William. 1974. "The state, the law and the definition of behavior as criminal or delinquent." In Daniel Glaser (ed.). *Handbook of Criminology.* Chicago: Rand McNally.

———. 1975. "The political economy of crime: A study of Nigeria and the U.S." In Ian Taylor, Paul Walton, and Jock Young (eds.). *Critical Criminology.* London: Routledge and Kegan Paul.

——. 1976. "Functional and conflict theories of crime: The heritage of Emile Durkheim and Karl Marx." In William Chambliss and Milton Mankoff (eds.). *Whose Law? What Order? A Conflict Approach to Criminology*. New York: John Wiley.

——, and Robert B. Seidman. 1971. *Law, Order and Power*. Reading, Mass.: Addison-Wesley.

Chiricos, T., and G. Waldo. 1975. "Socioeconomic status and criminal sentencing: An empirical assessment of a conflict proposition." *American Sociological Review* 40: 753-72.

Clarke, Michael. 1976. "Durkheim's sociology of law." *British Journal of Law and Society* 3: 246-55.

Cohen, Lawrence E., and James R. Kluegel. 1978. "Determinants of juvenile court dispositions: Ascriptive and achieved factors in two metropolitan courts." *American Sociological Review* 43: 177-98.

Cohen, Percy. 1968. *Modern Social Theory*. New York: Basic Books.

Collins, Randall. 1975. *Conflict Sociology: Toward an Explanatory Science*. New York: Academic Press.

Connor, Walter D. 1972. "The manufacture of deviance: The case of the Soviet purge 1936-1938." *American Sociological Review* 37: 403-13.

Coser, Lewis. 1962. "Some functions of deviant behavior and normative flexibility." *American Journal of Sociology* 68: 172-81.

Cottrell, Roger B. 1977. "Durkheim on law, development and social solidarity." *British Journal of Law and Society* 4: 241-52.

Dharendorf, Ralf. 1959. *Class and Class Conflict in Industrial Society*. Stanford, Calif.: Stanford University Press.

——. 1968. *Essays in the Theory of Society*. Stanford, Calif.: Stanford University Press.

Davis, Kingsley. 1959. "The myth of functional analysis as a special method in sociology and anthropology." *American Sociological Review* 24: 752-72.

Denisoff, R. Serge, and Donald McAugrie. 1975. "Crime control in capitalist society: A reply to Quinney." *Issues in Criminology* 10: 109-17.

Dentler, Robert, and Kai Erikson. 1959. "The functions of deviance in small groups." *Social Problems* 7: 98-107.

Devlin, Patrick. 1965. *The Enforcement of Morals*. London: Oxford University Press.

Douglas, Mary. 1966. *Purity and Danger: An Analysis of Concepts of Pollution and Taboo*. Middlesex: Penguin Books.

Durkheim, Emile. 1947. *The Elementary Forms of the Religious Life*. Glencoe, Ill.: Free Press. (Originally published in 1912.)

——. 1950. *The Rules of Sociological Method*. Glencoe, Ill.: Free Press. (Originally published in 1895.)

——. 1951. *Suicide*. New York: Free Press. (Originally published in 1897.)

——. 1957. *Professional Ethics and Civic Morals*. London: Routledge and Kegan Paul. (Originally published in 1950.)

——. 1964. *The Division of Labor in Society*. New York: Free Press.

——. 1973a. "Individualism and the intellectuals." (Originally published in 1828.) Translated by Mark Traugott. In Robert N. Bellah (ed.). *Emile Durkheim on Morality and Society*. Chicago: University of Chicago Press.

——. 1973b. "Two laws of penal evolution." (Originally published in 1899-1900.) Translated by T. Anthony Jones and Andrew T. Scull. *Economy and Society* 2: 285-308.

Empey, LaMar T. 1973. "Juvenile justice reform: Diversion, due process and de-institutionalization." In Lloyd Ohlin (ed.). *Prisoners in America*. Englewood Cliffs, N.J.: Prentice-Hall.

Erikson, Kai T. 1966. *Wayward Puritans: A Study in the Sociology of Deviance*. New York: John Wiley.

Evans, Edward P. 1906. *The Criminal Prosecution and Capital Punishment of Animals*. London: W. Hineman.

Farley, Reynolds. 1977. "Trends in racial inequalities: Have the gains of the 1960s disappeared in the 1970s?" *American Sociological Review* 42: 189-208.

Friedman, Lawrence M. 1975. *The Legal System: A Social Science Perspective*. New York: Russell Sage Foundation.

Genovese, Eugene D. 1972. *In Red and Black: Marxian Explorations in Southern and Afro-American History*. New York: Vintage Books.

Gibbs, Jack P., and Maynard L. Erickson. 1975. "Major developments in the sociological study of deviance." In Alex Inkeles (ed.). *Annual Review of Sociology*. Vol. 1. Palo Alto, Calif.: Annual Reviews.

Giddens, Anthony. 1971. "Durkheim's political sociology." *Sociological Review* 19: 477-519.

———. 1972. "Introduction: Durkheim's writings in sociology and social philosophy." In Anthony Giddens (ed.). *Emile Durkheim, Selected Writings*. London: Cambridge University Press.

———. 1973. *The Class Structure of Advanced Capitalist Society*. New York: Harper and Row.

———. 1976. "Classical social theory and the origins of modern sociology." *American Journal of Sociology* 81: 703-29.

Goffman, Erving. 1961. *Asylums*. Garden City, N.Y.: Doubleday.

Gold, David, et al. 1975. "Recent developments in Marxist theories of the capitalist state." *Monthly Review* 5: 29-43 and 6: 36-51.

Gouldner, Alvin. 1973. "The two Marxisms." In Alvin Gouldner. *For Sociology: Renewal and Critique in Sociology Today*. New York: Basic Books.

Greenberg, David. 1976. "On one dimensional Marxist criminology." *Theory and Society* 3: 611-21.

Gusfield, Joseph R. 1963. *Symbolic Crusade: Status Politics and the American Temperance Movement*. Urbana, Ill.: University of Illinois Press.

———. 1967. "Moral passage: The symbolic process in public designations of deviance." *Social Problems* 15: 175-88.

Hagan, John. 1974. "Extra-legal attributes and criminal sentencing: An assessment of a sociological viewpoint." *Law and Society Review* 8: 357-83.

Hempel, Carl. 1965. "The logic of functional analysis." (Originally published in 1959.) In Carl Hempel. *Aspects of Scientific Explanation and Other Essays in the Philosophy of Science*. New York: Free Press.

Hindelang, Michael. 1978. "Race and involvement in common law personal crimes." *American Sociological Review* 43: 93-109.

Hirst, Paul Q. 1972. "Marx and Engels on crime, law and morality." *Economy and Society* 1: 28-56.

Hopkins, Andrew. 1975. "On the sociology of criminal law." *Social Problems* 22: 608-19.

Horton, John. 1966. "Order and conflict theories of social problems as competing ideologies." *American Journal of Sociology* 71: 701-13.

Humphries, Drew. 1977. "The movement to legalize abortions: A historical account." In David F. Greenberg (ed.). *Corrections and Punishment*. Beverly Hills, Calif.: Sage.

Hyman, Hubert H. 1964. "England and America: Climates of tolerance and intolerance." In Daniel Bell (ed.). *The Radical Right*. Garden City, N.Y.: Anchor Books.

Inverarity, James M. 1976. "Populism and lynching in the South: A test of Erikson's theory of the relationship between boundary crisis and repressive justice." *American Sociological Review* 41: 262-80.

Kaiser, Guenther. 1976. "Recent developments in German penal policy." *International Journal of Criminology and Penology* 4: 193-206.

Keat, Russell, and John Urry. 1975. *Social Theory as Science.* London: Routledge and Kegal Paul.

Kelley, Clarence. 1976. *Crime in the United States.* Washington, D.C.: U.S. Government Printing Office.

Kittrie, Nicholas N. 1971. *The Right to be Different: Deviance and Enforced Therapy.* Baltimore: Johns Hopkins Press.

Lieberson, Stanley, 1971. "An empirical study of military-industrial linkages." *American Journal of Sociology* 77: 562-84.

Manning, Peter K. 1975. "Deviance and dogma: Some comments on the labeling perspective." *British Journal of Criminology* 15: 1-20.

Marcuse, Herbert. 1965. "Repressive tolerance." In Robert P. Wolff, Barrington Moore, and Herbert Marcuse. *A Critique of Pure Tolerance.* Boston: Beacon Press.

Marshall, T. H. 1965. "Citizenship and social class." (Originally published in 1949.) In T. H. Marshall. *Class, Citizenship and Social Development.* Garden City, N.Y.: Anchor Books.

Marx, Karl. nd. *Capital.* Vol. 1. New York: Modern Library. (Originally published in 1867.)

———. 1970. *A Contribution to the Critique of Political Economy.* New York: International. (Originally published in 1859.)

Matza, David. 1969. *Becoming Deviant.* Englewood Cliffs, N.J.: Prentice-Hall.

Merritt, Richard L. 1966. *Symbols of an American Community, 1735-1775.* New Haven, Conn.: Yale University Press.

Merton, Robert K. 1968. *Social Theory and Social Structure.* New York: Free Press.

Michalowski, Raymond J., and Edward W. Bohlander. 1976. "Repression and criminal justice in capitalist America." *Sociological Inquiry* 46: 95-106.

Offe, Claus. 1972. "Political authority and class structure: An analysis of late capitalist societies." *International Journal of Sociology* 2: 73-105.

Parsons, Talcott. 1960. "Durkheim's contribution to the theory of social integration." In Kurt Wolff (ed.). *Essays on Philosophy and Sociology by Emile Durkheim. et al.* New York: Free Press.

Pittman, David J. 1974. "Decriminalization of public drunkenness offense: An international overview." In Sawyer Sylvester and Edward Sagarin (eds.). *Politics and Crime.* New York: Praeger.

Platt, Anthony. 1973. "Towards a new criminology." Unpublished paper.

Poulantzas, Nicos. 1973. *Political Power and Social Classes.* London: New Left Books.

Quinney, Richard P. 1970. *The Social Reality of Crime.* Boston: Little, Brown.

———. 1973. *Critique of Legal Order.* Boston: Little, Brown.

———. 1977. *Class, State and Crime: On the Theory and Practice of Criminal Justice.* New York: David McKay.

Raymond, M. J. 1956. "Case of fetishism treated by aversion therapy." *British Medical Journal* 2: 854-57.

Richter, Melvin. 1960. "Durkheim's politics and political theory." In Kurt Wolff (ed.). *Essays on Philosophy and Sociology by Emile Durkheim et al.* New York: Free Press.

Rose, Arnold M., and Arthur E. Prell. 1955. "Does the punishment fit the crime? A study in social valuation." *American Journal of Sociology* 61: 248-59.

Roshier, Bob. 1978. "The functions of crime myth." *British Journal of Sociology* 29: 309-23.

Rossi, Peter, et al. 1974. "The seriousness of crimes: Normative structure and individual differences." *American Sociological Review* 29: 224-37.

Rubinstein, Jonathan. 1973. *City Police.* New York: Farrar, Straus and Giroux.

Rueschemeyer, Dietrich. 1977. "Structural differentiation, efficiency and power." *American Journal of Sociology* 83: 1-25.

Rusche, Georg, and Otto Kirchheimer. 1968. *Punishment and Social Structure*. New York: Russell and Russell. (Originally published in 1933.)

Scheff, Thomas J. 1966. *Being Mentally Ill: A Sociological Theory*. Chicago: Aldine.

Schelling, Thomas. 1963. *The Strategy of Conflict*. Cambridge, Mass.: Harvard University Press.

Schur, Edwin. 1965. *Crimes without Victims*. New York: Random House.

Scull, Andrew T. 1977. *Decarceration: Community Treatment and the Deviant—A Radical View*. Englewood Cliffs, N.J.: Prentice-Hall.

Scheleff, Leon S. 1975. "From restitutive law to repressive law." *Archives Européenes de Sociologie* 16: 16-45.

Smelser, Niel F. 1963. *Theory of Collective Behavior*. New York: Free Press.

Sorokin, Pitrim. 1937. "Fluctuations of ethicojuridical mentality in criminal law." In Pitrim Sorokin. *Social and Cultural Dynamics*. Vol. 2. New York: American Book Company.

Spitzer, Stephen. 1975a. "Punishment and social organization: A study of Durkheim's theory of penal evolution." *Law and Society Review* 9: 613-35.

———. 1975b. "Toward a Marxian theory of deviance." *Social Problems* 22: 638-51.

Steinert, Heniz. 1977. "Against a conspiracy theory of criminal law a propos Hepburn's 'Social Control and the Legal Order.' " *Contemporary Crisis* 1: 437-40.

Sternberg, David. 1972. "The new radical-criminal trials: A step toward a class-for-itself in the American proletariat?" *Science and Society* 36: 274-301.

Stinchcombe, Arthur. 1963. "Institutions of privacy in the determination of police administrative practice." *American Journal of Sociology* 69: 150-60.

———. 1968. *Constructing Social Theories*. New York: Harcourt, Brace and World.

———. 1976. "Marxist theories of power and empirical research." In Lewis Coser and Otto Larson (ed.). *The Uses of Controversy in Sociology*. New York: Free Press.

Stouffer, Samuel. 1955. *Communism, Conformity and Civil Liberties: A Cross-Section of the Nation Speaks Its Mind*. Garden City, N.Y.: Doubleday.

Sutherland, Edwin. 1940. "White-collar criminality." *American Sociological Review* 5: 1-12.

———. 1945. "Is 'white collar crime' crime?" *American Sociological Review* 10: 132-39.

———, and Donald Cressey. 1974. *Criminology*. 9th ed. Philadelphia: J. B. Lippincott. (Originally published in 1924.)

Szasz, Thomas. 1963. *Law, Liberty and Psychiatry: An Inquiry into the Social Uses of Mental Health Practices*. New York: Macmillan.

Taylor, Ian, Paul Walton, and Jock Young. 1973. *The New Criminology: For a Social Theory of Deviance*. New York: Harper and Row.

———. 1975. *Critical Criminology*. London: Routledge and Kegan Paul.

Thernstrom, Stephen. 1964. *Poverty and Progress: Social Mobility in a Nineteenth Century City*. Cambridge, Mass.: Harvard University Press.

Tigar, Michael. 1971. "Socialist law and legal institutions." In Robert Lefkowitz (ed.). *Law against the People*. Garden City, N.Y.: Doubleday.

Trubeck, David. 1977. "Complexity and contradiction in the legal order: Balbus and the challenge of critical social thought about the law." *Law and Society Review* 11: 529-69.

Tucker, Robert C. (ed.). 1978. *The Marx-Engels Reader*. 2nd ed. New York; W. W. Norton.

Turk, Austin. 1976a. "Law as a weapon in social conflict." *Social Problems* 23: 276-91.

———. 1976b. "Law, conflict and order: From theorizing toward theories." *Canadian Review of Sociology and Anthropology* 13: 282-92.

———. 1977. "Class, conflict and criminalization: *Sociological Focus* 10: 209-20.

Turner, Ralph. 1967. "Types of solidarity in the reconstruction of groups." *Pacific Sociological Review* 10: 60-68.

Unger, Roberto M. 1976. *Law in Modern Society: Toward a Criticism of Social Theory.* New York: Free Press.

Van den Berghe, Pierre L. 1963. "Dialectic and functionalism: Toward a theoretical synthesis." *American Sociological Review* 28: 695-705.

Vogel, Egon, and Norman Bell. 1968. "The emotionally disturbed child as the family scapegoat." In Norman Bell and Egon Vogel (eds.). *A Modern Introduction to the Family.* New York: Free Press.

Walton, Paul. 1973. "Social reaction and radical commitment: The case of the Weathermen." In Laurie Taylor and Ian Taylor (eds.). *Politics and Deviance.* Middlesex: Penguin Books.

Wellford, Charles. 1975. "Labeling theory and criminology: An assessment." *Social Problems* 22: 332-45.

Wenkert, Robert. 1961. "Reply to 'Some comments on working class authoritarianism.'" *Berkeley Journal of Sociology* 6: 109-16.

Wilson, James Q. 1968. "The police and the delinquent in two cities." In Stanton Wheeler (ed.). *Controlling Delinquents.* New York: John Wiley.

Wright, Erik O. 1973. *The Politics of Punishment: A Critical Analysis of Prisons in America.* New York: Harper and Row.

Young, Jock. 1975. "Working class criminology." In Ian Taylor, Paul Walton, and Jock Young (eds.). *Critical Criminology.* London: Routledge and Kegan Paul.

Afterword

Suggestions for the Study of the Political Dimensions of Deviance Definition

Pat Lauderdale and *James Inverarity*

THE DEFINITION OF DEVIANCE

The studies in this book are representative of a trend in the sociology of deviance toward examining the political processes underlying the creation of deviance. This focus on the politics of deviance entails the integration of the study of deviance with the study of other aspects of social organization, namely social movements, professional organizations, media, and the state.

The attention to the political aspects of deviance has emerged when the boundary between apolitical and political realms of social life has been similarly reconsidered in several substantive areas. For example, collective behavior (riots, social movements, crowds) has long been the exclusive preserve of social psychologists. Employing such concepts as relative deprivation and cognitive dissonance, they sought to explain the episodes of collective disorder in terms of nonrational motives of the individual participants. Recently, a number of investigators have sought to show how such supposedly apolitical collective action is, in fact, a form of political activity. Hobsbawm (1971), for example, views bandits and mafias as forms of prepolitical action, whereas Tilly (1969) and Gamson (1975) have examined political processes underlying such seemingly nonpolitical activities as food riots and urban riots.

In a similar fashion, the narrow view of political life advocated by pluralists has come under increasing examination. Pluralists contend that politics consists of conflict between organized interest groups over explicit issues. Against this view Bachrach and Baratz argue that another dimension of political life is excluded by the pluralist view, that is, issues that are "suffocated before they are even voiced; or kept covert; or killed before they gain access to the relevant decision-making arena; or, failing all these things, maimed or destroyed, in the decision-implementing stage of the policy process" (1970: 44).

Within the field of deviance this rediscovery of the political process has been slow and unsure. We have not yet established a coherent view of its nature, potential, and limits. In this book we have made an effort to clarify these issues by examining how the definitional processes taking place at various levels of analysis share common properties.[1] Chapters 2 through 5 are substantive efforts to spell out the ways in which definitions are formed at different levels of analysis. We have chosen to investigate changing definitions in a wide variety of substantive areas in order to illustrate the generic political character of the definitional process. Political analyses of forms of "deviance" involve essentially the following basic issues: (1) how the definition is created (e.g., legislation, medical nomenclature, mass media); (2) actors involved in the creation of the definition (e.g., charismatic moral entrepreneurs, social movements, professional organizations, the state); (3) how the definition is maintained or removed (e.g., enforcement by social control agencies); and (4) the effects of that definition (e.g., status reallocation).[2]

The studies in this book reveal certain similarities in definitional processes and suggest how future work might produce structures of similar definitional transformations. More research is needed on the ways in which definitions come to have a structure and on the transformations between legitimacy and illegitimacy that occur in regular patterns. Examination of these transformations will be useful in the search for the origins of institutionalized stigma, well-meaning interference, and the general control of behavior in society (Foucault, 1965 and 1977).[3]

In chapter 2, Parker and Lauderdale examine the transformation of definitions occurring in the American courtroom. They show that focusing simply upon the behavior of the supposed deviants makes it impossible to understand how the "deviants" were redefined as folk heroes instead of individuals who had gone astray. The study indicates how antiwar defendants, initially defined as criminals, were able to have themselves redefined as political deviants by their own shattering of the defendant role supported by the antiwar movement and an ongoing mass sentiment conducive to their interests.[4] The advocacy system of justice provides for due process under law, protecting the legal rights of the defendant against the overwhelming power of the state. The study shows how these individual rights have the latent function of depoliticizing courtroom trials, making it virtually impossible for individuals placed in the roles of defendants to redefine their action as beyond incrimination. Only by breaking out of the role of defendant is it possible for the accused to establish himself or herself as a political actor. This is very difficult to accomplish in liberal capitalist states because adherence to due process legitimizes the criminalization of deviants. The legitimacy of the trial makes it an ideal weapon of repression, for by charging political "troublemakers" with crimes the state can tie them down with extensive litigation (cf. Marx, 1970). Contrary to traditional approaches to political criminality based on the notion that certain crimes are unambiguously political in nature (e.g., Clinard and Quinney, 1973), chapter 2 suggests that the distinction between the criminal trial and the political trial is a product of a negotiating process that is dependent on a number of interrelated factors. These factors include the articulations of the defendants, the expertise of legal counsel, and the presence or absence of an external support movement (for more on this, see Rosett and Cressey [1976]). Future work regarding the symbolic definition of the defendants as political or criminal should explicitly consider variations in structures of the legal system (e.g., adversarial versus inquisitorial procedures) and levels of social support external to the courtroom.[5]

Lauderdale and Estep, in chapter 3, discuss another critical point at which definitions are negotiated, the mass media. The Columbia tradition of media research has debunked the popular notion that public opinion is at the mercy of mass media advertising and political appeals. At the other end, Marcuse (1964) and other social philosophers view the media as omnipotent, if not in creating demand for a specific product or candidate at least in creating false needs for the consumer society. Relatively neglected is how the media bestows the accent of reality on events (Schutz, 1964). Chapter 3 examines one instance of selective perception by the media. In this particular case, the actors who were attempting to be designated as political actors were not simply defined as deviant but were denied public existence altogether.[6] Future work should investigate not only the creation of media definitions but also the impact of such media portrayals on public opinion. We know, for example, that Roosevelt won elections despite overwhelming opposition on the part of mass media. Survey data (similar to the Harris and Roper polls) may serve to assess the impact of the media's presentation of the anti-Bicentennial protest and similar events, providing more closure to our understanding of collective definitions of deviance.

Although the area of political trials is troublesome because the research is typically based upon secondary data and explanations, the study of social movements is problematic because much of the social reality of the movements is created by the selective data presented via the mass media, organizational linkages, and so on. Chapter 3 suggests that the defendants in the antiwar trials were fortunate not only because support for their political articulations was created by an ongoing social movement but also because the movement's activities were brought before the courts and public via the mass media. An important question is to what extent actors who attempt to articulate political aims are ignored because they lack the support of a movement or media coverage of the movement. Following Gamson (1975), it becomes especially relevant to examine the actions of the "stably unrepresented," that is, the unorganized, unmobilized, and typically undefined mass. The boundaries between movement and "normal" politics have become hazy since the tactics of the two appear, on closer analysis, to be strikingly similar. That is, both normal political organizations (institutionalized movements) and emerging movements engage in rational decision making, operate on the scheme of means to ends, create useful ideologies, and calculate consequences. Therefore, it becomes increasingly clear that movements are simply politics by other means. The task remains to determine the explicit role of structural conduciveness in the emergence and possible institutionalization of nascent movements. Although some of the factors have been dealt with implicitly, the explicit role of conduciveness has only begun to be examined (see, for example, Gamson's [1975] initial attempt to show how violence is related to politics at the boundary).

In contrast to the previous chapters, Hallowell's study of hockey violence (chapter 4) examines the definition of behavior at a more institutionalized level. Certain definitions of deviance are the outcome of a political process involving negotiations between professional organizations and the state. Hockey violence (and sport violence in general) is a particularly strategic phenomenon to examine in understanding the political dynamics of definitional change. We tend in this society to think of violence as being *the* intrinsic property that distinguishes deviant from conventional behavior. It is often argued, for example, that society reacts less severely to white-collar crimes such as price fixing than to working-class crimes such as burglary because working-class crimes characteristically involve a much greater level of direct, personal violence. Yet personal violence is an intrinsic part of legitimate institutionalized professional athletics. Only occasionally do public or social control agents view violence in professional sports as problematic. Hallowell demonstrates that these occasional reactions have little to do with the actual behavior of the players; rather, societal reactions against hockey violence are consequences of political processes in the professional organization of the sport. This paper raises several questions that warrant further investigation.[7] How do other professions that engage in violence as part of their occupational routine (e.g., the police or the military) legitimize their use of violence? Do societal reactions against police violence also reflect the politics of professional organizations, rather than variations in actual police conduct? Are there common dynamics in the process of deviance definition among professionals? Could Hallowell's analysis help explain how medical associations discover drug abuse among physicians or why bar associations instigate disbarment proceedings against their members? Hallowell's dissection of episodes of problematic violence in the history of the hockey profession provides a new and challenging perspective on the politics of professions and the political bases of professionally defined deviance.

Bergesen's paper (chapter 5) looks at another locus of definitional change, the relationship between the local community and the national state. He provides evidence for the thesis that the destructiveness of riots is a consequence of police behavior rather than rioters' activities (cf. Marx, 1970) and suggests that the behavior of police is a consequence of their class relationship to the federal government. The intrusion of the central state into the local community has recurrently led to episodes of collective violence (Tilly, 1975). In the 1960s the intrusion of the federal government into urban programs and desegregation processes created a climate of resentment in the urban, white ethnic communities, from which the police and National Guard were recruited. Given the nature of the conflict between local community and nation-state, the occurrence of "police riots" came to be defined as the reaction of agencies of social control to race riots, thus legitimating behavior on the part of police that under normal circumstances would be subject to criminal prosecution. More systematic work is needed on the political determinants of definitions of deviance by social control agents.

In chapter 6, Inverarity seeks to provide a structural approach to deviance definitions based on the theoretic conceptions of law and society developed by Marx and Durkheim. The synthesis of Marx's contrast between feudal and bourgeois law and Durkheim's analysis of repressive and restitutive law begins to spell out the social-organizational conditions under which certain types of reactions to and definitions of deviance will occur. In considering social control in advanced capitalist societies, this paper emphasizes the similarities between Marx and Durkheim more than the differences. This synthesis sees the primary factor in such societies to be the complex division of labor that attentuates the repressive character and the integrative role of the criminal law. The importance of the individual in such systems is to be understood as a consequence of capitalism's market needs for freely contracted individuals. Chapter 6 reinforces the theme of the preceeding chapters that a variety of political processes underlie deviance definition and suggests that, by drawing on the ideas of these classical theorists, we can develop some understanding of the social-organizational conditions that facilitate, if not produce, variations in political processes of deviance definition.

TOPICS FOR FURTHER RESEARCH:
HEGEMONY AND INTERESTS

The studies in this book do not provide a complete solution to the problem of how definitions of deviance come to be formed and applied. In working through these related problems in several substantive areas, we have discovered two issues that seem to require more detailed consideration. The central question to ask about political phenomena is, of course, "Who benefits?" Who benefits from the designation of certain forms of harmful (or harmless) behavior as deviant when other forms of behavior are treated as normal?[8] The concept of interest and its relationship to deviance designation is ambiguous in the current literature. In this section we will review these problems and propose some solutions. First, we must recognize that the identification of interests served by stigmatizing does not necessarily imply an adequate explanation of it. The concept of *hegemony* is essential to an understanding of the role of structural factors that affect stigmatizing. This is a major *terra incognita* in the field of deviance. Second, we must clarify the concept of interest. Third, we must consider the circumstances under which relationships can be empirically investigated.

Hegemony

We might best understand the role of hegemony in the social definition of deviance by first considering an analogy. Most people perceive air travel as much more hazardous than automobile travel. The actual death rates of these two modes of transportation, however, suggest just the opposite. In 1977, the death rate per 100 million passenger miles was 0.65 for passenger automobiles on freeways but only 0.04 for scheduled domestic airplanes. The gap between perceived risk and actual risk exemplifies the distinction made above between subjective and objective interests. How can we account for the disparity? One possibility is that, for modes of transportation, the properties of the two types of accidents lead to differences in perceived risk. Automobile deaths are perceived as routine, small-scale events. When, however, American Airlines flight 191 from Chicago to Los Angeles crashed on takeoff, killing 273 on Memorial Day weekend in 1979, the story covered the front pages of newspapers for several days and was the subject of special TV news programs. During the same weekend far more people died in automobile accidents. Even though interest groups such as the National Safety Council and automobile insurance companies strive vigorously to dramatize the highway death toll, their efforts have never succeeded in having the impact of a single airline catastrophe. This contrast in public reaction illustrates the general principle that

> popular perceptions are no safe guide to the actual magnitude of a social problem. Ill-understood but partly known processes of social perception involve the patterned omitting, supplementing and organizing of what is selectively perceived in the social reality... perception seems affected by what we are better able to describe than to explain: the dramatic quality of unitary events that evoke popular interest.[9] The airplane disaster is perceived as a single event, although it is of course compounded of many occurrences that eventuated in the victims going to their death. In contrast, the hundreds of automobile accidents occurring on the same day, with their, say, 200 dead, comprise a compound event that can be detected only through the aggregation of cold and impersonal numbers. The import of this kind of thing is clear. Pervasive social problems that seldom have dramatic and conspicuous manifestations are apt to arouse smaller public attention than problems, less serious even when judged by the beholder's own values, which erupt in the spotlight of public drama. This is another reason that the sociologist need not order the importance of social problems in the same way as the man in the street. For,... even when we take, as we do, the values of the people we are observing as one basis for assessing social prob-

lems—in the present case, the sanctity of life and the tragedy of premature death—the public's perception of these problems is often found to be badly distorted (Merton, 1966: 713).

This fear of flying produced by infrequent but dramatic incidents serves the interests of the insurance companies that underwrite flight insurance policies. People feel the need to take out insurance before flying in an airplane, but not before driving in an automobile. The public reaction to airline crashes, then, serves the interests of the insurance companies, since they can sell more profitable policies. But, just because their interests are served, it does not follow that the insurance companies play a role in the creation of the public reaction. They are, in all probability, passive beneficiaries of a reaction that is produced by more complex causes than machinations of insurance agents.

Similar situations may be at the basis of social reaction to crime and deviance. For example, numerous observers since Sutherland have commented on the paradox of public reactions to white-collar or corporate crime. Despite the fact that the financial loss from white-collar crime greatly exceeds the cost of street crime, laws against the former are less stringent and less strictly enforced. In addition, public reaction is more fearful of and hostile toward street crime. Little attention has been paid to the possible hegemonic sources of this underreaction to white-collar crime. The fact that street crimes involve dramatic, unitary events with the threat or use of personal violence may account for some of the differential public and legal reaction. Thus, the underreaction in law and public opinion to white-collar offenses may result in complex ways from the structural differences between working-class and upper-class criminality. The police generally tolerate policy operations and other nonviolent forms of law violation in the ghetto. The differential legal and popular reaction to street versus suite crime may arise in part from the structural differences of the two locales, especially the fact that attacks on the street appear to entail more direct, observable violence (cf. Gordon, 1973). At present we know very little about how perceptions of seriousness of offense are structured or how hegemonic definitions change.[10]

Although hegemonic processes account for some public perceptions of harm, perceptions may in certain circumstances be directly manipulated by interests, the second issue requiring detailed consideration.

Interest

Analyses of law in terms of interest have frequently been tautological, but there is no reason that interest cannot be employed as a legitimate independent variable. One difficulty with explanations of stigmatizing in terms of the interests this process serves, however, is that the very concept of interest can be defined several ways. One crucial distinction is between objective and subjective interests. Subjective interest is articulated by actors in the form of political demands, opinions, beliefs, and attitudes. Objective interest is determined by some criterion that is not subject to the actors' frame of mind. All too frequently investigators of deviance definition assume that subjective and objective interests coincide. This can be a serious error. Heinz Steinert makes this point quite well in his critical review of Quinney (1977):

> [Quinney] good-naturedly believes what propaganda tells us, namely that "the corporate world is concerned and alarmed about the economic costs of crime" (p. 129). But as far as I can see, crime for capital interests is just another cost-factor (as far as plants, businesses, etc. are victimized), and not a very grave one, since it can easily be handled by insurance or by turning the costs over to the consumer. Where price-competition still functions it is in the interest of the single capitalist to reduce this as other cost-factors, but only if it is not [sic] reduced for all competing capitalists. And the reduction of this cost-factor must be balanced against the costs of its reduction. It is likely that capital can live with crime. It is the worker who is victimized most by crime either directly or indirectly, e.g., higher prices, and who, in addition is more likely to face criminalization. This latter fact puts the worker in a dilemma of interests, but primarily it is consumer and not capital interests that are furthered by a reduction of crime. Thus the "corporate world's" concern about crime is suspect (Steinert, 1978: 310-11).

The relative ease of gathering data on subjective interests, the proliferation of survey research techniques, and the training of most deviance researchers in social psychology have all contributed to the preoccupation with subjective interests and the lack of attention to measuring objective interests. A similar preoccupation among the idealist historians of his time prompted Marx to observe that

> while in ordinary life every shopkeeper is very well able to distinguish between what somebody professes to be and what he really is, our historians have not yet won even this trivial insight. They take every epoch at its

word and believe that everything it says and imagines about itself is true (Tucker, 1978: 139).

The first step in distinguishing social illusion from social reality is to spell out the possible combinations of subjective and objective interests. Balbus (1971), for example, develops the scheme outlined in table 14. The first situation, represented by cell 1, is not problematic. The actor is realistically aware of being affected by some phenomenon. The central problem in contemporary deviance research is the assumption that all cases fall into this cell. Cell 4 also is not problematic and, for our purposes, is trivial. Cells 2 and 3 represent two types of false consciousness. Cell 3 exemplifies the hypochondriac condition discussed by Steinert. Cell 2 represents perhaps the most common situation, in which the actor is harmed but is unaware of this harm or its source.

Table 14. Relationship between Subjective and Objective Interests

| | | Actor is Aware of Being Affected by X | |
		Yes	No
Actor Is Affected by X	Yes	1	2
	No	3	4

Once we understand the possible relationships between subjective and objective interests, we can decide how objective interests are to be assessed. But this requires the investigator to abandon, at least partially, the viewpoint of the actor and to impose her or his own assessment of the actor's situation. Middle-class academics generally have few inhibitions about pronouncing on the false consciousness of subordinated groups in the society, as Mills so trenchantly observed in "The professional ideology of social pathologists" (Mills, 1942). Sociology, however, must transcend the class values of the observer and develop an objective assessment of class interests. This is the task Marx set for himself in the first volume of *Capital*. Unfortunately, it is a task that has been neglected by sociologists studying the ways in which societies create deviance.[11]

Sociologists have avoided the tough empirical work required to assess interests and the correspondence between interests and definitions of deviance. We suspect that such analysis will tend to support the central arguments being made by conflict theorists. The present state of the art, however, reduces these complex issues to a fixed choice between a theoretical assumption of consensus and a theoretical assumption of dissension. The political analysis of deviance is removed from the realm of research and placed into the realm of ideology.

The question of who benefits from criminalization can be addressed at least partially by empirical data gathered for other purposes. Victimization data can, for example, be used as a starting point in calculating the costs and benefits of law enforcement. Representative examples of such data are presented in table 15. The general conclusion about crime from these statistics is that "the poor pay more." Taylor, Walton, and Young's (1973: 187) imagery of delinquents "redistributing private property" like latter-day Robin Hoods appears, on the basis of this evidence, to be unrealistic. This conception was no doubt fed by the Nixon-Agnew rhetoric that crime in the streets is a major problem for Middle America. While some change may have occurred in the sixties, it is nevertheless the poor, the black, and the disadvantaged who are the primary victims of the violent and predatory offenses defined as crime.

CRISES AS STRATEGIC RESEARCH SITES

If we do, in fact, live in a system in which important objective interests do not coincide with subjective interests and the dominant classes exercise legal and cultural hegemony, empirical support for assertions about the political processes underlying deviance designation will be difficult to find. As Bachrach and Baratz point out, it may be impossible "to determine empirically whether the consensus is genuine or instead has been enforced through non-decision-making" (1970: 49). The proliferation of tautological explanations of law in terms of interests, then, arises from the intractable nature of the relationship.

One resolution to this impasse may be to direct attention to the system in crisis. Although this strategy has not been explicitly addressed in the study of changing definitions of deviance, there are several examples in which it has been implicitly employed. The rationale for focusing on crisis situations is that crucial portions of the structure of a system obscured during its normal functioning will be exposed when it undergoes a crisis.

Balbus (1977), for example, adopts a view of the significance of crisis for revealing the central contours of the capitalist state. He examines the criminal justice system in three large American cities, not in terms of their day to day operations, but rather in terms of the way these systems respond to the crisis of urban riots. He uses his

Table 15. Social Distribution of Vicitimization

A. Homicide Victimization of Males Aged 25 to 34 by Race (Rates per 100,000 Population)

	Whites	Blacks
1959-1961	5.9	81.4
1969-1971	12.9	146.3

B. Victimization by Race (Rates per 100,000 Population)

Offenses	White	Nonwhite
Forcible rape	22	82
Robbery	58	204
Aggravated Assault	186	347
Burglary	822	1,306
Larceny	608	367
Auto theft	164	286
Total	1,860	2,592
Respondents	27,484	4,902

Source: The Challenge of Crime in a Free Society (Washington, D.C.: U.S. Government Printing Office, 1967: 39).

C. Victimization by Income (Rates per 100,000 Population)

Offenses	Income of Less Than $2,999	Income of $3,000 to $5,999	Income of $6,000 to $9,999	Income of $10,000 or More
Forcible rape	76	49	10	17
Robbery	172	121	48	34
Aggravated assault	229	316	144	252
Burglary	1,319	1,020	867	790
Larceny over $50	420	619	549	925
Auto theft	153	206	202	219

Source: The Challenge of Crime in a Free Society (Washington, D.C.: U.S. Government Printing Office, 167: 38).

three cases to argue that the American criminal justice system is engaged in a dialectic among three problems: organizational integrity, legitimacy, and maintaining order. Analyzing the crises allows Balbus to see the contradictions inherent in the system more clearly than examining the system under normal conditions.

Erikson (1966) empirically established a connection between solidarity and ritual punishment. He chose as a strategic research site three crises in seventeenth-century Puritan Massachusetts. The crises provided Erikson with extreme variation in the solidarity variable that he associated with corresponding variations in punishment.

A similar problem posed by Claus Offe has been to demonstrate the class character of the state in capitalist society, in particular the ways in which the organization of the state serves to reproduce the class system. He outlines a series of mechanisms by which the capitalist state guarantees the integrity of the system, both against opponents of the system and against parochial interest of individual capitalists. When the system operates normally, however, it is virtually impossible to demonstrate the class character of the state. The apparent neutrality of the state disappears when it faces a crisis. Only in crisis situations, when the state is forced to rely on coercion, does its bias become readily apparent (Gold et al, 1975).

Thus, the crisis situation appears particularly heuristic in gaining a relatively clear picture of hegemony and interests. We hope this strategy and the line of analysis presented in this volume will result in future theory and research not only on the definition of deviance but on related processes of social definition as well.[12] Such work will embrace a wider range of phenomena including labor relations, ethnic cleavages, global resources, and the collective recognition of social harm. This book is presented as a first step in that direction.

NOTES

1. The study of political processes should not be limited to those previously mentioned in this volume. For example, certain categories of deviance (e.g., traditional ones like drug abuse, sex abuse, and violence) are typically related to socially harmful individuals such as addicts, prostitutes, and murderers, whereas other categories with similarly harmful consequences are usually passed over or reacted to as only mildly (interestingly) deviant (e.g. business abuse).

2. It may also be useful to consider the following three views of deviance. Stigmatization may result from: (1) individuals crossing moral boundaries; (2) the creation of the boundaries, independent of the actions of actors; and/or (3) the movement of the boundaries, independent of the actions of actors. The first view notes that deviance may well be achieved but, as we have maintained, is overrepresented in sociology as well as the mass media, folklore, and daily conversation. The other two perspectives are essential to further research in deviance designation since they focus upon the ascribed aspect of stigmatization via enactment, enforcement, or reinterpretation of rules of conduct. One of the central issues emerging from this scheme is why particular boundaries are created and others ignored.

3. Foucault's works (1973 and 1977) equate many institutions with types of knowledge and space (knowledge with perception of a structure) and form a relation between the two.

4. The study also illustrates that not all laws that make things illegal create deviance and suggests the importance of explaining in further detail why certain criminal laws are enacted and then why only some are enforced (or, for that matter, why the enforcement of some, such as laws against speeding, income tax evasion, and jaywalking, does not necessarily lead to stigma.

5. Political crimes, we argue, ought not to be considered a separate species of phenomenon, tucked away in an obscure corner of typologies of deviant behavior. Rather, it should be looked on as a crack in the hegemonic facade.

6. It is interesting to observe that the more violent of the two protest groups, ROOB, did receive more publicity; however, it appears that the publicity was not sufficient to keep them from eventually being ignored.

7. Another plausible reason for the increase in perceived sports violence is the changing nature of the spectator. Recent work (cf. Clarke and Jefferson, 1976) suggests that sport is now being infiltrated with a new type of fan, one who is interested in the finer points of the game. This new spectator attempts to assess the game objectively and not simply to cheer for the home team. Clarke and Jefferson suggest that bourgeois spectators, unlike their predecessors, are more likely to define aggressive play as violent.

8. According to Merton:

> We have observed the difficulties entailed in *confining* analysis to functions fulfilled for "the society"; since items may be functional for some individuals and subgroups and dysfunctional for others. It is necessary, therefore, to consider a *range* of units for which the item has designated consequences: individuals in diverse statuses, subgroups, the larger social system and cultural system (1968: 106).

9. The role of "dramatic and unitary" events in changing public awareness of harms (and the consequent impact on legitimacy of legal change) independently of interests is illustrated by the history of federal legislation on adulterated foods and drugs. Around 1900, evidence of adulteration and outright poisoning of commercial food products had rapidly accumulated. Chief among the proponents of federal regulation of the industry was chemist Harvey Wiley, whose careful research revealed health hazards in many of the foods and drugs on the market. Despite the evidence and warnings, however, the public remained largely indifferent, and the industry was able to block reform legislation. In 1906, the socialist writer Upton Sinclair published an account of the "wage slaves of the Beef Trust" in the Chicago stockyards. *The Jungle* was the story of a Lithuanian immigrant, his daily encounter with exploitation, industrial accidents, and slum housing. Sinclair hoped the novel would increase the level of socialist consciousness on the part of his readers. In establishing the setting of his tale of class conflict, he described in detail the operations of the stockyard: tubercular pork was used in the making of sausage; poisoned bread was used to kill rats and the dead rats were dumped into the sausage grinder; workers occasionally fell into the open vats of boiling lard, and their bodies became an ingredient of "pure lard" sold at the corner grocery store. *The Jungle* had an immediate impact. Sales of meat dropped by half. President Roosevelt appointed a commission to investigate the allegations made in Sinclair's novel. When the commission reported the accuracy of *The Jungle's* portrayal of the stockyard conditions, passage of the Pure Food and Drug Act was quickly achieved. Sinclair later observed, "I aimed at the public's heart and by accident hit it in the stomach." By hitting the public in the stomach, Sinclair effectively raised awareness of a widespread harm and made it possible to use the law to regulate the harm. (A more recent example of the role of the writer in creating a dramatic focus for public awareness is Ralph Nader's *Unsafe at Any Speed* and subsequent works.) Without such dramatization, harms that are distributed across a large number of individuals will not have the psychological impact that relatively trivial, but dramatic, personal crimes will have.

10. The legal reaction may be reversed. In the Soviet Union theft of personal property is reacted to much less strongly than theft of state property (cf. Berman, 1963: 148-49). For other cases, see Starrs, 1961.

11. Much is to be gained by considering how this question has been addressed in other substantive areas. The research on who benefits from ethnic and sex discrimination in the labor market (Szymanski, 1976; McLaughlin, 1978; Villemez, 1978) may prove to be heuristic for sociologists interested in the role of interests in stigmatization. Lieberson (1971), as another example, addresses the thesis that the level of military expenditure can be explained in terms of the interests of the dominant corporations. To test this thesis empirically, he estimates the impact of government spending (military and nonmilitary) on corporate profits over a period of several decades. He discovers that corporate profits are more responsive to nonmilitary spending and that only a small segment of the corporations actually benefit from military spending. The advantage of Lieberson's study is that the causal variable (interests of the corporation) has been operationalized rather than mystified; it is in principle possible for the thesis that military spending serves corporate interests to be false. Unfortunately, in most discussions of the role of interests in the creation of deviance, there is no logically possible way for the interest hypothesis to be false: the actual interests of those who benefit are not spelled out, and whatever state of affairs happens to exist is "explained" by the interests of some omnipotent class.

12. Relevant studies include those on business and professional deviance (e.g., Johnson and Douglas, 1978) and those on the more subtle ties of Machiavellian behavior in small groups (cf. Goffman, 1956). Significant analyses could be undertaken in such areas as the day-to-day behavior of police (cf. Manning, 1977), psychiatric manipulation of dissent (cf. Medvedev and Medvedev, 1971; Bloch and Reddaway, 1977), terrorism and political witch-hunts (Bergesen, 1977), and official misconduct (Douglas and Johnson, 1977).

REFERENCES

Bachrach, Peter, and Morton Baratz. 1970. *Power and Poverty*. New York: Oxford University Press.

Balbus, Isaac D. 1971. "The concept of interest in pluralist and Marxian analysis." *Politics and Society* 1: 151-77.

———. 1977. *The Dialectics of Legal Repression*. New Brunswick, N.J.: Transaction Books.

Barnett, Ronald J., and Ronald E. Muller. 1974. *Global Reach: The Power of the Multinational Corporations*. New York: Simon and Shuster.

Bergesen, Albert James. 1977. "Political witch hunts: The sacred and the subversive in cross-national perspective." *American Sociological Review* 42: 220-33.

Berman, Harold J. 1963. *Justice in the U.S.S.R.* Cambridge, Mass.: Harvard University Press.

Black, Donald, and Maureen Mileski. 1973. *The Social Organization of Law*. New York: Seminar.

Bloch, Sidney, and Peter Reddaway. 1977. *Psychiatric Terror: How Soviet Psychiatry Is Used to Suppress Dissent*. New York: Basic Books.

Cantor, Robert. 1977. "New Laws for a new society." New York: Center for Cuban Studies 5 and 6.

Clarke, John, and Tony Jefferson. 1976. "Working class youth cultures." In Geoff Mungham and Geoffrey Pearson (eds.). *Working Class Youth Culture*. London: Routledge and Kegan Paul.

Clinard, Marshall B., and Richard Quinney. 1973. *Criminal Behavior Systems: A Typology.* 2nd ed. New York: Holt, Rinehart and Winston.

Douglas, Jack, and John Johnson (eds.). 1977. *Official Deviance: Readings in Malfeasance, Misfeasance and Other Forces of Corruption.* Philadelphia: J. B. Lippincott.

Epstein, Edward J. 1977. *Agency of Fear: Opiates and Political Power in America.* New York: G. P. Putnam.

Erikson, Kai T. 1966. *Wayward Puritans: A Study in the Sociology of Deviance.* New York: John Wiley.

Foucault, Michel. 1965. *Madness and Civilization.* Translated by Richard Howard. New York: Pantheon Books.

——. 1973. *The Birth of the Clinic: An Archaeology of Medical Perception.* Translated by A. M. Sheridan Smith. New York: Pantheon Books.

——. 1977. *Discipline and Punish: The Birth of the Prison.* Translated by Alan Sheridan. New York: Pantheon Books.

Gamson, William A. 1975. *The Strategy of Social Protest.* Homewood, Ill.: Dorsey Press.

Goffman, Erving. 1956. "The nature of deference and demeanor." *American Anthropologist* 58: 473-502.

Gold, David, Clarence Lo, and Erik Wright. "Recent developments in Marxist theories of the capitalist state." *Monthly Review* 5: 29-43 and 6: 36-41.

Gordon, David M. 1973. "Capitalism, class, and crime in America." *Crime and Delinquency* 16: 163-86.

Henry, Jules. 1963. *Culture against Man.* New York: Random House.

——. 1973. *On Sham, Vulnerability and Other Forms of Self-Destruction.* New York: Random House.

Hobsbawm, Eric J. 1971. *Primitive Rebels.* 3rd ed. New York: Praeger.

Jacobs, David. 1978. "Inequality and the legal order: An ecological test of the conflict model." *Social Problems* 25: 514-25.

Johnson, John M., and Jack D. Douglas (eds.). 1978. *Crime at the Top.* Philadelphia: J. B. Lippincott.

Lang, Kurt. 1972. *Military Institutions and the Sociology of War.* Beverly Hills, Calif.: Sage.

——, and Gladys Engel Lang. 1968. *Politics and Television.* Chicago: Quadrangle Books.

Liazos, Alexander. 1972. "The poverty of the sociology of deviance: Nuts, sluts, and perverts." *Social Problems* 20: 103-20.

Lieberson, Stanley. 1971. "An empirical study of military-industrial linkages." *American Journal of Sociology* 77: 562-84.

McLaughlin, Steven. 1978. "Occupational sex identification and the assessment of male and female earnings inequality." *American Sociological Review* 43: 909-21.

Manning, Peter K. 1977. *Police Work: The Social Organization of Policing.* Cambridge, Mass.: M.I.T. Press.

Marcuse, Herbert. 1964. *One Dimensional Man.* Boston: Beacon Press.

Marx, Gary. 1970. "Civil disorder and the agents of social control." *Journal of Social Issues* 26: 19-57.

——. 1974. "Thoughts on a neglected category of social movement participant: The *agent provocateur* and the informant." *American Journal of Sociology* 80: 402-42.

Medvedev, Zhores A., and Roy A. Medvedev. 1971. *A Question of Madness.* Translated by Ellen de Kadt. New York: Alfred A. Knopf.

Merton, Robert K. 1966. "Social problems and sociological theory." In Robert K. Merton and R. A. Nisbet (eds.). *Contemporary Social Problems.* New York: Harcourt, Brace and World.

——. 1968. *Social Theory and Social Structure.* New York: Free Press.

Mills, C. Wright. 1942. "The professional ideology of social pathologists." *American Journal of Sociology* 49: 165-80.

Mueller, Claus. 1973. *The Politics of Communication*. Oxford: Oxford University Press.

Nagel, Jack H. 1975. *The Descriptive Analysis of Power*. New Haven, Conn.: Yale University Press.

Pearson, Geoffrey. 1978. "Goths and vandals: Crime in history." *Contemporary Crises* 2: 119-39.

Quinney, Richard P. 1977. *Class, State and Crime: On the Theory and Practice of Criminal Justice*. New York: David McKay.

Reasons, Charles. 1973. "The politicizing of crime, the criminal and the criminologist." *Journal of Criminal Law and Criminology* 64: 471-77.

————, and Robert Rich. 1978. *The Sociology of Law*. Toronto: Butterworth.

Rosett, Arthur, and Donald R. Cressey. 1976. *Justice by Consent: Plea Bargains in the American Courthouse*. Philadelphia: J. B. Lippincott.

Schlesinger, Arthur M. 1973. *The Imperial Presidency*. Boston: Houghton Mifflin.

Schutz, Alfred. 1964. "Don Quixote and the problem of reality." In A. Bridersen (ed.). *Collected Papers*. Vol. 2. The Hague: Nijhoff.

Schwendinger, Herman, and Julia R. Schwendinger. 1970. "Defenders of order or guardians of human rights?" *Issues in Criminology* 5: 123-57.

————. 1977. "Social class and the definition of crime." *Crime and Social Justice* 7: 4-13.

Sinclair, Upton. 1906. *The Jungle*. New York: Doubleday, Page.

Starrs, James. 1961. "The regulatory offense in historical perspective." In Gerhard O. Mueller (ed.). *Essays in Criminal Science*. South Hakensack, N. J.: F. B. Rothman.

Steinert, Heinz. 1978. "Can socialism be advanced by radical rhetoric and sloppy data? Some remarks on Richard Quinney's latest output." *Contemporary Crisis* 2: 305-13.

Szymanski, Albert. 1976. "Racial discrimination and white gain." *American Sociological Review* 41: 403-13.

Taylor, Ian, Paul Walton, and Jock Young. 1973. *The New Criminology: For a Social Theory of Deviance*. New York: Harper and Row.

Thompson, Edward P. 1975. *Whigs and Hunters: The Origin of the Black Act*. New York: Pantheon Books.

Tilly, Charles. 1969. "Collective violence in European perspective." In Hugh Graham and Ted Gurr (eds.). *Violence in America*. New York: Signet Books.

Tilly, Charles, Louise Tilly, and Richard Tilly. 1975. *The Rebellious Century, 1830-1930*. Cambridge, Mass.: Harvard University Press.

Tucker, Robert C. (ed.). 1978. *The Marx-Engels Reader*. 2nd ed. New York: W. W. Norton.

Villemez, Wayne J. 1978. "Black subordination and white economic well-being." (Comment on Szymanski, *ASR*, June 1976.) *American Sociological Review* 43: 772-76.

Indexes

Name Index

Subject Index